The end of tradition

The end of tradition

Country life in central Surrey

John Connell

ROUTLEDGE & KEGAN PAUL
London, Henley and Boston

First published in 1978
by Routledge & Kegan Paul Ltd
39 Store Street,
London WC1E 7DD,
Broadway House,
Newtown Road,
Henley-on-Thames,
Oxon RG9 1EN and
9 Park Street,
Boston, Mass. 02108, USA
Set in 11/12 IBM Baskerville
by Hope Services
Clifton Hampden, Oxon
and printed in Great Britain by
Redwood Burn Ltd
Trowbridge and Esher
© John Connell 1978
No part of this book may be reproduced in
any form without permission from the
publisher, except for the quotation of brief
passages in criticism

British Library Cataloguing in Publication Data

Connell, John
The end of tradition.
1. East Clandon, Eng. — Social life and customs
2. East Horsley, Eng. — Social life and customs
3. West Clandon, Eng. — Social life and customs
4. West Horsley, Eng. — Social life and customs
I. Title
942.2'162   DA690.E1/   78-40675
ISBN 0 7100 8844 2

Contents

Preface	ix
1 Rural England	1
2 The past as prologue	10
3 Contemporary countryside	60
4 Migration and housing: élites and council tenants	97
5 Country life	132
6 Participation and planning: preservation and people	173
7 The end of tradition	205
Notes	215
Index	225

Maps and tables

Maps

1	Surrey: Metropolitan Green Belt and areas of outstanding beauty	11
2	Horsleys and Clandons, 1816—1970	40—1
3	Rateable values, 1970	93

Figure

2.1	Population change, 1801—1971	15

Tables

3.1	Occupational groups, 1961	62
3.2	Occupational groups, 1971	63
3.3	Socio-economic groups, 1961	64
3.4	Socio-economic groups, 1971	64
3.5	Social-class groups, 1966	65
3.6	Guildford Rural District Council housing types, 1970	78
3.7	Railway work trips from the four parishes, 1964	79
3.8	Work transport, 1971	81
3.9	Trips within Guildford Rural District	81
3.10	House prices, 1950—76	90
4.1	Age and population structure, 1961—71	98
4.2	Migration (1968-70) and social class	99
4.3	Migrant origins and destinations	102
4.4	Migration decisions	103
4.5	Workplace location: migrants	107
4.6	Workplace location: Total population	107
4.7	Council-house basic rents, 1970	118

Maps and tables

4.8	Council-house class structure, 1970	119
4.9	Council-house migration: All tenants	122
4.10	Council-house migration: New tenants	125
4.11	Central Surrey: Social-class composition	126
4.12	Housing stock, 1971	127
5.1	Social organisations, 1971	133
5.2	Social-class composition of voluntary associations	137
5.3	Church attendance	142
5.4	Recreation: all parishes	144
5.5	Local participation: Public house, church and social organisations	147
5.6	Do you think of yourself as a villager?	151
5.7	Do you think of yourself as a villager?	151
6.1	Horsley Countryside Preservation Society	180
6.2	Clandon Society	182
6.3	Desire for street lighting	199

Endpapers

Front: Ordnance Survey, Old Series, one inch to one mile map, Sheet 8 (1816). Back: Ordnance Survey, First Series, 1:50,000, Sheets 186 and 187.

Preface

Rural life has always provoked the interest of poets, painters, authors and sometimes even scholars; as the population has left the countryside, and as its distinctive characteristics have dwindled, that interest has increased and with it has grown an almost universal desire to live amongst fields and trees and recapture something of an idealised rural tranquillity. This book is an attempt to examine how life styles have changed in the last century in a tiny part of the English countryside: the four Surrey villages of East Clandon, West Clandon, East Horsley and West Horsley, close to London but isolated and protected from it by the Green Belt, but even so, closer to a great English city than any villages that have attracted earlier study.

The origin of the work lies in a thesis presented to the University of London and is based in part on a survey of nearly all the 500 households that had moved into and within the area in a two-year period. My greatest debt is to them and to a variety of local officials; I hope I have not done them an injustice. Since the thesis was completed the study has been continuously revised to incorporate subsequent changes, but inevitably it has not always been possible. In 1974 Guildford Rural District became incorporated into a new district council; a completely new organisation was born which affected numerous aspects of rural life, especially in the administration of local-authority housing. Consequently, this is an account of part of that rural district essentially as it was until the time

Preface

that it became incorporated into a larger and more urban district.

Inevitably theses are boring, overloaded with footnotes and jargon and too long. If the book has escaped at least a little from this it is in no small part due to all those who persuaded me that much of what I had written was unreadable and that the sobriety of the present could happily be condensed to make way for the variety of the past. They cannot be blamed for my errors and opinions. Substantial thanks are due to all those who, by providing data, tea and sympathy at crucial points, enabled the work to be finished.

The author and publisher would like to thank Richard Natkiel and *New Society* for permission to reproduce Map 1 and *Punch* magazine for permission to reproduce the four cartoons by Thelwell. The front endpaper is taken from Ordnance Survey, Old Series one-inch to one mile map, Sheet 8 (1816), by courtesy of the British Library; the back endpaper is taken from the present-day Ordnance Survey map, First Series, 1:50,000, Sheets 186 and 187, and is reproduced by kind permission of the Ordnance Survey, Southampton.

John Connell

CHAPTER 1

Rural England

> In a manner all south-eastern England is a single urban community; for steam and electricity are changing our geographical conceptions. A city in an economic sense is no longer an area covered continuously with streets and houses.
>
> H.J. Mackinder, *Britain and the British Seas*

Beyond the fringes of cities there have always been large and small villages stretching out in a panoply of shapes and sizes, each with its individual history and function. As the cities grew, many of these became engulfed; Highgate and Dulwich in London, Merrow in Guildford, and many others are distinctive places within the urban morass. Each retains just a little of its former village style and each in consequence is a little more exclusive than the more modern suburbs around it. Others have become metropolitan villages, shaped by the city but not yet, and perhaps never to become, a physical part of it. Still more seem almost oblivious to centuries of change.

As post-war planning increasingly put an end to the physical expansion of the city and, at the same time, car-ownership became more universal, so the villages beyond took on a new distinctiveness. Instead of becoming drowned in the tide of a huge metropolitan wave they retained much of their physical form: small houses remained surrounded by agricultural land, but within that shell the social and economic structure was changing rapidly. Urban growth spilled over, as 'infilling' or 'rounding off' into villages, old towns or planned New Towns. As Jones noted: 'suburbs have spread further still, compromising the countryside without creating new urban forms';[1] in Pahl's felicitous phrase, they are 'urbs in rure'.[2] The Second World War marked a particular watershed for metropolitan expansion, leaving in its wake the pieces of compromised countryside that are the present metropolitan villages, where social and economic changes are primarily a response to the requirements of a nearby urban centre. They are characterised above all by the daily streams of commuters setting out for town.

A new kind of countryman is being forged—with ties in both city and village. Simultaneously, mechanisation has diminished the numbers of agricultural workers and with them have disappeared the blacksmiths, coopers and agricultural craftsmen; as their numbers and status have declined so their children have sought urban employment using new skills and receiving higher wages. Some of them have left for the cities; few have wages high enough to enable them to commute. Within most villages in England, but especially those on the fringes of large cities, social and economic organisation has changed extremely rapidly. In many areas, the present century has seen the emergence of a new kind of village, often divided significantly between rich and poor, and with only superficial approximations to a village community.

These divisions are not new—at all times there have been social and economic hierarchies within English villages. Until the end of the nineteenth century the landowners moved in a national social circuit and had few economic worries; the agricultural workers were dependent on the landlord for their jobs and houses and rarely left the village. They were bound together only by the agricultural system. The landowner's wealth was partly produced from his land, and the workers were responsible for production. Few villagers were independent of the land. The shopkeepers sold goods to the workers and, with the permission of the squire, who controlled the living, the vicar preached to them. It would nevertheless be naïve to think of a simple society of employers and labourers: urban employment had always provided one outlet. Yet in the nineteenth century this simple system was being invaded. Gentlemen of independent means (independent in the sense that they relied on inherited wealth or city property and business) were building their own houses in the countryside. Although they moved swiftly towards the upper rungs of the village social hierarchy, they had no position in the parallel economic hierarchy: they were in the village but not of it. As Cobbett observed in 1830, these newcomers were not like the established gentry. They were:[3]

> a gentry, only now-and-then residing at all, having no relish for country delights, foreign in their manners, distant and haughty in their behaviour, looking to the soil only for their rents...unacquainted with its cultivators, despising them and their pursuits....The war and paper-system has brought in nabobs, negro-drivers, generals, admirals, governors...loan jobbers, lottery dealers, bankers, stockjobbers.

Cobbett complained that these new arrivals gave no leadership to the village, being interested in its social and economic life only in pursuit of their own ends. Nevertheless they, at least, were a minority and it was not until the end of the nineteenth century that urban residents began to leave the towns in any numbers and occasionally make their presence felt:[4]

> The advent into many villages of families from outside, usually of the professional or business classes, which we have seen was beginning during the close of the nineteenth century, has had some effect on the social life of the areas into which they have come...they frequently set about organising amusements in the villages in which they have settled.

This early intrusion into village life has grown and changed so fast that in many villages various kinds of newcomers are the majority: agricultural villages have become metropolitan villages and not all of the newcomers are welcome. Only a limited number organised amusements, and even fewer established villagers welcomed these distractions. In many areas the two groups were not simply in social antipathy but had presented a planning problem:[5]

> accommodation of industrial workers in non-industrial places has proceeded, hitherto, without any deliberate direction or conscious planning....Generally there has been no attempt to assimilate the newcomers to the old community. The new houses, run up as private speculations on land adjacent to the villages and sold to their occupants on the hire-purchase system, are housing estates in miniature in their siting, in their architecture and in their occupants. They are something entirely apart from the old village, and the only reason for their location is that the speculator has been enabled, by his choice of a site, to exploit whatever existing services there may be....Rarely, if ever, can the social advantages which should accrue from the larger unit of population, be realized under a planning scheme which segregates so completely the old inhabitants from the newcomers.

In Surrey these disparities and discontinuities are particularly striking and, indeed, the whole process has been going on much longer. Much of Surrey was long remote from urban and industrial influence. In the sixteenth century the manufacture of gunpowder and weapons was pioneered in the Tillingbourne Valley, between Guildford and Dorking, because of its remoteness and safety. Otherwise the Industrial Revolution largely bypassed Surrey. Its industrial archaeology mainly consists of picturesque disused lime-kilns, glass-furnaces and the Wey and Arun Canal; terraced housing and dirty factories are almost absent and even contemporary New Towns have avoided the county. Nor did London's presence assist agricultural improvement, as Daniel Defoe's description of Bagshot Heath as a 'mark of the just resentment shew'd by Heaven on the Englishmen's pride'[6] indicates.

Near London the trend for city workers to live in the countryside was early established. Aiding this process was the growth of such places as Epsom Spa, already fashionable in 1680, and later the races. A contemporary journal, *The Virtuoso* (1704), observed that Epsom was a suburban excursion for a 'sprucer sort of fellow'.[7] All over the country on the turnpike roads stately homes were constructed until, as Defoe noted: 'The ten miles from Guildford to Leatherhead make one continual line of gentleman's houses...and their parks or gardens almost touching one another.'[8] So extensive was the expansion of housing in the country between 1690 and 1730 that Nairn and Pevsner described it as 'suburbanisation'.[9] The gentlemen of this period were some of the first Surrey commuters and the exodus from London never lost its social status. It merely moved to different areas at different times, gradually moving away from central London. Bertrand Russell records that:[10]

> In the year 1883 my Uncle Rollo bought a house on the slopes of Hindhead....At that time there were no houses on Hindhead, except two derelict coaching inns, the 'Royal Huts' and the 'Seven Thorns'. (They are not now derelict.) Tyndall's house, which started the fashion, was being built.

Other famous migrants around this time included Tennyson and Lloyd George, both living at a safely aristocratic distance from London. The stockbrokers lived nearer and on the main line.

Only a very few southern areas of the county, in the nineteenth century as now, have to some extent remained aloof from this invasion. One of the factors that determined which villages received early long-distance commuters is indicated by Sydney Low: 'the decrease of population in Alfold is ascribed to its being a purely agricultural parish with no resident gentry.'[11]

Not all the newcomers built stately homes to live in but it was the locations of their homes which guided later arrivals:[12]

> The main army is preceded by an advance of villas... seizing a few picked positions....Then come the more solid ranks of the semi-detached...along the high roads and in the neighbourhood of railway stations.

Surrey was accessible, beautiful and comfortable and contains some of the finest scenery in the south of England. The old guidebook that described the Devil's Punchbowl as the 'Switzerland of Surrey' may have exaggerated rather wildly but it is difficult to know what to make of the statement by the country planner Fines that, in a scale of landscape values, the highest value found in Lowland Britain is 12·0, and that is 'the prospect from Newlands Corner near Guildford over the Lower Greensand Hills of Surrey and West Sussex'.[13] On the other hand there does seem to be a consensus about that particular scenery; Basil Cracknell also believes that there is no finer view and cites Matthew Arnold's letter to a friend in February 1876: 'as I looked at the landscape from the hills above Horsley, the backbone of England, I felt how pleasant a country it was, and how well satisfied I could be to remain all my days in it.'[14]

By the late nineteenth century the scenery and climate of parts of Surrey had become residential-location factors of some importance. The 1871 Census attributed the population increase of Witley, south of Godalming, 'to the attractions of the scenery, many artists having taken up residence in the district'.[15] The change that followed migration was recognised early on. George Sturt (writing under his pseudonym 'George Bourne'), in a number of books on rural life in north-west Surrey, commented on the speed of social change:[16]

> The old life is being swiftly obliterated. The valley is passing out of the hands of its former inhabitants. They are being crowded into corners, and are becoming as aliens in their own homes; they are receding before newcomers with new ideas, and, greatest change of all, they are yielding to the dominion of new ideas themselves.

Despite the general assumption that this kind of change is new, radical and continuing at an accelerating pace, it is quite clear that George Bourne was describing what he considered to be very rapid change. Moreover, the rapidity of that change at that time has meant that, in Surrey at least, present change is slower and much less substantial.

Even before George Bourne was mourning the demise of traditional rural life in Surrey, in the first decade of the twentieth century Maud Davies had carried out a very detailed survey of her own remote parish of Corsley, Wiltshire. There she found that increasingly there were two different social groups within the village with those at the top not always linked even economically with those at the bottom;[17] a study of a Surrey village at the same time would probably have found the links to be rather more tenuous. Increasingly, this emerging duality has been recognised in villages scattered over wide areas of England. If the authors of village studies were usually aware that a strict dichotomy simplified the existing state of affairs they were also aware that the dichotomy was becoming more marked, as two main contrasting groups became polarised in opposition and intermediate social and economic groups became less important. Specifically in central Surrey these processes were defined quite precisely and quite early by Jervis, who recognised in 1954 that:[18]

> Much has happened in south-west Surrey during the present century that is to be regretted. The new development, such as that at East Horsley, is competently built, consisting of houses individually pleasant to live in, but too often as a whole quite without coherent form or relation to the countryside into which it has intruded. The inhabitants are largely people new to the area and with no particular interest in it, often oblivious of the existence of an old-established social structure. It is almost as though there were two complete social patterns, each with its own outward physical form and inward social relationships: the old village structure, which has been evolving since prehistoric times, and laid on top of it the new twentieth-century pattern of 'desirable village residences', the social and cultural threads of which are often centred not locally but in London. The division is often reinforced by a difference in social class, for the new development is typically of upper middle-class type—those who can afford the daily fare to London and who can keep a car to avoid physical isolation.

In its way this was simply an echo of George Bourne's

observations but it could stand repeating and, independently, two years later MacPherson was again describing East Horsley:[19]

> The inhabitants, mainly middle class, do not mix easily. There is very little community spirit. There are several social sub-grades and it is difficult to move between them. The original people who built the houses having moved or died, a large proportion of the inhabitants have come post-war. They are not easily accepted by the pre-war community, so forming another division.

Thus a decade before Pahl had observed in 'Dormersdell', Hertfordshire, 'what now appears to be a polarized two-class division',[20] a rather more varied social composition had been reported from central Surrey. But the variety of the social composition was sometimes seen in different ways. Thus Basil Cracknell describes in the Horsleys and Clandons, 'a dreadful middle-class uniformity differentiated only by the particular train they caught each morning, and by the make, but not the size, of their motor car'.[21] Elsewhere, as Pahl recognised, the division was between established residents and newcomers. In central Surrey it had begun to go beyond that: the established residents were so few and the newcomers so many that they were no longer entirely a homogeneous group relative to the locals. Within the newcomers differences had begun to emerge; there were several kinds of newcomers, each with his own conceptions of rural life. The extent of intra-village differences is now well-known and indeed the split village has become a favourite of the media; not so long ago village life to some seemed like the following:[22]

> The place is divided into two distinct halves. At one end, it's lavender, medium sherry, the Daily Telegraph and what a wonderful job the Government's doing and at the other end it's broad beans, bicycle clips and what a lousy job Sir Alf Ramsey's doing.

In the Horsleys and the Clandons[23] life is not so nearly polarised yet the quotation conveys a sense of the scene.

Rural England

Country life in central Surrey may not be quite like this but then there are many myths about life in English villages which need to be re-examined. Divisions, real and imaginary, are at the heart of contemporary rural life.

CHAPTER 2

The past as prologue

No part of Surrey has changed more in a single lifetime than the northern edge of the chalk from Croydon to the Clandons.

Basil E. Cracknell, *Portrait of Surrey*

In the very centre of Surrey are the four adjoining parishes of East and West Clandon and East and West Horsley. All had historic centres at springs in the chalk, on what eventually became the Guildford-Leatherhead road, and like all the other parishes on the north-facing dip slope of the North Downs they were aligned north-south so that each had a part of three distinctive physical environments: sandstone, clay and chalk. Before the growth of agricultural markets each village could be self-sufficient, internally exchanging different products from the different zones. Indeed, Bronze Age settlements mined the chalk for flints, worked the clay for pottery and grew grain between. Farther north was once swamp. The porch of West Clandon parish church contains the reproduction of a mediaeval carving of a dog with the head of a dragon in its mouth. Legend has it that West Clandon was once terrorised by a dragon living in Send Marsh; naturally no names or dates exist.

The earliest settlements of Neolithic people on the chalk, there because of its properties of drainage and its light forest cover, began the process of clearing which by 1500 had

The past as prologue

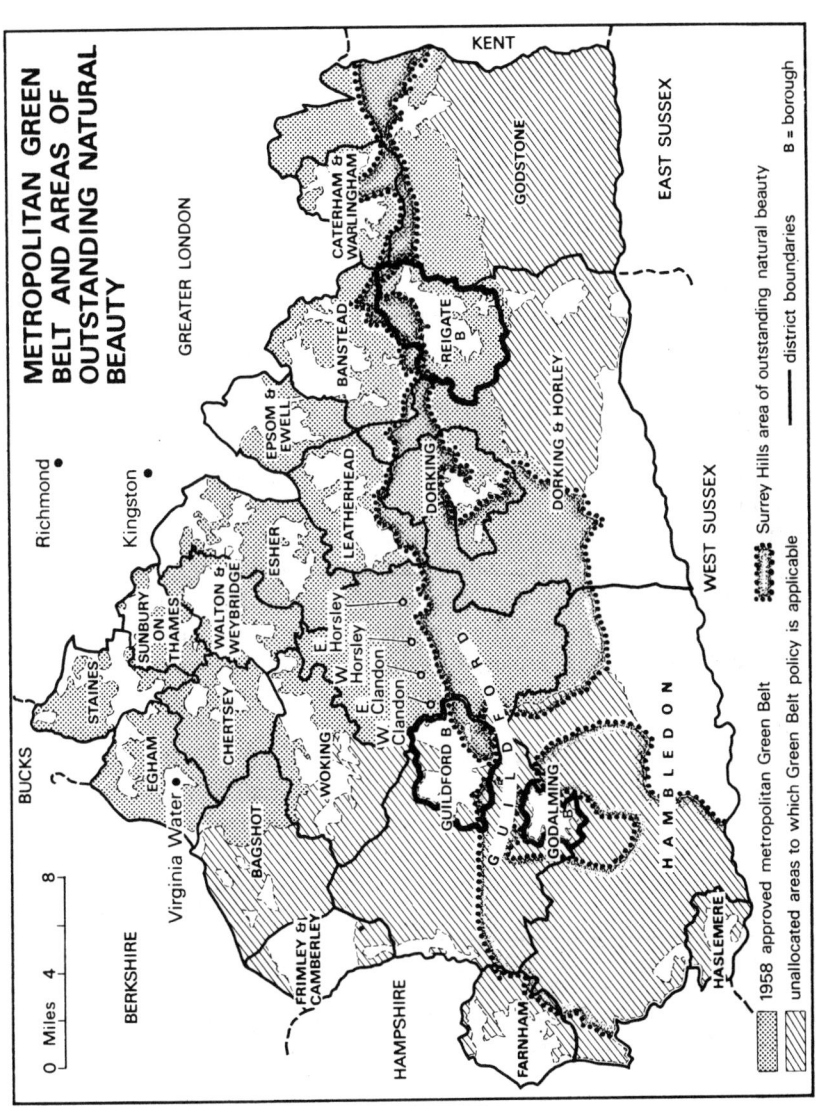

Map 1 Surrey: Metropolitan Green Belt and areas of outstanding natural beauty

The past as prologue

produced chalk downland pasture. This clearance continued in some areas until the sixteenth and seventeenth centuries and the local '-ley' place name originally meant a woodland clearing. Partly resulting from the local influence of John Evelyn there was some afforestation in the eighteenth century, often associated with the parallel development of large parks and estates on the main turnpikes. Conifers, none of which is indigenous to Surrey, are one of the most important new species in local plantations. More recently the Forestry Commission has also afforested parts of Surrey; since the Second World War, plantations south of West Clandon, towards Newlands Corner, have grown up whilst at the same time plantations were also developed in the south of both Horsley parishes. Their growth has significantly altered the character of the landscape to the extent that recent local opinion has opposed the extension of more plantations because of their supposed deleterious effect on local views. On the other hand, as Stamp and Willatts suggested, 'a "Surrey home" is a phrase with a considerable *cachet*; few such Surrey homes would be complete without a screen of trees, often exotic conifers, which may become a fragment of woodland'.[1] So far has the woodland cycle turned full circle that the considerable amount of woodland was thought to be sheltering an escaped puma in the mid 1960s; in subsequent years the Surrey puma was 'sighted' at regular intervals.

Each village is recorded in the Domesday Book, and by the middle of the fourteenth century East Clandon was already established as the smallest of the four parishes; two hundred years later the Lay Subsidy Returns show that there had been little change in population sizes. One change had

Parish taxes	1332	1334
Esthorsleigh	£2. 12s. 7d.	£2. 14s. 7½d.
Westhorsleigh	£2. 17s. 7d.	£2. 19s. 7½d.
Estclendon	8s. 5d.	4s. 10½d.
Westclendon	£1. 8s. 8d.	£1. 2s. 8¾d.

The past as prologue

Lay subsidy returns	1524 Number of taxpayers	1525 Number of taxpayers
Esthorsleigh	64	63
Westhorsleigh	29	24
Estclendon	26	30
Westclendon	38	34

occurred, however: the north-east of the county was becoming wealthier than the remainder, and for the sixteenth century Sheail attributed this wealth to the presence of London: 'The impact of London is clearer than in Kent. . . . North-east Surrey was densely settled and it is possible that the North Downs were the "place of most resort" for many who belonged economically to London.'[2] Although there is no supporting evidence for the presence of any kind of commuters it is clear that from the start of the sixteenth century Surrey was commonly to the fore in agricultural innovations, and its agriculture was efficient in comparison with neighbouring Kent and Sussex. London's market had first attracted Surrey's agricultural produce in the seventeenth century but local markets were dominant until the nineteenth century. Indeed Farnham, by the end of the seventeenth century, was the most important corn market after London. If Surrey's agriculture was generally responding to improved marketing opportunities it seems that this was scarcely true of the Horsleys and Clandons; they grew only very slowly as areas closer to London grew much faster. Arthur Young, travelling towards London in 1769, noted agricultural improvement only after Cobham.

A compensatory trend was a special form of suburbanisation; in 1730 Clandon Park was laid out by Capability Brown and the house was built by Leoni for the Earl of Onslow. Hatchlands in East Clandon was built for Admiral Boscawen during 1756-8. West Horsley Place has remnants of a fifteenth-century core and was once the seat of Sir Walter Raleigh's son; Raleigh's head is dubiously rumoured to be buried in the parish church opposite. In East Horsley, however, Horsley Towers was not built until the mid-nineteenth century, largely as a folly for the Earl of Lovelace,

The past as prologue

and at the same time the whole village was rebuilt in flint and bricks to harmonise with his estate. All these great houses, and some lesser houses, remain and with their associated large parklands stamp a particular character on the whole local area.

The nineteenth century: an age of agricultural improvement

According to the 1801 Crop Returns less than a third of the area of the four parishes was cultivated;[3] the heavy clays were the poorest agricultural areas in the county and inferior oats were as important there as wheat. The commons were spreading over part of this area and the agricultural depression coupled with lax administration of the Poor Law in the county provoked substantial unrest. By 1870 the worst was over; under-drainage of the clays and other agricultural improvements began to stem the migration of agricultural labourers and resulted in the gradual re-emergence of agricultural production for the metropolitan market.

The early nineteenth-century Censuses indicate both the dominance of agriculture in the parish economy and the low mobility of population in the area. Few people left the parishes; even fewer arrived. Social and economic change had penetrated the four parishes only through limited agricultural improvements and the development of gentlemen's houses with their associated service employment. This latter was insufficient to absorb agricultural unemployment and it is clear that there was some migration especially between 1841 and 1861. The 1851 Census recorded that 'since 1841 several large families have emigrated from East Horsley and West Clandon'[4] and the 1861 Census records the decline in population of East Horsley as a result of the rather mysterious 'reduction of a large establishment in the parish'.[5] The population was growing quite rapidly closer to London but in central Surrey the only new arrivals for some centuries had been the gentlemen. They had produced a curiously dichotomous society. As one observer commented:[6]

> A vast number of the aristocracy reside in the country from its proximity to town; and besides them there are

The past as prologue

only the farmers and their labourers; the servants of the
aristocratic establishments—a numerous and very peculiar
class; and the few tradesmen who supply the great houses.
The many gradations of rank and property which are found
in more trading, manufacturing and mixed districts
do not here exist

There was no middle class in central Surrey and in rural areas like this agriculture was no longer successful as it had been in the past. The middle of the century was therefore a time of substantial agricultural poverty, which produced the 'Captain Swing' revolts; it is strange that such a depressed period should preface the most substantial changes in the history of the Horsleys and Clandons.

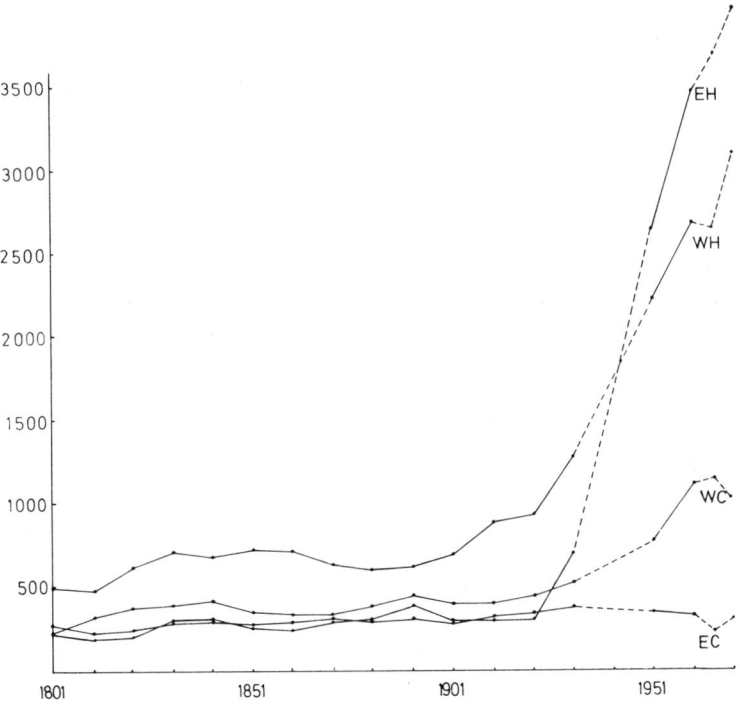

Figure 2.1 Population change, 1801-1971

The past as prologue

The Guildford-Woking railway line was built in 1844 and in 1846 the Reading-Guildford-Reigate line was completed through the Tillingbourne Valley. The London and South Western Railway extended the 'New Guildford Line' in 1885 from Stoke d'Abernon through to Guildford with stations being constructed at Effingham (Junction), East Horsley (then entitled Horsley, Ockham and Ripley) and West Clandon, through which the first trains passed on 20 February 1885. The existing local railway network was finalised in 1891 with the completion of the link line from Effingham to Leatherhead, giving a through route from Guildford to Leatherhead. The 'New Guildford Line' was situated near the northern end of the four parishes and only in West Clandon were any houses then near the station; although its presence was almost unnoticed for some thirty years, it quietly heralded a new era in the historical development of the four parishes. Initially the line served as a relief for through traffic to Portsmouth and until the First World War was as much concerned with the marketing of agricultural produce and the provision of coal as it was with passengers. Elsewhere in the county Haslemere and Woking were largely creations of the new railways; in Epsom the railway company actually provided twelve houses near the station to encourage commuters to live there, but no company provided houses or special fares for the Horsleys and Clandons. In several parts of Surrey the villages and towns grew rapidly, yet in the four parishes there was little change, the population of each remaining stationary throughout the century with that of West Horsley, the largest parish in area, consistently greater than the others.

Until the advent of the railways, available local evidence supports the view that the parishes of central Surrey were probably not very different from many other English lowland parishes. Village economic life revolved around agriculture, and social life was shaped in the same mould. Throughout the nineteenth century and earlier the most obvious characteristic of life for the agricultural workers and their families, who formed a majority in all the parishes at least until the last decades of the century, was a deep-seated poverty. Arthur Young, passing between Guildford and Ripley in the 1760s, noted that agricultural wages were 1s 2d a day in winter, 1s 4d in spring and 2s or even 2s 6d in the peaks of the harvest season. At the same time mutton was $4\frac{1}{2}$d a pound, beef 4d, bread 2d and butter 7d.[7] Young said little on how prices and wages might be balanced but generally this was a period when labourers had few clothes, little food, inadequate housing and poor health.

Forty years later Simond, travelling through Albury on the other fringe of the parishes, noted that:[8]

> the peasants look very decent in their manner, dress and appearance. No marks of poverty about them but they are certainly very diminutive and thin. They seem better clothed than fed; one might suspect a certain native pride in them disdains to wear the livery of poverty although they suffer in secret.

It is possible that the 'peasants' of Albury were better fed and clothed than their contemporaries in the other parts of England that Simond had passed through, yet some changes were already having a slight impact locally. Malcolm quotes wages in 1800 in the same area as 9s to 12s per week for a man, 1s to 1s 6d a day for a woman (which suggests that already they were irregular members of the labour force in the South East) 12s to 14s per day for shepherds.[9] Compared with other parts of Britain these were substantial wages. Andrew Meikle's threshing machine had been invented around 1784 and the reaping machine followed around 1828;[10] both had certainly made their presence felt in central Surrey before the middle of the century. Throughout the period 1801-81 the numbers employed in agriculture remained the same although the proportions fell slightly. In most rural areas it was not until the 1850s that migration to towns became important, and then it was usually only landless labourers and the older craftsmen whose manual skills had been superseded by urban machinery.

At the time when rural Britain was at last beginning to realise that it was indeed subsidiary to urban Britain Richard Drewitt, the agent for Lord Onslow, was providing evidence for the 1867 Agricultural Commission. Although the earl

The past as prologue

owned a considerable amount of land in Surrey his seat was at West Clandon and the evidence of his agent is certainly true of the parish:[11]

> Women are only occasionally employed on a farm of 4 to 500 acres, perhaps 4 or 5 women will be employed in raking and spudding couch grass, weeding corn, haymaking and harvesting. After harvest they are employed in picking tuffets off the sown wheat. They usually work from 8 to 5. I don't think that the wife's work is of much assistance to the family except during harvest. I am well acquainted with the country for ten miles around this place and what I say now applies to all that district. The farms are usually from 200 to 500 acres in extent. Girls very seldom work in the fields and it is not at all desirable that they should. Boys usually remain at school until they are twelve; their chief employment is to drive the plough; they are useful for that purpose at the age of twelve. Those employed in birdscaring and sheep or cow tending are usually twelve. They earn about 3/- a week at that age. Most boys can read and write. I can name one family that cannot but that is because they will not go to school. Lord Onslow subscribes £10 a year to the schools in each of the parishes in which he has property. It is a great mistake to suppose that all labourers earn the same. In order to be a good agricultural labourer a boy must begin work when young, but I think 12 is young enough to begin except during harvest. Gleaning causes more immorality than any other kind of work. The children go out 50 or 60 together to get so many handfuls and they go to steal the corn in order to complete their handfuls. Lord Onslow lets about 1½ cottages per 100 acres with the farms. He charges his tenants £3 per cottage and I endeavour to bind the tenant and let them to the labourers for the same sum as they pay themselves, but I cannot get them carried out. Lord Onslow charges 50/- a year for the cottages he lets to the labourers ....Every labourer who has only 20 poles of garden has an allotment of a quarter of an acre for which he pays 5/- a year. The usual rent of land is about 25/- an acre. The allotments are let subject to the conditions of the

occupiers keeping sober and going to church. They may not grow wheat on more than a quarter. The farmers do not object to the allotments. Almost all the labourers keep pigs. The cottages are conveniently situated with respect to the work to be done but there are not enough of them. I build 2 cottages for 100 guineas each, with two bedrooms and a small sleeping room for the children upstairs, and sitting room, kitchen and scullery downstairs, that sum included the water supply (a well) which can be easily obtained here and fences. On Sunday the shepherd is wanted during half the day, sometimes more; the housekeeper and stockman three hours each. I think a good labourer will earn £50 a year here, but here he can earn 30/- a week for 6 weeks by stripping bark. I have three under me now who earn about £40. I think it is desirable that boys go to school during a portion of their time after they begin to work, but they can only devote the evenings and Sunday to it.

This single description gives considerable insight into village life a century ago; naturally its emphasis is on agricultural life but there is not even a hint that other kinds of employment were possible. Compared with other parts of England it appears that the labourers on the earl's estates were reasonably well off: not all women had to work, children apparently did not start work until they were 12 and many labourers kept pigs. But this is not the complete story. The earl's agent almost certainly exaggerated since school records from the next decade show many absences to work in the fields. Moreover, in the 1850s in villages around Godalming wages for male labourers varied from 8s to 10s per week whilst women labourers received only 8d per day.[12] Wages changed little in that decade and unless the earl was much more benevolent than neighbouring landowners, which is improbable, the wages too are exaggerated. Other elements are certainly accurate: the overpowering paternalism that demanded sobriety and church-going to be worthy of an allotment and, perhaps most interesting, the presence of obsolete dialect and agricultural words such as 'spudding' and 'tuffets' even in the prose of the earl's agent.

Very little is written on Surrey dialect. Leveson-Gower noted in 1895 that 'it can hardly be said of Surrey that it had a dialect peculiarly its own'.[13] Nor could he detect much difference between rural and urban areas; the distinctive words and proverbs that he did collect were common to much of working-class speech in a wide area of south-east England. A decade later Gertrude Jekyll observed dialect only amongst the very poorest old folk. Interest in dialect post-dated its disappearance in much of Surrey. Gertrude Jekyll, however, did manage to collect one folk song that in 1905 was still sung in the Godalming area: 'The Ploughman's Song'.[14]

> Come all you Jolly Ploughmen with Courage Stout and Bold
> That labours all the winter in Stormy Winds and Cold
> To clothe the Fields with plenty, your Farm Yards to renew
> To crown them with Contentment behold the painful
>   Plough

The other six verses are little better but the song is apparently unique; I can trace no other folk songs from Surrey collected north of the Weald. Shortly afterwards George Bourne, writing of almost the same area, noted that there were no folk songs and no folk culture.[15] This aspect of traditional life had gone completely. The oral tradition perished long ago in central Surrey. It is even too late for revivalism.

Most of the nineteenth century was a prosperous period for agriculture until about 1873, when the Agricultural Depression began to have an impact on rural areas, even in the counties fringing London. Many tenant farms reverted to the estates, where at least most labourers could be sure of their jobs throughout the year, but the massive fall in land values led to considerable uncertainty as estates changed hands or were broken up. The last three decades of the century were times of considerable poverty and most local newspapers carried advertisements suggesting emigration to Canada, Australia or other colonies and this reduced the misery of a few rural families. Rural poverty became an established feature almost until the start of the First World War. In a Bedfordshire village in 1901 it was calculated that

41 per cent of the population lived in poverty, the sort of poverty that left biological needs unsatisfied, a result of inadequate wages rather than the absence of jobs.[16] At the same time life-expectancy for the working class was 30 years, compared with 60 for other classes. But in different parts of Surrey there were different conditions. George Bourne recorded that in the Farnham area in 1909 agricultural wages varied from about 14s to 24s but that summer hay-making wages might be as low as 2s 6d per day.[17] Albert Bennett, starting work in West Clandon on the Earl of Onslow's estate, in 1893 earned 3s 6d per week at the age of 11.[18] (Either times had become substantially worse, which is possible since this was the last depression year, or the earl's agent had indeed exaggerated.)

During the Depression period the role of women changed. Although in the 1870s many women did the same work as men but were usually paid only 10d a day compared with 2s for men, by the 1880s it was unusual in England to find women working regularly on farms. Jobs were no longer generally available and hence only the very poorest would seek out the badly paid jobs that did exist. Nevertheless seasonal work such as fruit- and potato-picking remained useful sources of income for many decades, but Gertrude Jekyll noted that by 1904 women were no longer even employed to glean.[19] George Bourne observed five years later that field work still employed some women but wages were low and numbers declining. In a few rural areas it was possible for women to take in out-work from urban factories but generally they simply reverted to domestic responsibilities; in economic terms women were increasingly being differentiated from men. A further effect of the Depression was the decline of rural trades; the blacksmiths, shoemakers, millers and tailors were almost all superseded by the towns as the purchasing power in the villages fell rapidly at the same time as industrialisation mass-produced the same kinds of goods whilst transport improvements brought them to the villages and small towns. The rich variety of rural occupations that had characterised most villages in the eighteenth and early nineteenth century rapidly diminished, never to reappear.

The past as prologue

Education and the village economy

Lord Onslow's agent stated that the earl subscribed £10 a year to schools in several parishes and that boys customarily stayed there until they were 12. If each parish had schools before 1870 then the area was exceptionally generously provided; education in England was the province of religion and the initiative remained with the voluntary church societies even after the famous Elementary Education Act of 1870 which ordered the setting up of local school boards to organise the construction of new schools where voluntary provision was inadequate. The voluntary schools were to continue and receive grants, whilst the 'board schools' were to fill the gaps. This massive change had one particularly useful result (apart from education): each school maintained a detailed report. From those reports[20] it is clear that scarcely any boys remained at school to the age of 12. In the 1870s many boys started work at the age of 8, probably doing jobs which required little energy, such as scaring birds from crops, and graduating through tasks such as weeding and stone-picking so that, as the earl's agent noted, by the time they were 12 they were capable of doing arduous tasks such as driving the plough.[21] However, in winter, when there was less agricultural work available, many boys did go to school and the records indicate considerable seasonal fluctuations in numbers. In 1873 the Agricultural Children's Act forbade the employment of children less than 8 years old on any kind of agricultural labour and a further Act in 1880 made it compulsory for children to go to school until the age of 10. (However, it was not until 1891, when free education was introduced, that this was possible.)

Local records show many of the problems and difficulties of rural education in the nineteenth century in considerable detail. In many areas, as around West Clandon, the school had been provided by the squire. After the initial benevolence his interest proved often to be disruptive. East Horsley school was continually being visited by Lady Lovelace and the rector, and their suggestions on the content of the curriculum were expected to be carried out. The school regularly purchased as many bibles and prayer books as exercise books and the church's influence pervaded most of the instruction. Despite the apparent surfeit of bibles, it was still necessary in March 1874 to record: 'George Giles sent home to fetch his bible.' The rector usually taught religion in the school but occasionally he attempted to do more. In East Clandon the headmaster reported in November 1883 that the 'Rev. G.H. Lee visited the school and expressed his intention of permanently taking part in the secular instruction of the School which intention I have respectfully asked him to forego.' Nevertheless, in his capacity as Chairman of the School Management Board, he continued to make frequent visits to the school and recorded in the report books his comments, usually unfavourable, on progress, discipline and attendance. He also won his battle with the headmaster and began to teach arithmetic. It must have been particularly difficult for young teachers, often beginning their careers in country schools, to weather the disagreements of squire and rector in the management of the school, especially when they disagreed with each other. In 1891 Mrs Rendel, the wife of the squire, presented pictures to the school and these were put up, but as the rector recorded in the report book: 'as the above was done without any communications with the Managers they have ordered the maps to be replaced on the walls.'

The teachers were not particularly well off, despite their considerable status within the village, and their urban counterparts usually did better (hence the rapid migration of teachers from all the villages). In nearby Churt the salary of the headmaster was only £45 in 1871 and although it soon rose to £60[22] this scarcely compared very favourably with the possible incomes the earl's agent thought labourers might obtain. Teachers were also paid partly from the school fees that each child had to pay. In families with one child the fee was 3d a week, two children paid 5d and three or more 6d; however, children 'above labourers' condition' had to pay 4d. Teachers' concern with attendance is easily explained and the turnover rate was high; almost every year saw a new village schoolmaster or schoolmistress. Each school usually had only one teacher, who was solely responsible for all children from 4 to 13; occasionally one of the older pupils might help with

The past as prologue

the infants and sometimes a pupil-teacher was appointed. Thus in East Clandon school in February 1883 'Alice Grover, aged 13 years 11 months, commenced her duties as Teacher of the Infants' School' (which usually ran from 4 to 7 years of age). She was a local girl and probably got the same kind of salary as the pupil-teacher in Churt, who in 1870 was getting £10 a year.[23]

School attendances give some insight into village life. In the two decades after 1870, absences for work were particularly common. The East Clandon book records several such cases. In September 1874 when a new term was starting there were 'Many away, not finished harvesting and some working in the fields'; in July 1878 'attendance very bad, so many of the children having to assist their parents in the fields'. But the most basic feature is the way in which agriculture dominated the village to the extent that the peak seasons determined the opening times of the schools: in July 1881 'school kept open a week longer since the harvest was delayed for at least a week', and the summer holiday was usually called the Harvest Holiday. As late as 1909 George Bourne described how the long holidays in the schools south of Farnham were deferred until September since children were then engaged in hop-picking (despite the rapidly declining acreage).[24] Absences at harvest times were commonplace; children were also recorded as going blackberrying or 'wooding' (with their mothers, who reported them ill). In both Clandon and Horsley children also left school to coverbeat; in November 1880 the East Horsley record reads: 'attendance low as elder boys engaged coverbeating for shooting party at the Towers.' The record implies that this was not unusual and again the interests of school and squire were conflicting.

Gradually, the Depression removed the need for childlabour whilst legislation prevented it. The 1880 Act made the employer of any child between the ages of 10 and 13 liable to a penalty if the child had not got a certificate of education. This was not always sufficient deterrent: the East Clandon record complained in September 1885 that 'Charles Strudwick knows neither his age nor can he count up to 20; he seems so low in intellect that it will not be advisable to present him for examination'. Exactly two years later: 'Charles Strudwick absent since hand disabled in oil-cake machine.' This is the last reference to child labour in the village record books;[25] for the children, education gradually became more important than agriculture.[26] After the First World War, unlike almost every other part of England, the school holidays were no longer determined by harvest time and children were not required for agricultural work.

Harvests were not the only reason for absences. Attendance levels were often as low in winter as in summer because illness, often brought on by inadequate food and clothing (since the head of the household had priority), continually diminished the numbers. The diseases that recur most commonly in nineteenth-century record books are mainly those that have now almost disappeared, remaining only in the poorest urban areas: scarlet fever, diphtheria, whooping cough and measles. The district health officers were often not very helpful. In July 1883 Dr Smith visited East Clandon school to make enquiries about the scarlet fever: 'He did not venture inside the school room neither did he examine any of the children.' In time, the occurrence of epidemics declined as nutrition and health care improved, but between the wars there are references to verminous children and children with head lice, again problems that now tend to be confined to the poorest urban areas. In winter, wet weather coupled with the absence of boots also conspired to keep the numbers down.

When the schools were able to operate normally the curriculum was fairly rudimentary. Apart from religion, the main subjects listed in East Clandon in 1884 were arithmetic, English, music, reading and drill. Music was a new innovation. Taught by the Tonic Sol-Fa method the children in 1883 learnt three new songs: 'Four Jolly Smiths', 'Whistle and Hoe' and 'To the Tap of the Drum.' Country songs were still maintained in the schools but were no longer part of the life of the community. In geography, which was only a minor subject, it had already been observed in the record book that 'comparison with familiar things in the locality helps'. The infants were less fortunate; they had object lessons and the records for November 1883 include a lesson that was more complex than usual in referring to village occupations. These were 'ploughing and sowing, harvest, carpenter, blacksmith and builder'.

In these ways at least, education was related to village life. Yet it was not a preparation for it; indeed, for a long time it was merely a hindrance to farmers waiting for labour. The first reference to school activities that might have been in this sense useful comes paradoxically at a time when village agriculture was declining; the Horsley records for September 1905 refer to proposals for the establishment of school gardens, and in March 1906 the first practical lessons in gardening were given. Numeracy and literacy, on the other hand, if only exceptionally directly relevant to agricultural work, had a different kind of value. Even at the start of the nineteenth century the English village was plainly not a backwater totally insulated from knowledge and contact with the more dynamic sectors of society. Occasional village radicals provided vital links; the literacy and intellectualism of village shoemakers was proverbial.[27] Had they, too, been isolated the Captain Swing riots of 1830 would have been incomprehensible, as would the substantial stirring of dissent that followed Joseph Arch's organisation of an Agricultural Labourers Union in the mid-1870s.

The records dutifully record the children who left to start work, and even, in one case (June 1876), the departure of a child whose parents were emigrating to New Zealand. Nowhere until June 1922 is there a record of any child going on to higher education. Then, an East Horsley boy was awarded a Junior Technical Scholarship in Guildford. Just as most boys left to work in agriculture so most girls left to go into domestic service as agricultural work disappeared. Until at least the time of the First World War, domestic-service workers were plentiful in rural areas, despite many leaving to work in the cities. In most villages it was considered a privilege to have one's daughter working for the squire, and the rector and schoolmaster ranked not far behind. Indeed, the daughters of estate workers were expected to go into service on the estate; whole families became dependent on the fluctuating fortunes of a single master. Those who left for the cities were important points of contact with a completely new world, a world they were too often ill-equipped to deal with.

The past as prologue

Education was partly responsible for bringing this urban world, and even the world beyond Britain, into some relationship with the village, but the links were often tenuous. Beyond Britain was an alien world with which the Empire gave little point of contact; only the most significant events broke into the village curriculum. The East Clandon records for September 1904 read: 'Reference made to the Cairo and Cape Railway'; in the following year the death of Stanley was also thought worthy of note. Perhaps the most substantial change was a result of the possibilities offered by better communications. In July 1906 the record reads: 'School to be closed tomorrow for the first annual excursion to "Southsea", this outing as far as possible to be of an educational character.' On the following day with money raised from a school concert the children dutifully visited Portsmouth dockyard and other sources of enlightenment; it appears to have been most successful.

Equipment in the schools was rudimentary and what little there was had to be paid for by the children. East Clandon school in February 1886 'received 1 box of slate pencils and 2 doz. copy books. The latter are now to be charged at 2d. each.' It is scarcely surprising that there were considerable conflicts between parents, who could scarcely afford the school fees, and teachers, whose salaries were dependent on attendances and the inspectors' reports. On the other hand, the number of pupils in any of the village schools could never have been more than fifty until after the First World War, so some measure of individual attention was possible. This may have compensated for a narrow range of subjects; in May 1923 East Horsley school still had only thirty-four children, which was apparently insufficient for there to be either domestic economy or handicrafts. Moreover, village activities were closely related to school activities, and this might spill over to adjacent villages; 20 July 1882: 'Being West Clandon Flower Show and haying about a great many children are away this afternoon', whilst there was no school either on 4 July 1881, 'it being the Village Club Feast'. Not all relationships with the village were so pleasant. In September 1885 an East Clandon farmer, Mr Smallpiece, threatened children in the playground to stay off his land and had to be forcibly

The past as prologue

ejected by the headmaster. The vicar of East Horsley was giving the scripture lessons in 1919, and probably long after that, and in June 1906 a local resident, Major Norman, visited the school to inspect the drill. For a long time education was dominated by village society and, although children were ready to take their places in it when they left school, their real education was in the village-job situation.

Charity and the relief of need

Although the school records are unique in their ability to throw some light on the position of poor people in the parishes around the turn of the century, they nevertheless give little data on the extent of poverty and inequality within the village and only one other source is enlightening. On 30 January 1628, at the age of 78, Henry Smith, a Wandsworth silversmith, died. After building up a substantial business, he had given it up to become a beggar throughout the length and breadth of Surrey. At his death he left to the poor of all the market towns in the county a sum of £50 per annum and to each parish except Mitcham (where he had been whipped as a common vagrant by the inhabitants) he left £6 or £8 per year. This was to be distributed by the trustees, the local churchwardens. The capital was originally invested in land and the rents of this land (which in East Clandon in 1973 had risen to £90 per year) have been distributed annually for the relief of aged, poor or infirm people. Because of the size of this charity, when parish councils were established they usually took over as trustees and in central Surrey the parish councils have for some time administered it.

The earliest parish council minutes[28] give some idea of how this was done. In April 1895 in East Horsley the 'rector submitted a list of above 30 deserving people whose weekly wage did not amount to £1. It was resolved that they should each receive their proportion in either calico or flannel as had been the custom for the last thirty years, the amount to be given this year was £4. 13s.' In East Clandon, in the same year, the necessary qualifications are unclear but thirty-six people were given bread and groceries ranging in value from 2s 9d to 5s 6d (altogether £10 14s) from shops in the village;

in the following year clothing became a regular part of the charity there too. In 1901 there were thirty-one recipients for the charity, which then had a value of £14 6s and was given in 'bread and warm clothing', while in 1902 it was 'bread, flour and warm clothing' to a value of £21 18s. In East Horsley in 1910 there were twenty recipients, all of them listed and containing several names that are those of present residents. Between them they received 163 yards of calico (costing 6d per yard) and 17 yards of flannel (at 1s per yard). After that the council minutes no longer record the number of recipients but the structure of the charity remained the same until 1921 when the groceries and provisions were still obtained from East Clandon shops but clothing had to be purchased in Guildford. Urban shopping had started. By 1936 little had changed and 'it was resolved to distribute the Smith's Charity in the same manner and to the same persons as last year with the substitution of the name of Mrs. Jones for that of Mr. Godfrey....The clerk was instructed to see that the 10/- allotted to Mrs. Jones was spent on clothing or boots for the children.' It seems that poverty was entrenched among a small group of parishioners.

After the Second World War the administration of charity was beginning to become something of an embarrassment to some of the parish councils even if it remained of some value to the poorest parishioners. In 1971 in East Clandon nine vouchers for £9.50 and six for £3 were donated and one further change had occurred. The closure of the village shop meant that they had to be spent at Guildford Coop, which was the only shop that would deliver to East Clandon. In 1972 in West Clandon twenty-five vouchers for groceries were given to the value of £5 each; much was spent on coal. In some of the parishes it is now quite difficult to find 'deserving people', or more exactly, to differentiate between deserving and undeserving.[29] The councils are happy to leave the distribution in the hands of their own trustees, who in East Horsley contain the clerk, the vicar and the council chairman who are happy to rely on customary procedures, which invariably means that the vicar determines the recipients, now about fourteen or fifteen parishioners.

But Smith's Charity is far from the only one of local

importance; East Horsley, for example, has two other charities and only East Clandon seems to be dependent solely on Smith. Thus in East Horsley the Bishops Mead and Common Field charities are jointly administered and the same principles apply. In December 1896 'all persons in the village earning less than £1 per week in wages shall be recipients of Bishops Mead and Common Field Coal Charity' and receive at least one sack of coal. In 1910 there were eighteen recipients of £4 13s 8d worth of coal which meant that each could have 4 cwts; but by 1922 there was discrimination between the poor and the poorest—some received 4 cwts and others only 2 cwts. At the same time the trustees of the Smith's Charity gave some families 8 yards of calico and others 12 yards; unfortunately there is no way of determining how they then defined need.

The other charity, that covers both Horsleys, is Lady Noel Byron's Nursing Charity,[30] but since 1954 it has not been administered by the parish council and its present status is unknown. The first reference to it in the minutes of the council comes in March 1910 when the annual expenditure was given; the details are of some interest:

Expenditure		
	Nurse Marsh's salary	£70
	Rent of cottage	£14
	Nursing requisites	£2. 10s. 9d.
	Nurse's Cycle Repair	£2. 0s. 3d.

The nurse herself must have been only just above the charity level set for Smith's Charity and nor did her salary improve greatly in the following years. Somehow it had fallen to £69 7s in 1913 and to £65 in 1915. By 1916 it reached £70 again and in 1921 leapt to £125; from 1923 to 1933 it was £140 and in 1934 it was £145. Perhaps the trustees were diverted by the problems her bicycle faced; repairs of more than £2 in the single year 1910 were obviously excessive although in 1915 they reached £5 8s 3d. In 1929 she received a new cycle which, with repairs, cost £9 1s and in 1934 another, this time costing £11 10s. The low salary was not the only hazard of rural medicine—in 1929 she was 'laid up and suffering severely with a bad knee, caused by her bicycle being upset by a dog'.

The past as prologue

Even if the charities have now become anachronisms, in that they tend to supply wants rather than needs and have been bypassed by the welfare state, they were in the past a significant source of finance and health for the village poor. Food, representing possibly half a week's wages, was very valuable in the nineteenth century. George Bourne, writing of the Farnham area around 1910, concluded: 'all the calculations suggest that a majority perhaps of the labouring folk endure a less intense but chronic poverty, in which, at some point or other every day, the provision for bare physical need falls a little short.'[31] There is no reason to suppose that in central Surrey conditions were very different. Moreover, the charities helped to emphasise the church's role at the centre of the parish; they were a means of social control. It is not entirely coincidental that the role of the church and the role of parish charity have declined simultaneously. Villagers were not solely dependent on external sources of charity—rich landowners could be relied upon at particular times of the year, or at particular crisis points for their own employees, to assist in village welfare, and the villagers had their own benefit societies and clubs in which they could pay weekly or monthly instalments and be partially insured against illness or injury; the club, too, might organise an annual dinner and maintain a band. In 1880 the Blue Bell Inn, West Clandon, was converted into a working man's club which contained residential accommodation for thirteen men; the earl's estate could scarcely have justified these numbers much longer and indeed the earl closed the club, probably in 1884, when it became the Onslow Arms. Nevertheless by the turn of the century village welfare societies were disappearing as they gave way to national organisations such as the Ancient Order of Foresters. Control was moving away from the village and becoming more impersonal.

The emergence of parish councils

For much of the nineteenth century the territorial unit for most villages was the parish. It was a very real unit in the lives of the poor and for them it was an inescapable cage. Inside there was security; beyond they were at best tolerated foreigners, at worst deportable paupers. Hobsbawm and Rudé suggest that in the first half of the century the parish boundary was more important than the county boundary and much more important than the frontiers and shores of England.[32] But the parish was not the only unit in their lives; some labourers worked outside it, others married outside it. There were other links beyond to markets and hiring fairs, for example, but none of these gave the sense of place that came from the parish. Inevitably, society was parochial; there was no lack of interest in general affairs but priority was attached to one's neighbours and their affairs, kinship and family history, vestiges of which still remain in the local newspapers. Illiteracy tended to channel life inwards. The administrative centre was the parish church, and government of it was by a local committee of the rate-paying wealthier parishioners, who administered the parish, organised the maintenance of roads, and so on. The establishment of parish councils (and rural district councils) in 1894 did not end the age-old dominance of squire and clergy in village affairs; the civil functions of the vestry meeting were transferred to the parish council. For a long time afterwards the parish councils, as successors to the church council, retained a similar social composition and the introduction of formal democracy had little impact on the village, especially because of their limited power and financial resources.

In 1894 there were five candidates for election to the five places on East Horsley Parish Council; they were the rector, a solicitor, the Countess of Lovelace, a merchant of the manor, and a carpenter. The countess resigned in 1895, possibly in exasperation at the trivia that came to her attention, and her place was taken by a banker. The rector died in 1896 and to fill the vacancy the council considered that a Mr White of Forest House (whose occupation is never given) was 'a very eligible and fit person to submit for that office'. He was proposed, seconded and elected and the clerk was 'requested to inform him of that fact'. The council had what seems to be very much its token manual worker, and members could continue to select and re-elect themselves in an appropriate manner. However, by 1904 the new rector was on the council along with a vice-admiral and the carpenter had gone. When Lord Lovelace joined the council in 1906 in another fitful attempt at participation by the gentry, the council became even less representative of the parish. But there is no evidence that this was in any way resented; when Joseph Arch urged agricultural workers to take over their parish councils he could not then have been aware of what limited powers they would have. In 1913, when there was the first election for parish councillors, five of the six candidates received 4 votes and one received 3 votes. Participatory democracy had not taken a hold on the parish.

In West Clandon, lower-class participation seems to have been consistently more substantial. In 1896 when the first nominations are recorded five candidates were returned unopposed. They were a carpenter, a barrister, a bricklayer, a labourer and a grocer. In the following year the labourer had become an engine-driver whilst a timber merchant and the postmaster had taken the places of the carpenter and the barrister. Two years later the council consisted of the original bricklayer and grocer plus the schoolmaster and two 'gentlemen'. Between then and the First World War the composition continued to fluctuate. Councillors with such varied occupations as gardener, farmer, contractor, innkeeper and coal merchant came and went. These occupations were obviously not representative of the village structure but do indicate that there was a considerable range of occupations quite unrelated to agriculture and that the council consisted of a group of people, only a few of whom were dependent on the land. The vicar never joined the council but chaired the annual parish meeting which, just as in Horsley, was not well attended. The 1901 meeting must have been a particularly dismal affair: 'present Mr. Goacher [parish councillor] and G. Barnes [clerk]. After waiting an hour and a half and no-one else attending the meeting closed without any election or any business being done.' In 1919 the Countess of Onslow became the first member of the aristocracy and the first woman to sit on the council, but she stayed no more than two years. In 1946, when the occupations of the councillors were thought worthy of inclusion for the last time, the council consisted of a garage proprietor, a company director,

33

a builder and undertaker, a retired insurance official and the rector. At the same time, in East Clandon it consisted of a farmer, a farmer's wife, a gentleman, a retired civil servant and a land agent.

Although the range of occupations, which may then have been at its greatest[33] in the parishes, indicates that few parish councillors were directly involved in agriculture, it gives little indication of the range of activities in the village or the proportion of villagers that might have worked elsewhere. There were London railway commuters before the First World War but their influence is exaggerated by the rather vague letter from East Clandon PC in March 1908 to the Guildford postmaster complaining of the 'lateness of the morning delivery which does not reach the P.O. in the Village or thereabouts which is very inconvenient for persons wanting to catch early trains'. None the less there was in 1855 (and probably earlier) a daily return coach service from the Duke of Wellington (East Horsley) to London, leaving at 7.55 a.m. and returning at 8.00 p.m. Unfortunately the details have perished.

In November 1911 a letter from the manager of the Guildford labour-exchange asked East Clandon Council if it could assist by placing a weekly list of vacancies on the village noticeboard. Since the council went to the trouble of purchasing a board specially for this notice it must have considered the effort useful since there was then a high unemployment rate and men were often searching for work in the vicinity of the village. Apart from the train, which was expensive, public transport did not yet link the villages with any town, so that commuting far beyond the parish was in its infancy and was certainly restricted to the upper classes. One substantial change had, however, begun to remove the isolation of the working classes: the invention and introduction of the bicycle. Before its introduction countrymen travelled on foot and the heavy demands of agricultural work and inadequate food or boots effectively limited the usual range of contacts. The bicycle transformed this situation, although its history is unclear. Before 1885 cycling was a wholly middle-class and mainly urban activity and even then the cheapest new bicycle cost almost £10.[34] In the 1890s the use of bicycles by rural police and postmen became established and a secondhand market followed so that by the turn of the century a significant number of rural labourers owned bicycles. Work could thus be found at greater distances and, equally important, labourers could reach fairs and shops far beyond the village. Indeed, the most substantial impact of the bicycle may have been its role in encouraging courting and marriage across parish boundaries.

To understand the apathy with which most parishioners treated the affairs of the parish councils it is necessary to examine their workings in the first years of 'democracy'. Their limited powers restricted them to the affairs of the parish and these affairs were of the most trivial kind; the only positive activities were the maintenance and construction of footpaths, stiles, fences and hedges, the provision of adult education and administration of charity and the provision of lighting, although naturally the council attempted to influence decisions made elsewhere. The rapid turnover and despondency of most councillors, together with village apathy to their achievements, must have been a measure of the impotency that they thought should not have resulted from this devolution of government.

In its first six years of existence the East Clandon Council did little more than maintain the footpath to West Clandon and fence the recreation ground. Even these activities presented considerable problems. In July 1900 'it was proposed...that the Chairman, Joseph Linger, should write to Byron Noel, Esq. to obtain the consent of Lord Lovelace for the Parish Council to keep the footpath from East to West Clandon in repair by using flints on the Lane part as required and Ashes on the field part.' Two months later Noel replied that he would 'bring the matter to his Lordship as soon as possible'. Finally, two more months later, a letter was read giving consent. The council was to remain dependent on the earl—whose land it was—for some time; however, when the council asked him to increase the size of the recreation ground in 1906, no answer was received for two years. The pace of rural life was not to be hurried.

Of the activities the council could be involved in, the provision of adult education is perhaps the most interesting.

The past as prologue

East Horsley formed the somewhat grandiosely titled Technical Education Committee in 1895 which organised classes for men and women; unfortunately it is not until 1905 that these are listed. The approved subjects then were horticulture and carpentry for men and dress-making and home nursing for women. East Clandon was slower off the mark and it was not until January 1905 that the clerk was instructed to write to the clerk of the county council 'to obtain the necessary forms for holding Technical Lectures on Dressmaking, Cooking and Horticulture'. It is now too late to learn how often such lectures were held, who gave them and how useful they were for families who were almost certainly hampered more by poverty than by lack of expertise in any of these fields. The age of improvement disregarded these kinds of problem.

From time to time the outside world intruded into the affairs of the parish. At the start of 1897 the clerk to Surrey County Council wrote to each parish on the subject of the Indian famine; the letter no longer exists so his requests or suggestions are unknown. In any case East Clandon took no action although East Horsley decided to hold a church collection. In 1900 the county clerk sent another circular, this time on infant mortality, 'showing an alarming average of deaths per 1000...which drew remarks from the meeting [East Horsley] at such an unsatisfactory account of infant existence'. None of the parish councils felt it could assist on this problem. Medical attention was almost certainly inadequate since two years later the clerk to East Horsley Council had to write to the trustees of the Lady Byron Charity pointing out that the nearest qualified medical practitioner lived about four miles away from East and West Horsley, therefore asking if they could 'see their way to modify the present role with respect to cases of childbirth in such a way that the Nurse may be allowed to be called into attendance in all such cases'. There is no indication of the answer but infant mortality began to decline.

One further intrusion proved to be less desirable and that was traffic. The invention of the motor car soon resulted in the more wealthy country gentry taking pleasant spins through the uncrowded country lanes and it was not long before the villages resented their presence. East Horsley

The past as prologue

Council requested in 1903 that a speed limit of 10 mph be placed on the main road from Guildford to Epsom and in the same year East Clandon Council had put up warning boards at each end of the village. By 1907 the whole county had become alarmed at the rate of increase in traffic and Blechingley Parish Council had circulated a set of resolutions to all other councils; East and West Clandon at least were amongst those that endorsed the resolutions and forwarded them to the county council. They were:

> (1) That in this Council's view the development of motor traffic, with its attendant evils, calls for immediate attention
> (2) That urgent representation be made to the County Council and District Council asking them to take joint action to ensure:
> > (a) the limitation in speed in passing through villages and other populous places
> > (b) an increase in the amount payable for a motor licence and such a readjustment of the system as will ensure that the amount received for licences is available for the maintenance of the roads in such a condition as will enable the general public to use them with a moderate degree of safety and comfort.

Both parishes added to this their own requests for a speed limit of 10 mph within the village centres. In this and other ways the villages were becoming increasingly influenced by the world beyond. By 1911 the East Clandon Council opposed new road proposals since 'from an aesthetic point of view the Eastern approach to the village would be spoiled'.

Village social life

The benefit societies were probably the first organised societies within the villages but, towards the end of the nineteenth century, a number of recreational clubs was starting, implying that at least some villagers had the time, energy and cash to engage in new activities. (It would be wrong to think, however, that there was much affluence then, since the average wage rate of the ordinary male agricultural worker

The past as prologue

before the First World War was only 18s and until 1916 some workers were earning no more than 14s a week. Moreover, the cost of living rose almost in parallel.) There are no records of the dates when societies began but there seems to be a general pattern. East Clandon had a cricket club by 1897, since it then asked the parish council to provide a ground, and the other parishes almost certainly had clubs. The organisation of football clubs seems to have been more haphazard, probably because the wealthy villagers were unwilling to become associated with this particular form of physical activity (and therefore finance it). Fox-hunting and shooting were still popular with the wealthy, so that cricket was the main form of contact, outside the relationship of work, between rich and poor—so much so that in the Hertfordshire village of Little Munden, Pons describes the founding of the village cricket club as 'the beginning of the new or modern order in the life of the parish'.[35] In addition, the clubs had to look well beyond the parish boundaries to compile their fixture lists and, although there had been public houses in the villages from about 1830, it was the first time that social life escaped from the confines of the household.

More obviously, cultural activities followed a little later; the benefit societies had become working men's clubs but were no more than a benevolent version of the public-house system. West Clandon may have been exceptional in having a brass band in the 1870s but in 1877 there was a Merrow and West Clandon Gardeners' Show; since prizes were given for vegetables and flowers, honey, plain needlework, bread, copybooks, rustic baskets and collections of wild flowers, it seems that the show was far from being the preserve of the gentry. In East Horsley there was in 1908 a Smallholders and Allotments Association, and the village had a reading room before the First World War. Other villages may also have had libraries before then[36] but in East Horsley a formal lending library was not started until 1925.

It was a long time before the place of women was allowed to be outside the home, and the first reference to specifically women's activities in central Surrey comes in 1913 when a letter to West Horsley Council requested the use of the hall fortnightly 'for the purpose of giving some kind of recreation to the women of the village'. In 1914 another letter requested the use of the hall for dancing classes and in 1916 the Girl Guides were using it. Nurtured by the demands of war the first Women's Institute was founded in Wales in 1915, based on Canadian models, and the movement spread rapidly. In 1919 the East Horsley WI was founded and those in the other villages began at much the same time, heralding a new era in village affairs. The institutes lessened the isolation of village women and drew them into community life. Their life became richer and fuller and they learnt improved standards of health and diet.

Early Ordnance Survey maps show how village housing expanded between 1870 and 1919 (Map 2). For half a century there was only the slightest change in West Clandon as a few individuals' houses were built; in East Clandon there was no change. Indeed, the only substantial change, after years of discussion, had been the diversion of the main road which had run through the village centre, leaving it even quieter than before. Even so, in 1919 only five houses (apart from the two special groups at Snelgate Cottages and St Thomas's Cottages) that are there now, had not been built. Less than half a dozen houses were built in the half century to the end of the First World War. By 1897 in East Horsley the only visible effect of the railway was the construction of the Railway Hotel and a group of four railway houses close to the station, all of which were for railway employees. By 1919 there had been nothing more—not a single new house had been constructed. Similarly at Effingham Junction the only houses in 1919 were a cluster of five railway houses, whilst the path from the station to Effingham village had not yet been made up into a road. West Horsley, at a greater distance from a station, was likewise unaffected and although the population rose steadily between 1881 and 1921 this was largely independent of the railway. In that part of the parish north of the railway line (West Horsley North) eight houses were built on Ockham Road and three on East Lane during the whole period, but then it was only in the present century that the severe drainage problems that had prevented housing development on the London Clays were finally solved. In terms of housing development and population growth the

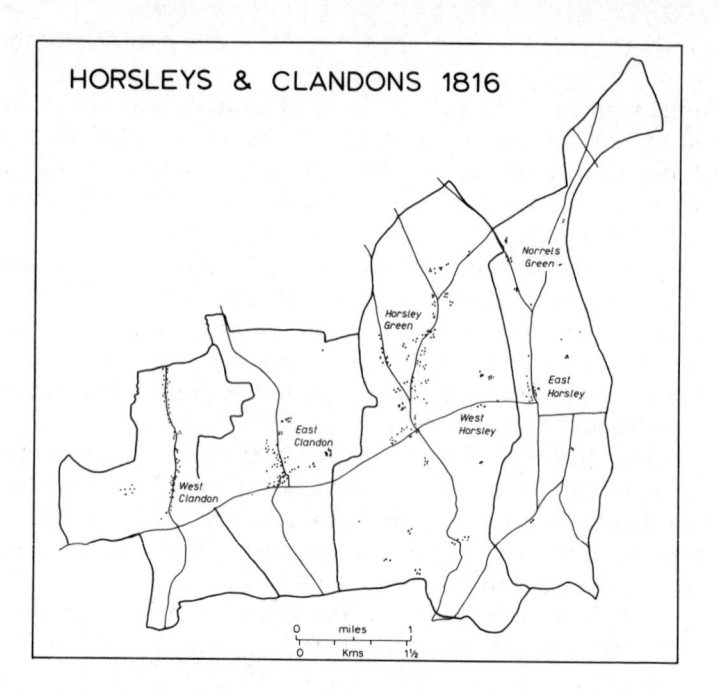

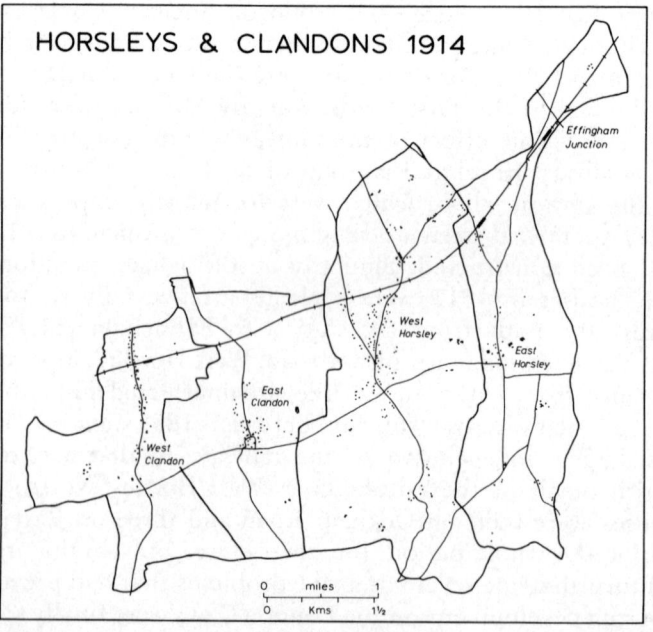

Map 2 Horsleys and Clandons, 1816-1970

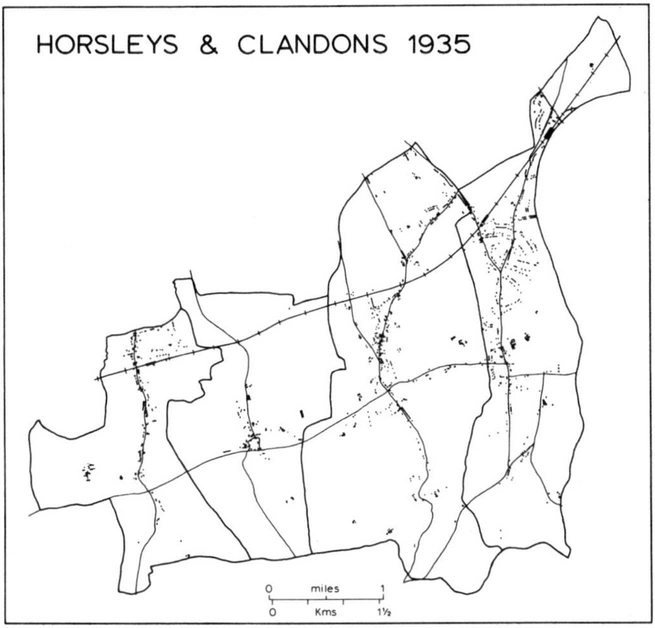
HORSLEYS & CLANDONS 1935
0 miles 1
0 Kms 1½

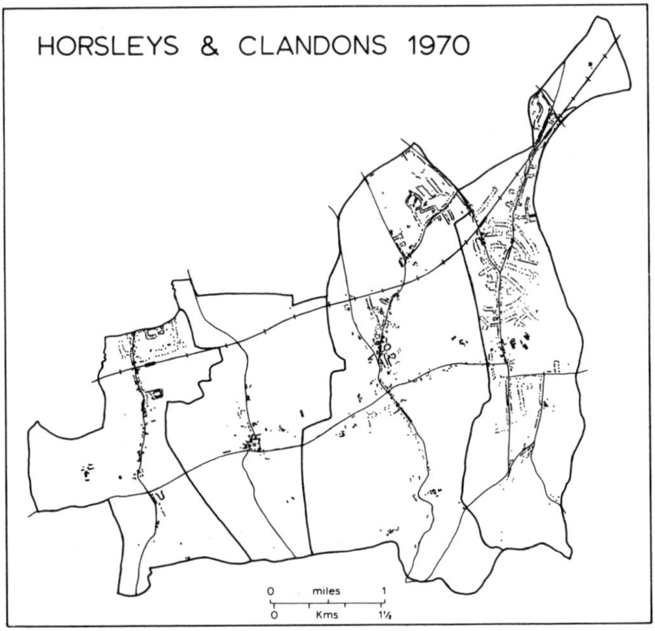
HORSLEYS & CLANDONS 1970
0 miles 1
0 Kms 1½

four parishes had almost completely failed to respond to national and regional changes; the insignificant growth that is attributable to external influences merely emphasises the rural nature of the four villages until the end of the First World War.

In many different ways the villages were coming into the sphere of influence of the towns. Increasingly their services were being provided from outside. In 1878, for example, telephones were connected to Clandon Park so that the gentry at least was in touch with the metropolis and in 1881 the Woking Water and Gas Company was formed and began to supply water to West Clandon and later to the Horsleys. About the turn of the century the Guildford Fire Brigade served all the villages; Ripley, which had its own brigade, competed with Guildford for the custom and therefore the funds of East Horsley parish, but was finally turned down in 1920 since it only had manual engines compared with the steam engines of Guildford. Men began to work outside the village and women shopped more often in the towns. There were always visitors to the villages; gypsies, tinkers and harvest labourers, often from Ireland, were familiar sights but the coming of the car brought different kinds of visitors. So, too, the village was becoming a part of the national sphere; national institutions were more obvious in the village. This was only part of a continuous process—even in the Middle Ages the nation taxed the village, made military levies and began to encroach upon the manorial courts. Later it brought the new religion of Protestantism, enclosed the village lands and introduced a post office and a school. Increasingly trade has brought from many parts of the world things that might be sold in the villages and has always been prepared to purchase the produce of village land. In 1884 the Representation of the People Act gave countrymen the vote and an increased interest in the relevance of national affairs; the parish councils gave them a start in democracy which, like most other influences such as public health, housing and education, filtered down, sometimes quite slowly, from the towns and cities. On the whole the villages have never been isolated in historic times and the fluctuations in their social and economic history have often been more a response to external than internal events; location has tended to influence social composition whilst the national economy has influenced the rise and fall of agriculture and the village economy.

For all that, in many people's eyes the Horsleys and Clandons around the time of the First World War remained excellent examples of untouched country villages. Morris, writing in 1926, describes 'East Clandon...whose aspect is singularly primitive and pleasing' and quotes a comment made on a part of East Horsley in 1878: 'In all my wanderings never have I seen in a civilised land such a deserted tract as this.'[37] As late as 1929 Home considered that East Clandon and West Clandon 'offer perfect backgrounds for pictures of ideal rustic life',[38] whilst according to Moul and Thompson in 1902 West Horsley was:[39]

> a village not yet prospected by that outpost of expanding London the builder. It is still one of the most typical and old-fashioned hamlets within easy reach of the metropolis. Half-way through the village is an old brick building still called THE WORKHOUSE, though now converted into cottages. Still it casts its reflection in the rural pond in front and still it bears an old-time look of comfort and protection.

Nevertheless in 1912 the parish council requested the rural district council to tar the main road through the village 'in accordance with other villages in the vicinity'. East Clandon was notably the least responsive to changes; in 1909: 'Everything in East Clandon is what it ought to be and everybody does what he ought to do',[40] whilst nearby Ockham, a mile north of Horsley station, was in 1900 'our little village... only 21 miles from Hyde Park Corner; it still remains what it was nearly a thousand years ago, a hamlet of oaks'.[41] Especially to those with perhaps a vested interest in the preservation of picturesque village society, the whole local area at the end of the First World War remained as it had been for decades, and the significant features of the villages were their rurality and their preservation from the alien influences of the capital. The changes that had gone on in the villages remained undetected in the superficial glances of visitors and tourists.

The First World War brought a new stage in the history of the parishes. In itself it resulted in several villagers joining the Services and experiencing a new range of social and economic conditions. The aircraft industries that the war fostered demanded labours of a new and well-paid kind and public motor transport at last emerged. Although the war encouraged change it can most usefully be regarded as a watershed between different patterns of rural life.

Perhaps the most significant of the inter-war changes was the continued social-welfare legislation which increasingly began to have an impact on the countryside. Some of this had preceded the war. In 1907 and 1908 Small Holdings Acts were passed nationally to enable parish councils to provide smallholdings (now allotments) for tenancy and purchase. In East Clandon, 'The Small Holdings Act was discussed and the letter read that had been written to the Board of Agriculture saying that as most of the people had large gardens and quite sufficient for the needs of tennants (*sic*), there were no Small Holdings required.' In this way, whether the letter reflected the real situation in East Clandon or, more probably, glossed over some local land shortage, the local decision was similar to that made by parish councils in most parts of the country. An Act that attempted to provide for agricultural labourers to have some subsistence production in their own hands met local opposition and was generally unsuccessful. This is the single most obvious example of how the local alliance of gentry, working through the parish council, could prevent the passing of a national measure that would have brought substantial relief to many rural areas.

One unusual development (especially in view of subsequent history) was the decision of East Clandon Council to erect a village lamp near the church in the village centre. In 1911 it was decided to raise the money for this by voluntary subscription; the cost came to 25s, of which 10s was donated by Lord Rendel and 5s by the council chairman, the Rev. A.P. Glyn. This early venture cannot have been very successful— perhaps paraffin proved too expensive, for in the December 1924 council meeting 'it was resolved that the lamp post be sawn off'. How long it operated and who benefited from it cannot be known. Possibly it would have been more useful in a different part of the village since in March 1912 'It was resolved that A. Mitchel be engaged at one pound to keep the footpath between East and West Clandon clear of cow droppings for one year.'

Indicative of the way in which the villages were beginning to share in the aspirations and culture of the cities and towns was the decline in country customs and manners. Just as the wooden plough had almost gone by the turn of the century so, too, had gone such rural industries as cider-making, copse-cutting, carting and thatching. Even in the most rural parts of Surrey other traditions had already perished: 'men and women wore a real country dress...more or less till near 1860, a date when much of the old traditions, in many different ways, was dying.'[42] Such dress had consisted of Sunday bonnets, pattens (sandals on a metal hoop to rise above the mud) and smocks. By the end of the nineteenth century many folk traditions had already been once revived; beating the parish bounds had gone but Maypole-dancing certainly existed again in West Clandon, at least at the end of the century. Already in many parts of England some villagers had become conscious that tradition required resuscitation if it was to survive even in artificial form. Rural ways were responding to urban and national demands.

Between two wars

After the First World War the history of central Surrey became set on a new course. A wave of new migrants reached the parishes and orientation towards London and other towns became an increasingly important fact of life for them and the established residents. The range of occupations continued to dwindle and agricultural land declined in area and importance. But although the changes could be summarised under the reasonably accurate title, 'the impact of urbanisation', few occurred at a single point in time; almost all were gradual, and sometimes almost imperceptible.

The most formal links came with the use of new transport modes and the spread of urban amenities. The gradual orientation towards the railway was not without its teething problems and East Clandon Council complained to the Guildford postmaster in June 1925: 'Since the parcel post has been conveyed by rail from Clandon Station instead of by pony and cart by road there as (*sic*) been constant complaints of the damage done to parcels which come in a broken or crushed condition and I should be glad to know what remedy you can propose.' But the roads were not always in good condition: in 1916 Silkmore Lane, West Horsley, was 'overgrown with bushes and impassable'. The parishes were only slowly coming to terms with rapid transportation.

Urban amenities continued to be absorbed into the countryside. Possibly the most substantial of these was mains electricity, which had reached West Clandon in 1921 and the other parishes at about the same time; it meant that the wireless, too, could arrive and increasingly lessen the isolation of the villages. Equally substantial was the arrival of village libraries. For example, in November 1925 the East Horsley village library was set up and the county librarian wrote to the parish council and 'promised to endeavour to supply about 100 good books to suit all classes'. Less than six months later, attention was drawn in the council to the difficulty experienced by working men in obtaining library books, because of the opening hours, and in 1926 the Men's Club took over the library. Despite their limited size, such village libraries were invaluable in helping to widen the horizons of the poorer villagers.

But not all urban amenities were welcome. The East Horsley Council discussed the problem of refuse disposal in February 1926 and decided it was unnecessary to collect refuse from houses since 'a fairly large area of land is attached to every house thus providing means of disposal of refuse'. However, by 1928 unsightly piles of rubbish were collecting and the council had to contract out monthly refuse collections at 2d per house on the basis of 250 occupied houses; indeed it was not until 1963 that the rural district council began regular weekly refuse collections in the district. Drainage, too, lagged behind and in February 1933 East Horsley and West Horsley councils objected strongly to any drainage scheme on the grounds of cost. During the whole of the inter-war period the parish councils dragged their heels whenever the threat of development emerged and, in this, they were rarely out of sympathy with the local electors. There were of course, minorities that desired change; at a 1933 village meeting to discuss the drainage scheme Frank Chown, in his capacity as a local government elector, stated that the parish council 'wanted Horsley to remain a rural district, but it was not possible. They had to move with the times and they were not far from London.' In the end he proved to be quite right. Sewerage operations began in 1937.

Despite the number and pace of these changes there is no doubt that many were little more than a veneer on what was still very much a rural area. In March 1920 a letter was read to the East and West Horsley councils from neighbouring Ockham, stating that during the past year a reward of 2s per dozen rats' tails was offered (compared with 1s in the previous year), with the result that they had received nearly 2,000 tails in the year compared with 600 in the previous year. Their co-operation, by offering a similar reward, was required. West Horsley agreed to pay the same sum but East Horsley, already perhaps conscious of a difference between the parishes, thought it was unnecessary because there were official county-council rat-catchers. Nevertheless in 1934 the East Horsley Council sent a letter to the county's Rat and Weed Inspector, requesting his assistance with weeds at White's Hill. Otherwise the parish-council minutes are unconcerned with the countryside in which, between the wars, agriculture changed little. In 1918 the minimum legal agricultural wage was 30s 6d but the wage rate for ordinary agricultural workers in Surrey was only 32s 3d for a 50-hour week in 1926;[43] during the Depression years it altered little. The façade of urbanism that new amenities could bring was still essentially marginal to the lives of agricultural workers; the difference was that their numbers and local importance were declining rapidly. Agriculture in the Home Counties declined substantially between the wars and the number of agricultural labourers diminished too, as agricultural wages improved little. Surrey wages in 1926 were 7d more than the national average; naturally many workers found urban jobs

The past as prologue

if they could. Those that could not or would not remained in poverty and until the 1930s 'girls, as they have always done, disappear into domestic service'.[44] Until then at least one-third of all houses had at least one domestic servant and many in central Surrey had several.

Perhaps the most substantial intrusion of all into the parishes was rural district council housing. Prior to the 1919 Act, however, it is clear that some parishes already had a very small number of houses which they were able to allocate to deserving tenants; for example, at the March 1915 East Clandon Council meeting: 'The Tenancies of the Year were put before the Council and passed.' Yet none of the parish councils was in any way enthusiastic about the new council housing for two main reasons: it was an intrusion (however small or justified) of mass-produced urban-type housing into rural areas, and they would not have any power to determine the occupants of the houses (and consequently the social composition of the parish). In 1918 the East Clandon Council met the rural district council and explained that four cottages would be sufficient but in 1926 the district council built twelve houses in the village. Throughout the detailed minutiae of the parish-council minutes of the 1920s and 1930s there is not one reference to these houses. The social composition of the council, and the social composition of the council houses, ensured that they remained beneath contempt. In East Clandon they were, and still are, out of sight and out of mind.

Other parish councils took a more active stand against the new housing; none liked the idea, but they were unable to substantially influence district council decisions. East Horsley Council received a letter in May 1928 from a resident in Longhurst Road,

> on behalf of a number of residents in the parish to protest against Council Houses being built opposite the Duke of Wellington Hotel. It was considered that the residents should have some control of
> (1) choice of site
> (2) design of buildings.

Their reasons for objection to the site were listed as:

(1) the inevitable fall in rateable value of the surrounding property
(2) detriment to the development of better class property
(3) the lowering of the general amenities of the district
(4) the subsequent depreciation in the value of the property of present house owners with its resultant heavy financial loss to them
(5) that a suitable alternative site could be found.

The council agreed 'that a copy of the letter be sent to the Guildford Rural District Council with the hearty support and approval of the East Horsley Parish Council'. This is possibly the first substantial objection to local planning decisions recorded locally; it set the tone for an increasing number of subsequent objections and, like them, it also failed. Wellington Cottages were built.

The parish councils had little control over how many houses were built or even where they were built; most decisions were determined by the general needs of the district and specifically the availability of land suitable for housing. However, in the inter-war period they retained the power to influence the allocation of these houses but even this was slipping away. In 1929 almost all East Horsley's recommendations were accepted but by 1939 the council had to request that the rural district council provide a list of those housing applicants who were *bona fide* workers in the parish. In 1924, at the start of the local-authority housing system, parishes were entitled to appoint two representatives to meet representatives of the district housing committee to select tenants for new houses being built in their parish. This was purely a concession that was not subsequently repeated, since in 1935 the rural district council was unwilling to give the West Horsley Council names of applicants for council cottages in West Horsley and in 1938, when the parish council attempted to recommend to the rural district council 'the names of eight applicants considered by the council to be the most suitable and deserving', it was informed that it could not do so. In the end applicants were interviewed and selected entirely by the rural district council. By 1945 the rural

The past as prologue

district council was reported to have instructed its members not to disclose any information as to the council's proposals for housing in the whole district. In 1947 the West Horsley Council was unable even to find out whether the houses then being built at Nightingale Avenue were for the council or for private disposal. It was still concerned over the selection of tenants and in October 1947 requested 'that the Parish Council should be asked to assist in selecting the tenants'. It was not asked, and so ended the last attempt by any of the parish councils to participate in housing provision and allocation. Another source of power had gone beyond the parish, and one group at least was pleased; as Scott, in his belatedly titled book *The Dying Peasant*, observed: 'the labourers can scarcely believe their good fortune when they find that the farmers have no say in the letting of the council cottages.'[45] The housing market had become wider and less subject to local influence.

Council housing was just one facet of the urbanisation of the area. Between the wars new housing estates were rapidly built in East Horsley and followed more slowly in West Clandon and West Horsley. In 1927 the East Horsley Council attempted to retain enough land for a recreation ground but the matter was left in abeyance and even Chown's draft scheme for a village green opposite the Duke of Wellington never reached fruition. Consequently East Horsley still has no public open space. Two years later the planning system had obviously moved into a higher gear: under the heading 'Town Planning in Rural Areas' the East Horsley minutes record a visit from members of the rural district council in which 'a coloured plan of the District was exhibited and explained' and Captain Jocelyn Bray, the Chairman of the RDC 'was confident the Parish Council would appreciate the efforts of the District Council in their endeavour to maintain the beauty and amenities of the district'. Unfortunately the 'coloured plan' no longer seems to exist.

There were other symptoms of urbanisation—continued requests were made for post times and train times to coincide with commuter movements. With the growth of population came new problems: traffic grew faster, noisier, more polluting and more dangerous. The newcomers were rich and the East

Horsley minutes of October 1930 record a spate of burglaries such that an extra constable had to be borrowed and it was 'agreed to seek information from the Chief Constable as to the steps to be taken by a Housholder if disturbed by a burglar'. (His reply is, unfortunately, not recorded.) There were other disturbing trends. In the same year the council complained about 'itinerant vendors' of ice-cream and Messrs Wall replied that instructions had been given to their salesmen to cease bell-ringing on East Horsley rounds. New shops were built at both ends of the parish despite solid objections from 'a large number of influential residents'. Indeed, from the late 1920s onwards the minutes continually record the grievances of 'influential residents' and there is little indication that the council ever took time to consider the needs of the local under-privileged.

Times were also changing in other ways. When the East Clandon Parish Council suggested a collection to mark the coronation of King George V in 1937 the vicar wrote to the council: 'It's no use your suggesting a collection inside the church as most of the people in the parish never pass through the front door.' Although he was, of course, a biased witness the churches were no longer the social centres of the parish and there was nothing to take their singular place; decisions were increasingly taken outside the parishes and recreation was increasingly found there also. It was no longer possible to insist that villagers take their regular place in church.

Post-war change

The same trends continued after the Second World War—the parishes continued to lose control of what little economic and social life was conducted within them and the parish councils continued to fight a rearguard action against the processes of development. The population grew more rapidly and each parish was swept into a quickening rate of change.

Inevitably vestiges of a rural life remained; in 1948 seating was provided under the West Horsley Village Oak but it was becoming difficult to maintain these symbols of a now departed village unity. There were no rural craftsmen available any more to do the odd maintenance jobs that the councils

The past as prologue

required, whilst in East Clandon it was impossible to keep the grass cut in the recreation ground—in the past villagers with horses had cut it for hay or let their animals graze there. In the decade after the Second World War the community life in the villages reached its last peak when Peace Celebrations occurred in each parish. In May 1945 in West Horsley, for example, there was a dance from 7 p.m. until 1 a.m. with music from the boys' club gramophone, a children's party, a fancy-dress parade and a bonfire in Glebe Meadow.

The coronation of June 1953 physically united each village for the last time. In each parish the celebrations took a slightly different form but in each the squire and his estate were at the centre of festivities. In West Horsley Sir Eric Bowater invited the entire village to Dene Place and a television was set up in the village hall;[46] some streets had their own coronation parties, notably the tiny council-housing estates of Farleys Close and Woodside. This is the last trace of community organisation in any of the local council estates. In East Horsley, predictably, the celebrations hit a slightly higher note; despite the balloon race and carnival the highlight was probably the open-air concert in the grounds of Horsley Towers, provided by the Nomad Players and Horsley Choral Society. If East Clandon's celebrations 'were not on so lavish a scale as in some other villages nowhere was there more enjoyment. Only a mere handful failed to turn out for the bumper tea which had been arranged.'[47] Later there was a fancy-dress competition and fireworks in the grounds of Hatchlands. West Clandon Council drew the following cheques to meet the costs of celebrations:

faggots for fire	£ 8		
fireworks	£41	4s	
grass seed for green	£ 8	6s	
hire of hall		12s	
pelmet		10s	6d
fixing flagpole and posts	£ 9		
flag	£ 1		4d
provisions for tea	£ 2	18s	1d
television aerial	£14		
printing	£ 3	15s	

The past as prologue

mugs	£16	3s	
oak tree	£ 1	2s	11d
post, phone, etc.	£ 3	9s	10d
	£110	1s	8d

Some other costs, especially for food, were met by the Women's Institute. It was the most expensive function ever organised by the parish. Everywhere the bonfires and dances in the grounds of the estates, and the televising of the ceremony, were the central attractions. Since then three things have happened: the local population has grown steadily, the squires have declined in number, wealth and importance and television sets are almost ubiquitous. No comparable celebrations occurred for the marriage of Princess Anne and the next coronation will not witness such celebrations in the streets or the parishes. Dramatic occasions no longer foster a sense of community.

The parish councils continued their struggle to maintain the local quality of life—not always successfully. In 1941 the chairman of West Horsley Parish Council was 'very distressed at the way young girls in the village were conducting themselves at the present time and felt that something should be done in the matter. It was agreed that the advice of a Moral Welfare Society be obtained.' In West Clandon the council protested in 1958 about the plot size for new housing at Woodstock, which 'was so small as to be entirely out of keeping with surrounding development'. More seriously in the same year the council organised a public meeting to protest against a county council proposal to convert the isolation hospital into a 'reception centre for tramps'. A year later the council was still concerned about the hospital—despite its being almost a mile from the nearest house—"not only over the menace which *would* be occasioned by any escapees but by reason too that the proposed new building would seriously contravene the metropolitan Green Belt proposals for the area on which the site is situated' (my italics). Nevertheless since the council proposed more suitable alternatives, namely a children's home, a convalescent home or a home for the aged, its objections were clearly against the character rather than the location of the residents. (It finally became a detention

The past as prologue

centre for juvenile delinquents.) Ironically, as the powers of the parish councils moved away their role reverted to what it had been some seventy-five years earlier. A concern for the beautification of the countryside and the concern of the council with flooded ditches, over-hanging trees, footpaths and rights of way gives the minutes an unjustified rural image. Yet most decisions are essentially superficial; what little economic powers the councils have had to shape the quality and structure of life in the parishes have been replaced by trivial cosmetic powers.

Some village social activities also declined. In 1952 the West Horsley Council noted falling attendances at the film shows and dances in the social hall. The former limped along at least until 1954 but probably not long after. But there were compensations: as social activities that could once have united the whole village declined so small groups emerged with specific interests to compete for village interest and support. The few remaining parish institutions declined or disappeared. West Clandon's village policeman retired in 1968 and was not replaced. East Clandon's primary school closed in July 1968, as East Horsley's had done a few years earlier, and in 1973 Clandon telephone numbers became Guildford telephone numbers. A year later a metropolitan district council emerged to take over from the rural district council.

For the past century East Clandon was, and still is, quite distinct. Until the 1960s it was an estate village and Maurice Wiggin has indicated vividly the extent to which the development of the village was controlled entirely by the squire, Harry Stuart Goodhart-Rendel of Hatchlands. Thus in 1950:[48]

> East Clandon under squire's aegis was still an almost feudal village. Not quite of course; the hairline cracks in the dam were just visible, modernity was seeping in: there were four cars and one television receiver. But by and large it was a village where time had stood still. Squire lived in the great house, Hatchlands, and though he didn't own the entire village he owned so much of it that his word was virtually law. I had thought our 'economic rent' very economical at £150 p.a., but when I realised that most of the cottages were let at rents of the order of 1s 6d

(7½ new pence) a week, some actually free, some half a crown (12½p) and so on, I began to see the light.

Wiggin observes how although the squire himself was not entirely opposed to change, his stepfather, who then lived with him, had replied in response to the suggestion that bathrooms and modern sanitation be installed in some of the cottages, 'Do the peasants really want bathrooms?', and it was his influence that ensured that the council houses stayed outside the village. Nevertheless there were very few changes. Maurice Wiggin and his wife were for a long time the only strangers to intrude into the village. 'The village consisted of three independent farmers with their satellites, and an Anglican (bachelor) rector...the squire and his household, and an extraordinary assortment of outworkers known as the estate staff, who looked after not only the big house, park and gardens, but all the dependent cottages.'[49] So it remained until 1961 when the squire died. At the same time Maurice Wiggin left the village having refused to pay £7,500 for his cottage, which in 1971 sold for some £18,250. Hatchlands became a superior girls' finishing school and, distinct only by distance, changes slowly became apparent within the village.

When Albert Bennett died at the age of 90 in West Clandon in 1972, the parish council 'received the news with great sadness. For many of the older residents he personified the village of West Clandon, which he served throughout his life both as a councillor and a garage owner. His death is the passing of an era.' But what was the era? Throughout the social and economic histories of English villages eras are always ending, usually at exactly the point where the author concludes his story. The past is different, always in some immeasurable way seemingly better than the present.

The 'organic community' was always dying. As George Bourne noted in 1912: 'in another ten years' time there will not be much left of the traditional life whose crumbling away I have been witnessing during the twenty years that are gone.'[50] He blamed the changes on enclosure and the decentralisation of an urban population. Lord Ernle, too, was not enthusiastic about the direction of change: 'medieval villages enjoyed a fullness of corporate and individual interest which, compared with today, is as a flowing river to a stagnant pond.'[51] Others, too, decried the changes[52] but often their accounts were sentimentalised, the retrospective views of people who had moved away from village life. Yet none of those who looked back on earlier, happier times ever satisfactorily pointed to a single period in history. In her detailed study of the Gloucestershire village of Bledington, M.K. Ashby suggests that there were two short periods of 'happy, realised sense of community': late in the fifteenth century and again towards the end of the nineteenth century, in both of which periods there were two shared characteristics—religious inspiration and popular enjoyment of art.[53] Yet these seem no more than brief times in which the social divisions were relatively few and a temporary unity prevailed; it is indeed possible to celebrate a feudal order but the community of peasants and landowners was often far from happy, especially for those at the bottom, where poverty was built into the expected order. Nevertheless the village community has always been a memory of the past and a hope for the future; in the January 1960 St Mary's parish magazine the vicar of West Horsley somewhat optimistically observed: 'The village of West Horsley has reached saturation point in its development. By the end of 1960 the parish should be pretty well established and will be able to settle down as a community with a community life.'

Green-Belt county

During the course of the twentieth century Surrey became inextricably tied to London, although never to quite the extent of Middlesex, which eventually disappeared completely. The erosion of its borders began with the creation of the London County Council in the nineteenth century and dramatically escalated in 1965 with the re-organisation of local government in London which turned several Surrey districts, including the centre of Surrey's own government, Kingston-upon-Thames, into new Greater London boroughs. A decade later Kingston remains the administrative 'centre' of Surrey; finance problems have prevented a possible move to Guildford.

The past as prologue

This gradual incorporation of country into city has rarely gone completely unchallenged although most challenges have proved to be ineffective. As early as 1580 a proclamation of Elizabeth I established a *cordon sanitaire* three miles wide around London in an attempt to limit the effects of plague, and no new building was allowed within that area. A further attempt to contain London was made by the Commonwealth Parliament in 1657 but it was not until the end of the nineteenth century that fresh plans for some sort of green belt began to emerge.[54] The feeling strengthened that it was essential to prevent the unrestrained growth of London; there was a need to preserve pleasant open spaces for recreation and for visual amenity.

In the inter-war years, in spite of the Depression, the south-east of England, together with London, continued to grow, and it grew in relation to the rest of the country by virtually whatever measure was used. The population grew faster, total employment rose and unemployment was less severe than in other parts of the country. Inevitably, concern was again felt over the growth of London. In 1924 the London County Council passed a resolution that called upon its town planning committee: 'to consider and report whether or not the preservation of a green belt...within the boundaries of or adjacent to Greater London is desirable and practicable and, if so, what steps can be taken to effect this.'[55] This was the first time that the term 'green belt' had been used although, once again, there was no significant response to the resolution.

Around London some counties were making progress on their own since they had substantial amounts of undeveloped land for which planning schemes could be drawn up under already existing legislation. Thus in the late 1920s there was already a number of small-scale regional plans covering most parts of Surrey. Most of these recommended routes for new roads; zoned land for agricultural, residential and industrial use; and designated proposed open spaces. Although these open spaces were intended to provide recreation and amenity they were also indirectly aimed at limiting London's growth. The Home Counties already had cause for concern.

In Surrey the first tentative regional plans were followed

by the acquisition of substantial tracts of land, following the Surrey County Council Act of 1931, by the county council (assisted both by the London County Council and by local district councils). In some areas control of development was exercised by voluntary schemes, such as the North Downs and Leith Hill planning schemes. In different ways some land was excluded from immediate development but it was clear that it would be difficult to preserve much of this land permanently; consequently the London County Council was forced to introduce a Bill which became, in due course, the Green Belt (London and Home Counties) Act 1938. For the first time the green-belt idea had legal backing.

After the Second World War the need for a continuous green belt, rather than the scattered patches that had previously been preserved, was recognised and the whole ideology of planning also changed. Instead of having to purchase land to preserve it the larger local authorities were given power to simply refuse development permission where it did not accord with their plans or wishes. This apparently minor provision of the 1947 Town and Country Planning Act, the basis of post-war planning, was the start of the effective establishment of the London green belt. Like the other Home Counties Surrey then began a period of extensive surveying and by 1958 when the Surrey County Development Plan was approved a wide area of the county, loosely defined as a stretch of land fifteen miles across at its widest point, extending from Woking and Guildford eastwards across the county to Redhill, became part of the Metropolitan Green Belt. This was an enormous stride forward from the scatter of copses and meadows that had previously been protected; only the remotest parts of the county, south of the North Downs, were excluded from the Green Belt. A period of rigorous control had begun.

Green-Belt legislation was so effective in controlling unscheduled development throughout the South East that most counties were continuously pressing to extend the area of their sections of the Green Belt. After more than a decade of uncertainty, whilst different governments made their own appraisals of the policy, these proposed extensions were finally improved in 1973 so that the Green Belt now covers

The past as prologue

virtually the whole county. Moreover, even those small areas that are excluded from the official limits of the Green Belt are still regarded by the county council as a part of the belt and effective legislation now covers the whole county.[56] Surrey is an entirely Green Belt county. In the history of British planning no other planning issue has received the same degree of general acceptance simultaneously coupled with enormous pressure upon it. With the current population stability of Greater London the future of the Green Belt is assured; in Surrey, at least, it has become sacrosanct. The Horsleys and Clandons are apparently insured against physical change.

CHAPTER 3

Contemporary countryside

Merridale is one of those corners of Surrey where the inhabitants wage a relentless battle against the stigma of suburbia. Trees, fertilized and cajoled into being in every front garden, half obscure the poky 'character dwellings' which crouch behind them. The rusticity of the environment is enhanced by the wooden owls that keep guard over the names of the houses, and by crumbling dwarfs indefatigably poised over goldfish ponds. The inhabitants of Merridale Lane do not paint their dwarfs, suspecting this to be a suburban vice, nor, for the same reason, do they varnish the owls; but wait patiently for the years to endow these treasures with an appearance of weathered antiquity, until one day even the beams in the garage may boast of beetle and woodworm.

John le Carré, *Call for the Dead*

Before the end of the First World War the villagers of central Surrey were largely employed within their own parishes, with a high proportion working in agriculture. After the war there was a further agricultural decline and, at the same time, the start of the influx of population. Local employment opportunities rapidly became relevant only to a small proportion of local workers, whereas regional economic growth became crucial. After two decades of near stagnation economic expansion began in the South East in the 1920s and between

1921 and 1951 three-quarters of the net increase in employment in England and Wales took place in the South East,[1] where the so-called 'growth industries' were heavily concentrated. Industry first moved into the London suburbs on a substantial scale in 1920, mainly to the north and west so that even in 1960 southern Surrey (and Kent) were rural backwaters on the wrong side of London for the bulk of the national market. Before the Second World War, despite some movement to Guildford and other towns in the Home Counties, economic development in the South East was still largely concentrated in a restricted area within fifteen miles of Charing Cross.

The rapid rate of growth since 1951 in areas between ten and thirty miles from central London may partly be attributed to the effect of the decentralisation of firms from central London. Surrey was exceptionally popular for this kind of short-distance move because of its good road and rail connections with London. Apart from offices and industries a substantial employer was the University of Surrey, which during the late 1960s gradually moved from Battersea to Guildford. Despite this kind of decentralisation, which generated a considerable increase in local employment, at the end of the decade half the total employment in the South East was still in Greater London. The major manufacturing industries of central Surrey were established early, the two large transport industries, the British Aviation Corporation (Weybridge) and Dennis Brothers (Guildford), being there from before the First World War. However, the majority of local industry is composed of small, often component industries using a minimum of raw materials and depending on a skilled labour force. Consequently, the only industry in Surrey that has a significant labour catchment area more than ten miles in radius is the British Aviation Corporation, because of its large size and its requirement for large numbers of skilled technical workers.

In the four parishes of central Surrey there is almost no local employment. In 1964, when it was last officially recorded, there were only five employers with a labour force of more than 20: the Central Electricity Generating Board, East Horsley (72), which is exceptional since it consists of

Contemporary countryside

trainees from many parts of Surrey temporarily resident in Horsley Towers; a garage (26); two builders (32 and 20) and one school (22). There were sixteen other units employing five or more persons and almost all of these were farms or shops. The situation was much the same a decade later; moreover, the immediate employment of the area is declining and is insufficient to cater for more than a tiny fraction of the local labour force, and since a high proportion of this is in shops most of the local jobs are for females. Symptomatic of these changes is that before the Second World War the parish councils employed labour—West Horsley, for example, had a full-time joiner. None does so now. By 1971 both East and West Horsley had only 27 per cent of their work force working inside the whole rural district; West Clandon had 43 per cent and East Clandon, continuing to differ, had 60 per cent.[2] Gradually, but especially since the First World War, the whole of central Surrey has become part of a much wider regional labour market and less of a purely local system. New residents in the district are quite unlikely to work there.

The employment situation in the parishes during the period 1961–71 is summarised in Tables 3.1 and 3.2. For the four parishes agricultural employment has almost disappeared, being only 5 per cent of total employment in 1961 and less than that (3·5 per cent) in 1971—even lower than the national average. Production (or manufacturing) employment is generally concentrated in urban areas and only a

Table 3.1 Occupational groups, 1961

		Agriculture	Mining	Production	Services	Defence	
East	M	1	—	—	4	—	7
Clandon	F	—	—	—	2	—	
West	M	3	—	12	24	1	51
Clandon	F	2	—	1	8	—	
East	M	2	1	36	62	2	150
Horsley	F	1	—	14	32	—	
West	M	5	—	32	39	1	109
Horsley	F	2	—	3	26	1	
		16	1	98	197	5	317

Source: 1961 Census, Scale 'D' Returns (10% sample).

Table 3.2 Occupational groups, 1971

	Agriculture	Mining	Production	Services	Defence & government	Transport	
East Clandon	1	–	1	3	1	–	6
West Clandon	2	–	11	30	3	2	48
East Horsley	1	1	33	119	22	10	186
West Horsley	8	–	29	71	16	8	132
	12	1	74	223	42	20	372

Source: 1971 Census, E.D. Returns (10% sample).

third of the local employed population is involved in manufacturing. Service employment such as banking and accounting is much the most important section, covering more than half the total employment and two-thirds of all female employment, whilst all the parishes contain twice as much employment in services as in manufacturing. Service employment is much the most rapidly expanding category and most of this group work outside the parishes. At the same time as office employment has increased so the historic variety of Surrey industry has steadily declined. Because of assumed economies of scale there are no longer any small breweries left in Surrey; amalgamations and closures have removed many companies, including the famous Lagonda car manufacturers, whilst gunpowder is no longer made in the Tillingbourne Valley and woad no longer grown in the Wey Valley.

Local variations in the pattern of employment are more clearly visible from the distribution of socio-economic groups (Tables 3.3 and 3.4). The Census information is organised into six broad categories of socio-economic status, ranging from professional workers through managers and the semi-skilled to unskilled manual workers and the armed forces. Professional workers, managers and employers represented 38 per cent of the population in 1971; in East Horsley 44 per cent of the employed population came into this category, much the highest proportion in any parish. Conversely for the groups at the other end of the scale–

Contemporary countryside

Table 3.3 Socio-economic groups, 1961

	East Clandon	West Clandon	East Horsley	West Horsley	
3.4 Professional workers	2	1	13	6	22
1.2.13 Employers and managers	–	14	50	19	83
8.9.12.14 Foremen, skilled manual workers	3	13	8	20	44
5.6 Non-manual workers	1	8	31	26	66
7.10.15 Semi-skilled manual workers	2	6	6	11	25
11.16.17 Unskilled manual workers, armed forces and others	2	5	10	8	25
All	10	47	118	90	265

Source: 1961 Census, Scale 'D' Returns (10% sample).

Table 3.4 Socio-economic groups, 1971

	East Clandon	West Clandon	East Horsley	West Horsley	
3.4 Professional workers	–	2	27	12	41
1.2.13 Employers and managers	1	9	45	31	86
8.9.12.14 Foremen, skilled manual workers	–	10	19	18	47
5.6 Non-manual workers	3	8	55	33	99
7.10.15 Semi-skilled manual workers	1	13	10	15	39
11 Unskilled manual workers	–	1	3	4	8
16.17 Armed forces and others	–	–	5	6	11
All	5	43	164	119	331

Source: 1971 Census, E.D. Returns (10% sample).

agricultural workers, the armed forces, workers in personal services and the unskilled (Groups 7.10.15.11.16.17)—East Horsley has rather less than the other parishes. The same general patterns are distinguished in the experimental 1966 social-class data (Table 3.5), with the slight distinction that West Clandon appears closer to East Horsley at the upper end of the social-class spectrum. Almost half of all household

Table 3.5 Social-class groups, 1966

Social class	1	2	3	4	5	Unclassified
East Clandon	–	1	2	2	–	–
West Clandon	4	15	10	8	3	1
East Horsley	19	61	30	8	–	8
West Horsley	9	17	47	15	1	3

Key
1. Professional, etc., occupations
2. Intermediate occupations
3. Skilled occupations
4. Semi-skilled occupations
5. Unskilled occupations

(Cf. Census 1966, *Classification of Occupations*, pp. 130-7.)

Source: 1966 Census, Scale 'D' Returns (10% sample).

heads are in social classes 1 and 2, the professional and intermediate occupations. Unfortunately none of this can be placed in a historical context; how long this may have been true and how fast it is changing is unknown.

The definitions employed in the Census are never totally satisfactory groupings; the range of categories involved in differentiating social groups at different times and in different places is almost infinite. Nevertheless the exercise is unavoidable.[3]

> We can't help putting people into categories; we see this as the only practical way of managing human relationships, because to grasp all the complexities and contradictions of all, or even several of the people we know, would make life too difficult. We even put ourselves into categories; we invent ourselves, and then use this invented self as a working hypothesis to cover the facts of our lives.

Here, the simple expedient of adopting the Census classification of social classes, based primarily on occupational differences and made in the belief that 'each category is homogeneous in relation to the basic criterion of the general standing within the community of the occupations concerned',[4] has been used. It is quite crude (yet so are several stated occupations) but it has some value in enabling a classification of migrants. Overall it provides a useful comparative framework but is an inadequate classificatory system. Since it is obviously unjustifiable to equate styles of life with either occupation or income, in some cases a separate distinction has also been made between the two main housing classes: 'owner-occupiers' and 'council-house tenants'. Occasionally, too, 'middle class' is also used, mainly for comparative purposes, and always, in the usual paradoxical way, referring to an amalgam of the official social classes 1 and 2. It would be unwise to make too much of these divisions; indeed, as Karl Marx himself pointed out in *Capital* more than a hundred years ago, in the class structure of England 'middle and transition stages obliterate even here all definite boundaries'.[5]

Agriculture

Conspicuously visible in central Surrey is the agricultural economy, yet agriculture has generally fared badly in the twentieth century. Until the Second World War the decline in arable land in Surrey, which had started in the nineteenth century, continued but was not always accompanied by a proportionate increase in permanent grassland. The quality of the pasture land was also declining and it supported fewer animals in the 1930s than it had in 1900. The Second World War altered the degeneration: the amount of arable land expanded rapidly under the plough-up campaign, even on the heavy London clays, and, after the war, continued to increase in some areas whilst improved and intensified animal management allowed an increasing number of animals on a declining acreage. In the mid-1940s as a result of the war the agricultural labour force actually reached its highest figure this century. Nevertheless two-thirds of the total farm area of Surrey is in grass; most farms have advanced technical apparatus, and modern methods are being adopted rapidly on expensive land. In the last decade many farmers have given up milk-production and switched over to beef and arable crops, further reducing their labour force. Those whose farms are most suited to dairying have found it necessary to increase their herds to more than 100 in many cases, injecting a considerable amount of expensive capital and equipment to keep them viable. Consequently the local farm worker is increasingly a skilled technician.

Contemporary countryside

There has been no marked decline in the total agricultural acreage since the end of the Second World War and in the case of West Horsley there has been a large increase. At the parish level conversions of good agricultural land to housing land are negligible; most land for housing has come from areas of rough grazing within the village boundaries that have been most likely to receive planning permission and most likely to be converted. Farming in these few confined areas has been 'farming to quit',[6] whence agricultural improvements have not been made because it is assumed that the land will soon be developed for housing. Outside these areas crop acreages have actually increased since the Second World War as the apparent permanence of Green Belt policy has severely reduced the probability of planning permission ever being granted for other than a very limited number of obvious locations. Despite this the Surrey branch of the National Farmers' Union remains alarmist:[7]

> it would be true to say that in ten or fifteen years time the amount of agricultural land from a line drawn from Aldershot through Guildford, Dorking, Reigate and Oxted northwards, will become a mass of south orbital roads and future developments. . .it has been suggested that the southern part of Surrey could well become a rather large lavatory as it is situated at a convenient (*sic*) spot when travelling out of or into London.

Yet since the Second World War there has actually been a significant increase in acreages under wheat and barley in all four parishes and to a smaller extent this is also true for vegetables and horticultural crops. In most areas, away from village centres, there has been a considerable intensification of agricultural production and, far from 'farming to quit', farmers are investing substantially in mechanical aids to enable reasonable profits on high-cost land.

The most significant post-war agricultural changes are not, however, in acreages and crops but in organisation and management. The South East had the fewest agricultural workers per hundred employed persons in 1951 and this proportion continued to decline in the next two decades so that the parishes now have a total of only 94 farm workers, a figure which includes absentee owners and part-time workers. As early as 1911 the Ministry of Agriculture found that the percentage of holdings actually 'farmed for business' as opposed to pleasure was lowest in the South East, with Surrey having the lowest proportion of any county, a position which has subsequently been maintained. Many of the Surrey hobby farmers previously farmed at a loss[8] and some of the most neglected farms were found to have changed hands every two years or so after being held temporarily to gain the benefit of remission of estate duty. Moreover, the introduction of salaried farm managers and modern technology has tended to result in rapidly improved agriculture, often of highly specialised kinds such as pedigree cattle. The ending of remission on estate duty in 1969, at least temporarily, has slowed the growth in numbers of hobby farmers but has produced a different kind of social change: individuals buy farms but do not farm the land themselves, hiring it out instead to adjoining or nearby farmers. Indeed, Owen Silver found that in the adjoining parishes of Effingham and Abinger all but two of the remaining farms had their original farmhouses as private houses with the land let off.[9] The farmhouse has become a home and not the centre of a farm.

Thus agriculture within the four parishes, and probably within other parts of the Green Belt, too, is economically successful and this success is almost entirely a result of the permanence of the Green Belt. The agricultural landscape is more or less maintained, with only slight changes in crop combinations; the only visible change is the now complete substitution of machinery for horses. Coppices and hedges, in the way of mechanised agriculture, are zealously guarded by the village preservation societies.

With the decline of agriculture has also gone the associations of agriculture; there was until recently perhaps one horse and cart in central Surrey, maintained in a gesture of defiance by one of the oldest residents in East Horsley, but farm horses generally have gone. In 1897 there were well in excess of 10,000 horses in use in Surrey agriculture, in 1947 there were 2,112, and in 1958, the last year that the Ministry of Agriculture bothered to collect these figures, there were a mere 459.[10] Hay meadows and wild flowers disappeared with them;

more than forty plant species have become extinct in Surrey in the past century.[11] Gone, too, are the blacksmiths, but The Forge, East Clandon, makes a distinctive home. The stable agricultural acreages make it possible to claim that agriculture is still an important component of the local scene, yet it is essentially marginal: there are few farm labourers, the agricultural production is almost entirely for a national market and the major local significance of agriculture is environmental. At least the claim can be made.

Modern housing

1 East Horsley

Until shortly before the First World War almost all of East Horsley was part of the Lovelace Estate, which also covered parts of adjoining parishes, including Ockham, Effingham and Abinger. In 1906 the third Earl of Lovelace sold the estate to Mr T.O.M. Sopwith (of the Sopwith Aircraft Company) and shortly after the war, in 1920, he in turn sold it off. Only two pieces of land close to the station were not sold at this time, having already been detached from the estate, but the rest of East Horsley was still part of the Lovelace Estate.

Until the First World War both the restrictive policy of the earl, but more particularly the distance of East Horsley from London, had prevented its break-up for residential development. The profit would not have been very great in any case since between 1850 and 1914 land values scarcely changed in the rural fringe of London. Hence, in the absence of planning restrictions elsewhere, there was no demand for housing for other than aesthetic reasons at this distance from London.

Apart from regional and national changes after the First World War, such as the rapid growth of London and the rise in real wages, two local changes were of great significance. These were the break-up of the Lovelace Estate following its sale in 1920, and the electrification of the railway in 1925. Details of the sale of individual parts of the estate are not all known but the property was described in the sales catalogue as 'an important country seat. Together with practically the whole of the village of East Horsley'.[12] The total area was

2,085 acres and there were 45 lots of which the largest was the 414 acres of Horsley Towers Park itself. Lot 45 consisted of a railway siding at Horsley Station 'for the sole use of the Earl of Lovelace, his heirs and successors'. It has long been disused. The estate fell into various hands and land came on the market at intervals after the initial sale. By the time that Manor and Place farms came on the market in 1925 the land was no longer offered in large units, as in the Lovelace sale, but was in lots ranging from 3 to 0·7 acres, which were sold for prices between £100 and £300. They were catalogued as 'excellent sites for the erection of good class houses.'[13] Some land was still available for purchase after the Lovelace sale but its potentialities for housing were obviously soon recognised and even in the inter-war years the rural district council had some difficulty in obtaining sufficient land for the erection of council houses.

The major benefactor from all the sales of land was Frank Chown, a local architect and surveyor, who managed to buy the majority of the lots from the Lovelace Estate. Furthermore he bought almost all the plots between the station and Guildford Road but bought very few plots elsewhere; all these sites were the most immediately suitable for housing development. Lots where old village houses already stood were largely bought by their owners, where those owners had the means; Horsley Towers itself was sold to the Misses Maufe and Isaacson, who ran it as a 'high class ladies' school' until it was sold in 1936 to the Electricity Board. The housing development that followed the estate break-up in East Horsley was heavily dependent on Chown's use of his land and, in particular, upon the restrictive covenants he imposed on housing layout and style (and which are still partially maintained). The decisions of one man have been the major influence on the historical development of East Horsley.

There were actually three 'groups' of developers: Chown himself, Horsley Estates Ltd and Mr J. B. Bower. Chown opened two estate offices at Guildford Lodge and Horsley Station and, through two groups of builders, built direct to his own plans and layout. Horsley Estates Ltd was a separate company but one of the directors was Chown and there were probably no more than two other directors. Bower obtained land from Chown and built houses initially through a Hampshire builder—Meech—and subsequently through Burbridge Builders. His proudest boast, which could equally be applied to Chown, was that he never built two houses alike. Effectively the three groups were one, since Chown and Bower worked closely together to prevent what they regarded as 'jerry-builders' buying land to put up houses of inferior quality. Further, apart from the basic network of roads (Ockham Road, Forest Road, Epsom Road, Green Dene and Chalk Lane), all the present service roads, most of which are culs-de-sac, were also constructed by firms working for Chown. Where Chown did not own all the land the old field boundaries are maintained in the housing layout; no roads cross the field and lot boundaries of the Lovelace Estate.

Housing developments started in the mid-1920s; Chown was responsible at least for The Warren, Pine Walk, Farm Lane, Woodland Drive, Nightingale Road, Hooke Road (part) and Cobham Way. Bower's first development was Pennymead Drive and Lynx Hill, followed by Glendene Avenue, High Park Avenue, Highfields, Oakwood Drive and The Highlands. The first houses on Bower's estates at Pennymead Drive, Lynx Hill, Glendene Avenue and The Highlands, all of which were detached, and many thatched, were advertised probably around 1926 at prices ranging from £1,250 to £3,000, including a plot of a quarter of an acre, and with 'each house different in elevation'.[14] Equally important, times and prices of trains to Waterloo and the advantage of a late train back were stressed as advantages. Burbridge Builders pointed out that it would be 'a large sum of money spent with wisdom and forethought'.[15] The time to develop had been chosen well: throughout the 1930s the health value of a house in the suburbs was repeatedly stressed and the wooded slopes of the Horsleys and Clandons were ideal. Not far away, for example, Costains were pioneering large-scale estate development at Selsdon Heights and advertising the attractions as:[16]

> the highest home centre within easy reach of the metropolis, 500 feet above sea level, free from fog and dampness. When neighbouring lowlands are shrouded in mist, the

Contemporary countryside

> Selsdon Heights stand out in clear, brilliant air...chesty people find new relief on this naturally drained chalk soil.

Chown set certain conditions on the housing developments but it is no longer clear what these were; only garbled versions remain. The restrictive covenants known to exist were that he wanted his own roads to remain as private roads for the sole use of the residents; no house could be below a certain size and no huts were allowed to be built in the house gardens. Since Bower acceded to these policies they were virtually universal for the whole of East Horsley. Moreover, the legal situation remains such that changes to the first and last clauses can only be made by reference to Chown's executors; consequently most of the culs-de-sac in East Horsley are private roads and are not maintained by the rural district council. Nor are there many garden huts. The present legal legacy is unimportant compared with its historical effect in restricting the kinds of houses built to those of a type and cost that could only be afforded by very affluent commuters. Even more important, the large extent of Chown-inspired construction determined the future residential character of the parish. None of the other three parishes was developed with the single-mindedness of Frank Chown; none has quite the same exclusive residential character.

There was no conception of overall planning for East Horsley despite the detailed consideration of individual roads and houses. Development was largely piecemeal as individual fields were released on to the housing market, whilst there was no need, and indeed a positive desire not, to cater for through traffic—hence all the roads are either private roads and/or culs-de-sac. No shops were built since it was Chown's intention that East Horsley be entirely residential, and until after the Second World War there were only two old-established village shops in East Horsley. If shops were unwanted, anything larger was anathema. Hence when a cinema was proposed for nearby Claygate it was coyly justified as a means of putting the housewife 'on equal terms with the housewife of more urban localities in the matter of securing the domestic treasure of which she dreams'.[17] In this sense, at least, development was extremely unbalanced, favouring high-quality, low-density residential development at the expense of everything else. In the absence of effective planning legislation the concentration of the power to make decisions was almost solely in the hands of a single individual. This influence was clear and unequivocal, producing a remarkably homogeneous layout over a potentially, and previously, varied landscape.

2 West Horsley, East Clandon and West Clandon

The inter-war period in the history of housing in East Horsley has been documented more fully because of its greater size, because of the remarkable planned homogeneity of high-status development, and because of the greater availability of information following the break-up of the Lovelace Estate. Both East Clandon and West Horsley had a different recent historical evolution because of their distance from a station, whilst the relevant information on the break-up and sale of estates in West Clandon cannot be traced.

In 1888 the Hatchlands Estate was sold, described in the sales catalogue as 'nearly the whole of the villages of East Clandon and West Horsley'.[18] Also part of the estate were two pieces of land in West Clandon, south of the Guildford Road. Despite the distance of this land from the railway station, Britain's Farm, West Horsley, was described as 'near the railway station of that name', whilst the value of Horsley Station was further stressed: 'Not only does the Estate possess a high Prospective Value for development as a Residential Property but an increased Agricultural Value has been thus acquired by reason of the better facilities for the transit of produce & c.'[19] There was not then even the prospect of residential building; the only prospective development was of the house itself and the agriculture associated with it.

In the inter-war period West Clandon developed in the same way as East Horsley, with similar housing styles but with little growth away from the railway station. It is probable that this was not only a result of its greater distance from London but was primarily a result of much potential residential land remaining in the ownership of large landowners

Contemporary countryside

(especially the Earl of Onslow) who were uninterested in profiting from the sale of land for residential development but would, in any case, have been in competition with the attractive new housing in East Horsley. Because of their distance from the railway East Clandon and most of West Horsley were not subject to this kind of residential development. They grew slowly in the inter-war period and, when more rapid growth might have been expected to occur, were restricted by the imposition of Green Belt regulations following the Second World War. Nevertheless by 1930 the parish councils of both the Horsleys were concerned over the standard if not the amount of building around their villages. One parish councillor in West Horsley suggested that '...they should register a protest against the erection of any poor kind of building in the parish'.[20]

West Horsley north of the railway was virtually a part of East Horsley with the important proviso that it was not part of the Lovelace Estate. Bower developed Heatherdene, Meadow Way, Nightingale Avenue and Nightingale Crescent—hence the East Horsley developers played some part in the expansion of West Horsley. Significantly, however, Bower also built the vastly inferior semi-detached houses in Woodside and Longreach and hence all the inter-war residential development in West Horsley (North) was his. It is interesting that the standard of construction fell as distance from East Horsley increased. Although all the land developed was near the station, its availability and purchase by determined developers was the key to the type and speed of residential growth. Even the success of such early developers as Bower and Chown proved not to be a catalyst for West Clandon's development.

The combined effects of remoteness and post-war planning controls are clear in East Clandon, where almost all of the present village was built before the First World War. The tiny size of the village allowed little scope even for infilling and rounding off under Green Belt regulations. By any available definition East Clandon has long been the most rural of the four parishes, with the smallest number and proportion of commuters and the largest proportion of agricultural workers and sub-standard housing.

3 Post-war

The more comprehensive development of East Horsley between the wars resulted in the steady spread of fairly homogeneous, high-quality, residential development, leaving a very limited area for subsequent housing development; few valuable sites were available for the post-war building of anything more than individual houses. Because of the imposition of planning restrictions few large estates were constructed in any of the parishes and in all four the majority of post-war building has been no more than small clusters infilling or rounding off. Consequently the other three parishes have retained a more rural character than East Horsley.

Infilling and rounding off have proceeded to the extent that there are now virtually no sites available in any of the parishes for housing development. Almost all plots in almost all streets have been built upon, and there is strong opposition to the sub-division of gardens—hence future building depends largely on the release of new land, presently protected under current planning legislation, for housing development. The present low level of housing construction distinguishes the four parishes from most other metropolitan villages and, unless present policies change almost totally, the current stability will be maintained for some time.

Despite the covenants of Chown, development standards have declined since the Second World War, with the construction of smaller houses on smaller plots of land, sometimes in the gardens of the largest houses. Even so throughout the four parishes (with the exception of a few small parts of West Horsley) all private residential development has been of detached houses which have commanded high prices in the housing market. The decline in standards is only relative to the high standards of the inter-war years. Together with infilling and the decreasing size of new houses there has been an increase in population density and with this the incursion of hitherto urban characteristics such as traffic, street lighting, sewerage, noise and shops. A few large houses have become institutions of different kinds; one or two have been sub-divided into flats.

Throughout the area, housing development has been

essentially piecemeal with no overall planning for any parish until after the Second World War, when it was entirely restrictive. Immediately after the war proposals were made by the London County Council for a 'Horsley New Town', which would have included the two Horsley parishes. Plans were drawn up in 1947 which would have involved an increase in population from 4,000 to 16,500 with 65 acres allocated to light industry, but the scheme was rejected by the rural district council and the Surrey County Council. The unanimous opposition of the parish councils was not required. So the largest overall plans were for estates only; consequently local development has been haphazard, the result of unplanned grafting of new on to old, and yet since there was so little of the old in East Horsley and so little of the new elsewhere the results are not completely disastrous. The major problem, common to all such rapid unplanned settlements, is that shopping and community facilities have not been designed for the local population but have only followed, if at all, after a time lag. As planning restrictions have increased they have not been allowed to follow. It is a familiar story for metropolitan villages: a continued dependence on beyond.

Council housing

At the same time that Chown was starting work on his grandiose schemes for East Horsley, in a much smaller way successive national governments were starting to implement the legislation that eventually brought to the four parishes a rather different sort of housing from that which Chown was insisting upon. Although local authorities had first been given the power to build houses by Shaftesbury's Act of 1851 municipal building made almost no impact until after the First World War and certainly none in rural areas. Through the Housing, Town Planning, etc., Act of 1919 local authorities were obliged to prepare plans to meet local housing needs and, as a result of this Act, the first few council houses were quickly constructed by Guildford Rural District Council in the same year and the housing stock of the council grew to more than 600 by the Second World War. Within the four parishes the distinctive Addison Cottages were built: in West Horsley, Fulkes Cottages; in East Horsley, Wellington Cottages, and in East Clandon, Snelgate Cottages. Each small group was quite separate from the rest of the village; in East Clandon the squire insisted that the estate be outside the village, and so it remains, a distinctive component of the rural landscape.

In the first post-war decade, local-authority house construction had been more or less twice the pre-war rate whilst private house building declined to less than the pre-war rate. The peak years nationally for the rural district were between 1947 and 1953 and in those six years just less than half the complete stock of houses was built. Subsequently, with the exception of 1960, which was the last year that council houses were built in central Surrey, the local housing completion figures have declined considerably but house types have increased in variety (see Table 3.6).

Acquisition of sites for council-house construction is subject to the same restrictions as for private housing. Attempts to match supply and demand are more difficult for a local authority, catering as it does for less mobile tenants. In addition there is a conflict between land shortage, planning policy and government housing subsidies to local authorities.[21] Choice and development of sites is becoming extremely difficult, especially since the demand for council housing is increasingly coming from older people and homes for them must be close to shops and other facilities. Almost half the present demand comes from people more than 60 years of age, so that local-authority housing in central Surrey is gradually becoming a special problem of catering for old people, with developments much more like residential homes. Consequently the problems of new development are enormous.

Transport and commuters

As a result of the 1921 Railway Act the Southern Railway was created and the plans for electrification of the tracks of the constituent companies were implemented almost immediately afterwards. On the 'New Guildford Line' electrification was completed to Guildford in 1925. As one railway historian wrote: 'It was a bold venture, for the areas

Contemporary countryside

Table 3.6 Guildford Rural District Council housing types, 1970

	Date of construction	Total no.of units	1970 pop.	No. of bedrooms			
				1	2	3	4
East Horsley (65)							
Old Lane, Cobham	(1953)	8	15	—	8	—	—
Wellington Cottages	(1959)	12	57	—	—	12	—
Kingston Avenue	(1950-1)	45	106	—	39	6	—
West Horsley (151)							
Mount Pleasant	(1947-8)	28	90	6	2	20	—
Fulkes Cottages	(18 in 1924; 2 in 1959)	20	75	—	2	18	—
Shere Road (2) and School Cottages (1)*		3	7	—	1	2	—
Farleys Close	(14 in 1938-9; 18 in 1950-1)	32	104	—	16	12	4
Nightingale Crescent	(44 in 1948; 4 in 1957)	48	182	—	—	48	—
Northcote Close	(1958)	8	12	—	8	—	—
Woodside	(1952)	12	36	—	8	3	1
West Clandon (111)							
Glebe Cottages	(12 in 1936; 10 in 1946-7)	22	73	—	—	22	—
Meadowlands	(58 in 1948-54; 31 in 1960)	89	272	1	53	34	1
East Clandon (12)							
Snelgate Cottages	(1926)	12	45	—	—	12	—
		339	1,074				

* The two houses in Shere Road were taken over from Surrey County Council in 1967 and the third in 1968.

Source: Guildford Rural District Council, Records, 1970 (unpublished).

served were still largely rural. But the expected traffic came.'[22] Between 1925 and 1929, and following the electrification, receipts on the Dorking and New Guildford line increased by 38 per cent, whilst on the steam-worked line from London to Guildford (via Woking) revenue had decreased by 25 per cent.[23] In 1930 third-class season tickets from Clandon to Waterloo were 13s per week and from Effingham Junction 11s 9d. The improved railway service both fostered and served the rapidly growing local population. Subsequently the organisation of the railways through the four parishes has scarcely changed in terms of number and times of trains. Even the reorganisation of the Southern Region timetable in 1967 and the closure of the Guildford-Cranleigh-Horsham line in 1965 had no local effect. For most people the only

Contemporary countryside

real changes since 1930 have been in the economics of commuting.

Current use of the three railway stations in central Surrey shows how completely the railway is orientated to its task of taking people out of the area and into London, rather than catering for local movements. Table 3.7 shows that for a sample survey held in the region some 87 per cent of all work trips were to destinations in London postal districts, with the majority of the remainder to Greater London boroughs.

Table 3.7 Railway work trips from the four parishes, 1964

	Destination	East Horsley	West Horsley	West Clandon	East Clandon	Total
London	SW1	31	8	5		44
	W1	19	5	4		28
	EC2	18	5	4		27
	WC2	13	7	4		24
	EC3	12	6	3		21
	EC4	10	7	2		19
	WC1	10	4	3		17
	SE1	7	6	2		15
	EC1	4	4			8
	NW1	2	2			4
Guildford		6	3	3		12
Leatherhead		2	2			4
Elsewhere		21	7	5	1	34
Total		155	66	35	1	257

Source: *BR Southern Region, 1964, Passenger Travel Enquiry South-Western Division, Report No. 2, London Road (Guildford)—Hinchley Wood*, Economic and Traffic Intelligence Section, Waterloo (London) October 1965, (mimeo), n.p.

This was further emphasised through the analysis of all tickets issued from Horsley Station in the month of December 1969. Then, more than 55 per cent of all final destinations were Victoria or Bank stations. However, a much more local pattern emerged with a significant number of trips to Guildford (17 per cent) and even within the parishes to Effingham and Clandon. Shopping journeys (especially in the pre-Christmas period), and especially schoolchildren, considerably reduce London's dominance of this section of the rail network.

At the same time as the electrification of the railways there were two other major transport changes that finally removed the bicycle from its unique position of importance in the rural areas. First, there was the gradual emergence of the motor car as an alternative mode of long-distance travel and, later, there was the development of local bus services. The early bus routes, such as that which started through West Clandon around 1917, running between Guildford and Epsom, generally focused on the towns but although this first bus service through the parishes provided no link between the old village centres and the new railway station some distance away, the Guildford-Leatherhead service that wound its way through the villages began only four years later. Bus services remain infrequent, yet, unlike more remote rural areas, almost every part of the parishes is covered every day. The infrequency of bus services, the skeletal nature of the route system and its lack of linkage with regional systems, have all partly encouraged the growth of car transport and sown the seeds of the system's decay. Increased personal mobility for car owners has helped contribute to the contraction of the public facilities on which less affluent members of society rely. The 'vicious circle' of public-transport provision so familiar in urban areas (services decline, the number of passengers falls, fares rise, numbers fall further and the services decline further) is repeated in the countryside, too, where its decline is an even greater social problem than that of its urban counterpart.

The railway, the catalyst of residential development in the area, not surprisingly is crucial for commuting. Central Surrey depends on the railway for work trips to the extent that 87 per cent of all trips by public transport outside the rural district are by train (Table 3.8). The image of the metropolitan villager, a bowler-hatted commuter standing on a railway platform waiting to travel to The City, is quite true here. Within the rural district the position is completely different, with the train and the bus quite inferior to walking or cycling whilst the car covers the remainder of the work journeys (Table 3.9). Four out of five households in the parishes own a car and in East Horsley as many as 36 per cent of all households owned at least two cars in 1971; these are exceptionally high figures, especially for two-car families, both for Surrey and for the whole country.

The railway network has been the main determinant of the pattern and process of population change in the area; the

Table 3.8 Work transport, 1971

	Train	Bus	Car	Other (including none)
East Horsley	63	7	70	50
West Horsley	42	10	55	29
East Clandon	1	—	4	1
West Clandon	19	2	11	16
	125	19	140	96

Source: 1971 Census, E.D. Returns (10% sample).

Table 3.9 Trips within Guildford Rural District

	Train	Bus	Car	Other (including none)
East Horsley	0	2	10	33
West Horsley	2	3	9	19
East Clandon	—	—	2	1
West Clandon	5	—	3	9
	7	5	24	62

Source: 1971 Census, E.D. Returns (10% sample).

rapidly growing villages around the railways have been counterbalanced by decline in villages remote from the railway network, and it is only in the post-war years that the road and cars have been able to counterbalance this influence. The historic road system that developed at the same time as the earliest 'spring-line' settlements has passed through a short period of relative decline, but with the increasing rate of car-ownership it is emerging again as an important route system, especially where it links to the dominant railway network. The railways have brought development; the roads have belatedly spread this development more widely. The spring-line has been superseded by the railway line as a focus for local settlements.

Amenity

One of the more distinctive ways in which villages differ from suburbs or towns is in the provision of social amenities.

Contemporary countryside

Even the most basic amenities such as the public utilities—water, sewerage, gas and electricity—are rarely fully extended to all rural areas. But conversely, because of their function as central places, villages may have a much greater range of clubs and associations than suburbs of the same size. Each of the four villages has mains electricity and only extremely remote houses are not connected to this grid—and so it has been at least since the Second World War. Mains gas supplies also extend to the parishes but many houses in the southern fringes are not connected to the mains. Similarly, only remote houses have no mains water; 3 houses in East Horsley and 2 in West Horsley depend on rain water, and a group of 9 uses a well.

It is in the provision of sewerage that the villages compare least favourably with urban areas. Most of East Clandon has only recently been connected to a mains sewerage-disposal system; previously it was completely dependent on cesspools, septic tanks and ultimately the rural district council's bi-monthly night-soil collection service. Indeed, this was a major reason preventing approval being given by the rural district council for new housing-estate construction: existing facilities could not cope with a significant increase in output. In the other parishes only outlying houses are not served. Since there, too, planning permission has consistently been refused for areas more than the legal limit of 100 feet from a sewerage system, the extent of the sewerage system is an unusual but considerable constraint upon rural development.

Indicative of the possible problems attached to rural residence is the absence of substantial educational and health provisions. Surrey County Council organises the main facilities and all the main hospitals and most specialised clinics are in Guildford. West Horsley and East Clandon have no doctors; both are dependent on group practices centred elsewhere. East Horsley is the only parish to have both a dentist and a chemist. It is medically wise to live in a large village or close to Guildford.

Until 1960 the only public-library facilities in the four parishes were small village libraries but most of these had fallen into disuse. That in West Horsley was broken up during the Second World War; some books were given to the

Contemporary countryside

Red Cross and the rest used for salvage. Libraries like this were open only one or two days per week and were quite unsuitable to the needs of a growing population, and so in 1959 the county council proposed to set up a travelling-library service with a greater number and variety of books. But the proposal was not everywhere welcomed. West Clandon Parish Council[24]

> were of the opinion that the existing service met the needs of the parish adequately and that the proposed travelling library would not be welcomed enthusiastically by parishioners who used the present facilities. Most of them would not think a greater choice of books would compensate them for the loss of the weekly opportunity to discuss in the warmth and comfort of the hall communal and personal affairs afforded to them by the existing service.

Nevertheless in May 1960 a travelling-library service was set up by the county council. This has grown steadily: in 1964 there were 211 stopping points within Surrey (and 7 vehicles based at Esher) and in 1969 there were 320 stops. Within the four parishes the library now stops at 7 points in a weekly route that also covers the fringes of Woking, Leatherhead and Dorking and other rural areas between. This is the largest of the county travelling libraries, with more than 7,000 books. Ashby found that each Surrey area had its own particular interests; the Horsleys were apparently especially interested in art books.[25] Subsequently in 1966 a new branch library was built in East Horsley and is open five days a week; this has resulted in a reduction in demand on the travelling service from both East and West Horsley, despite the earliest fears of the rural district council that 'it was important that the Travelling Library should not be allowed to undermine the success of the Branch Libraries'.[26] The wheel had turned full circle.

The only other statutory provision is education, provided by the district council. Curiously, neither East Horsley nor East Clandon has a primary school; both have closed since 1964. West Clandon Primary School (founded in 1872 by

83

the Onslow family) serves both Clandons, and the more recent Raleigh School in West Horsley serves almost all East Horsley. However, there are two private preparatory schools in East Horsley, Glenesk House and Parkside. Because they are more central they take more than 200 local children and set a particularly distinctive style. Glenesk House charges fees of £100 a term, takes children from 4 to 12, and aims 'to provide a sound preliminary education, to develop character and to prepare the boys and girls mentally and physically for the public school'.[27] Parkside, established in East Horsley since 1934, takes 175 boys, including about 40 boarders (usually with parents overseas). It charges boarders £300 per term and day boys £180 per term. Their curriculum is designed to prepare them for the common entrance examination to public schools and also eventually for the old boys' association hockey team, the 'Pussdogs'. In the early 1970s there were only two local secondary modern schools and no grammar schools, nursery schools or comprehensives within the rural district; grammar-school children must travel to Guildford. By 1976 comprehensive schools existed almost alone throughout the country but it was still unknown what system would finally prevail in the Guildford area where children were still going to the few remaining grammar schools. The most obvious feature of local educational provision is still lack of choice. The only nearby secondary schools are secondary modern schools; consequently, Roman-Catholic families and families who insist upon grammar-school education are less likely to choose to live in this area.

East Horsley has the only important collection of shops within the four parishes and is the only parish where shopping facilities have expanded since the Second World War. In 1938 in East Horsley proper there were 31 shops and a further 2 in Effingham Junction. At the same time there were 12 shops in West Horsley, 2 in West Clandon and 1 in East Clandon. The 3 in the Clandons were all general stores and remained so until the summer of 1969 when that in East Clandon closed, leaving, temporarily, only the post-office section in operation. Then, as now, there were 2 public houses in West Horsley and West Clandon, 1 in East

"What on earth do you mean—no stuffed olives?"

Clandon and 3 in East Horsley. There are now 55 shops in East Horsley proper and a further 3 in Effingham Junction. Many have been built since 1956 when there were 35 in East Horsley and 3 in Effingham Junction. There are also several specialist shops, including 2 banks, a dry cleaners, 3 estate agents, a solicitor, a carpet-and-furniture shop, an antique shop and also 2 restaurants. Despite this profusion of shops which serves most possible needs (if not price ranges) there are still mobile shops operating within East Horsley, but more particularly in the other three parishes. West Horsley is now reduced to only 8 shops.

East Horsley is an important shopping centre. The number of shops places it well above the other three parishes (and other neighbouring parishes) in services offered and in an intermediate position between these and the urban shopping centres. Its success is at least partly responsible for the decline of West Horsley's shopping facilities; like the Clandons these now tend to cater almost entirely either for occasional (often forgotten) wants or for a limited number of persons for whom travelling is very difficult. For them the situation can only get worse. For some goods, and even specialist services, Horsley offers competition to larger regional centres such as Guildford and Kingston. The distinction between Horsley and the towns is in prices; there is a distinct gradient in prices, which increase from large town to small village. In central Surrey prices are as high as any in Britain.

The lack of choice that is present in educational provision and to a lesser extent in shopping services is present also in religion; in the same say, this lack of variety operates in favour of the middle way. Minority groups are less well catered for in both education and religion and those who require a particular kind of school or a particular church are unsatisfied locally. Thus all four parishes and Effingham Junction have an operational Church of England, whilst West Horsley has one main church and a daughter church in the newer north of the parish. These were for centuries the foci of social life and welfare action within rural villages; the social, legal and political role of the parish church has continued to decline throughout the present century yet the church is still often regarded as one of the leading foci of social activity. The churches are still the centres of parish religious activity in terms of numbers in attendance; and, additionally, they generate a small number of semi-independent social organisations: St Martin's, East Horsley, for example, has a mothers' union, a young wives' group and a good-neighbour organisation, and had, until late 1969, the Adventurers' Youth Club. The Horsley Floral Decoration Group is also closely linked to the church. Within the parishes there are also several churches of other denominations: there is a Methodist church in West Horsley, a Catholic church in West Horsley (North), and an Evangelical church in East Horsley which is unique enough to be a minor influence on migration. In Guildford there is a range of possibilities, yet even so some religious organisations are not present in Guildford or Leatherhead and this, too, operates in favour of social conformity and homogeneity within the rural district.

Apart from village social activities (Chapter 5) there are other amenities above and beyond parochial activities. Local newspapers come either from Guildford or Leatherhead; the monthly *Surrey Villager* which is now published in Guildford was first published in December 1964 in East Horsley. Coverage of local parish activities was then much less detailed, although the January 1967 copy boasted: 'people read *The Villager* because they, like us, believe in the community spirit of Village Life.' The nearest cinemas are at Leatherhead and Guildford, although until recently there was also one at Cobham. There are theatres at Leatherhead and Guildford. For those with more esoteric social demands or even, in this context, an interest in Labour-Party politics or trade-union activity, all activity is beyond the parish boundary. The range of available social activity is naturally small, as would be expected in any rural district, and not unexpectedly the range of activities is broadly those that are acceptable to large groups of people; the fringe activities and interests that are available in urban areas find insufficient support in rural areas.

By any criterion East Clandon is by far the worst served of all the parishes. Mains drainage was completed in 1971 but in the past five years both the village shop and the village school have closed, whilst the population has declined and become higher class. Additionally it is the smallest and most remote from transport of the four parishes. The restrictions on growth in the village, coupled with an incursion of mobile commuters, have speeded the decline of amenities, yet for many of the new residents the village provides a perfect rustic prop to an urban way of life. With the council houses tidily out of the way, the twelfth-century church and the numerous old agricultural cottages (ideal for renovation) provide the fabric of the 'traditional village' in the heart of central Surrey.

Administratively the four parishes were still rural areas until 1974; the local government then consisted of parish councils, leading up to the rural district council and the county council. Because it was a rural area, the postmen were empowered to carry postage stamps to serve areas remote from post offices. The main social organisations are WIs rather than townswomen's guilds, and the Young Farmers' Club even has a branch in East Horsley. The local edition of the *Surrey Advertiser* is the 'Horsley and Villages' edition, suggesting a slightly different status for East Horsley, and conventional usage is to speak of 'the villages', whilst each parish usually enters the annual Surrey Best-Kept Village competition. Although all the parishes contain essentially nucleated villages, many houses are more than a mile from the old village centres and 'the village' is not synonymous with the parish; areas like Woodcote, West Horsley, have no real links with any of the villages.

At the start of the long debate on local-government reform in 1971, the rural district council proposed that all the rural district be linked with Guildford as a single unitary authority. A council meeting in March 1972 indicated strong opposition to this; several rural areas, especially West Clandon, did not wish to join Guildford on the stated grounds that only rural districts could effectively preserve rural areas and Green Belts properly. Thus in March 1971 the chairman of Guildford Rural District Council proposed that the authority should amalgamate with Hambledon in order to stay rural and prevent urban encroachment. At this meeting the councillor for Send stated: 'The countryside is best administered by those who live and work there. Country folk do not want to be run by townsmen.' The councillor for

Contemporary countryside

Albury suggested: 'We would almost look on main drainage coming along as a form of urban pollution.'[28] Nevertheless following the Boundary Commission proposals of April 1972 a Guildford District Council was established, unifying the urban and rural authorities, and a joint committee proposed seven rural and seven urban wards. Both West Horsley Parish Council and Horsley Liberal Association objected to the division of West Horsley so that its northern section fell in a different ward. Each claimed that the parish had no links with Ripley or Send but that it shared shops, transport and doctors with East Horsley and was linked to East Horsley and Effingham in the Five Villages Association (see Chapter 6). West Clandon Parish Council strongly objected to the proposed link with Shere and Albury, considering that its connections were with the Horsleys and Effingham, again especially through the Five Villages Association. Thus the parish councils, and most other parish organisations, have always considered that the parishes are essentially rural and that this should as far as possible be maintained. In the event their objections were ignored and the merger of city and rural district was swift and surprisingly smooth.

The rise of distinctive residential areas

The general availability since 1961 of social data for areas (Enumeration Districts) even smaller than parishes makes it possible to see how different parts of the same parish vary, and especially how the parishes differ. Thus the central area of East Horsley between Lynx Hill and the station is differentiated from both Effingham Junction and the area to the south by having: the lowest persons per room density, a social-class composition much more weighted towards the higher classes, the highest rate of car-ownership and the greatest proportion of 'qualified' people (those with qualifications higher than GCE A level).[29] This combination of characteristics suggests that the area built almost entirely by Chown and his associates is much the most exclusive part of the four parishes. Outside East Horsley none of the other parishes, or parts of parishes, can rival it.

Information on house prices and rateable values produces

Contemporary countryside

the same sort of regional variations. Examination of the prices asked by advertisers in the *Surrey Advertiser* shows the rapid upward movement of prices (Table 3.10), especially at the start of the 1970s when demand for housing in central Surrey was so great that very few houses needed to be advertised for sale. In the first half of 1972 there were more advertisements wanting houses in the area than there were for houses for sale. Already by 1970 prices had become very high and when the last house in West Clandon to be sold for less than £10,000 was advertised at £9,250 it was then described as being 'in need of decoration and maintenance'. Until

Table 3.10 House prices 1950–76

	East Clandon	West Clandon	East Horsley	West Horsley
1950	—	6,170 (6)	5,096 (24)	4,893 (7)
1962	—	8,507 (22)	7,773 (64)	6,243 (14)
1966	10,700 (4)	11,341 (33)	10,875 (61)	7,913 (48)
1970	10,160 (5)	15,270 (27)	13,632 (64)	10,936 (46)
1972	—	36,000 (18)	27,875 (44)	22,120 (23)
1974	25,833 (3)	37,355 (37)	34,218 (58)	25,309 (32)
1976	27,000 (1)	36,657 (23)	36,625 (54)	25,708 (32)

Note: The number in brackets is the number of cases.

1973 it was still possible to purchase houses for less than £10,000 in West Horsley, where there are some small semi-detached houses. Now it is no longer possible and all the parishes have become quite exclusive: the first priority for a potential resident is a high salary and, especially since 1970, an existing house somewhere else. No first-time buyer could normally expect to afford a house in central Surrey.

In many ways the different social composition of the four parishes is most accurately understood by the estate agents involved in making local sales. A composite account of the four parishes from the observations and knowledge of local agents reflects the variations present. Proximity to a picturesque village centre is always a good selling point—hence East Clandon represented a 'market in itself' and gave higher prices than similar property elsewhere; a house sold there in 1975 for £25,000 would have sold at about £20,000 in the other three parishes. The basic selling point is the railway station, and consequently quite a distinct housing market exists to the south of the Downs, where direct rail access to London is impossible. A Horsley address was considered to be third or fourth in the Surrey 'league table', following St George's Hill, Esher and possibly Cobham. West Horsley was a 'poor man's East Horsley' but it did provide some old property that appealed to those who contemplated do-it-yourself repairs. The social gap between East and West Horsley was felt to result both from the existence of some housing in West Horsley that sold for little more than £10,000, hence lowering the tone of the parish, and from West Horsley's greater distance from the railway station, which meant that identical houses cost slightly less there. Effingham Junction was 'almost jerry-built', with no control of development; consequently it was 'a starting place for cheap people' with a few retired people mixed in. No one, apart from some of those who lived there, ever considered it to be part of Horsley, although the estate agents themselves always advertised it as such. The local area was considered to be more important than the house itself, especially for those buying a house costing more than £30,000; the particular combination of accessibility to London and the countryside being 'the first village down the line situated behind fields', was crucial to the popularity of the area. Consequently, East Horsley is an exceptionally big village with a large area of high-status housing. This sort of exclusiveness was considered to be highly desirable; the almost complete absence of new estates and council houses in East Horsley was again a most important selling point. Only in East Clandon was it possible to sell the idea of living in a 'community', but everywhere it was possible to advertise 'set in delightful surroundings' and 'beautiful views'.

Local rating-valuation practice indicates current official attitudes to housing, which are little different from unofficial private attitudes. Council houses are looked on extremely unfavourably:[30]

> The important factor which must not be overlooked in the valuation of council houses is that the normal council housing estate is not the most desirable locality in which to live. The houses are often built to set patterns and lack

any individuality; furthermore, often due to slum clearance and other causes types of persons necessarily housed on an estate do not always tend to elevate the character of the neighbourhood. It follows therefore the level of value will not be quite as high as for reasonably comparable private houses.

Nevertheless the assigned rateable values are a useful indication of how, administratively, different kinds of houses are considered to be superior and inferior. The lowest rated properties (less than £50) are almost all farm cottages which are old, with few amenities, and often remote. The lowest rated of all are Round Tree Farm Cottages, West Horsley, and Butt and Ben Cottages, West Clandon, all at £27. Comparison of the valuation between 1956 and 1970 shows how many properties of low value have been removed from the lists by demolition or improved in the past decade. The highest rated properties are the largest houses in the parishes, notably Clandon Regis (£700) and Temple Court (£700) in West Clandon, Hatchlands (£740) in East Clandon, and West Horsley Place (£850). Without exception these were built earlier than the present century. East Horsley, however, is unique since all three properties there rated at more than £500 were built since the First World War; two inter-war houses in Pennymead Drive and The Warren are rated at £520 and £570 respectively. The highest rated houses of the 1950s and 1960s are also in East Horsley. None of the other three parishes has twentieth-century houses rated at more than £500, and few rated at more than £400. The overwhelming concentration of high-rated streets is at the centre of East Horsley (Map 3) and it is precisely because so many of them are there at the centre that the ethos of opulence tends to characterise the whole parish.

The physical structure of each parish is, in some measure, a reflection of its social structure, and *vice versa*. The distribution of population is not haphazard or random but follows a more or less conscious plan and this plan alone depicts some of the unities and divisions in the social structure of the village. People who are close to each other in the social system, such as it is, tend to live side by side; people

Contemporary countryside

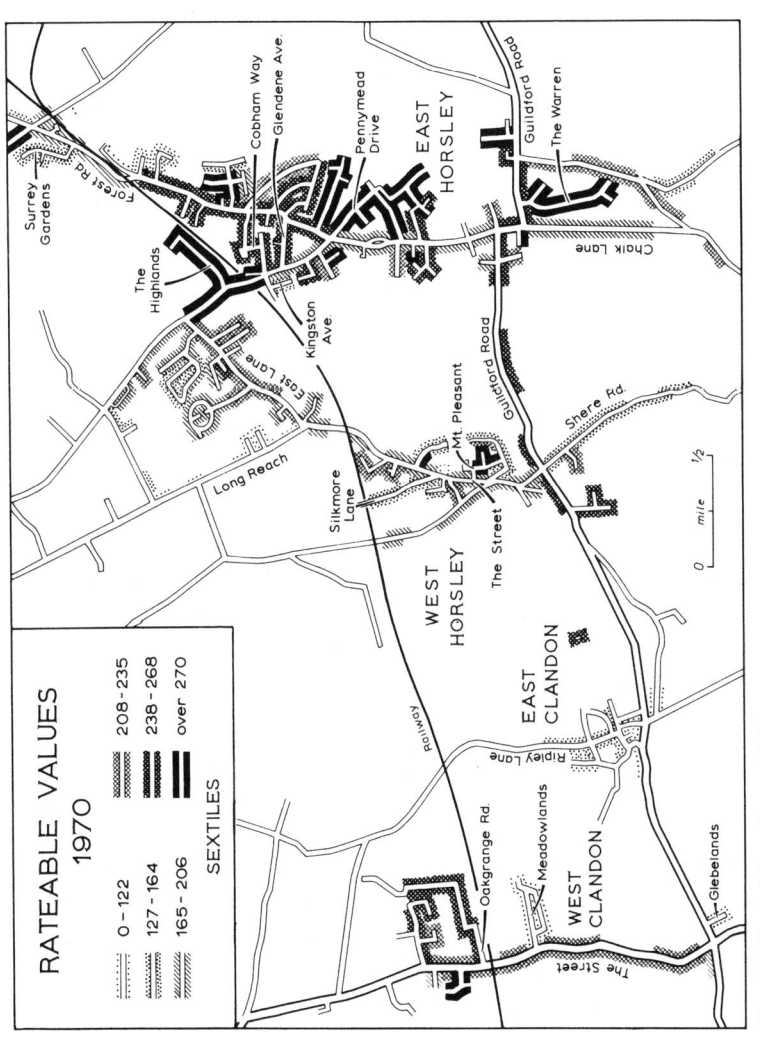

Map 3 Rateable values, 1970.

whose social positions are widely different live apart. The parishes have certain clear territorial divisions to which social values are attached; the most significant of these divisions is the general isolation of the council estates, an isolation that is still encouraged officially and unofficially. Thus a recent book on village planning suggests that council-house estates should be separated and 'screened' from the rest of the village.[31] East Horsley is distinct in a separate sense: 'it is an enormous and very respectable residential area, expensive, smooth and making valiant efforts to retain some sort of historical unity, whether it be by the line of mock-Tudor shops or by the wrought iron name signs that hang at the crossroads.'[32]

Local political variations are unknown, since parish and rural-district-council elections are not fought under political colours and in parliamentary elections the four parishes are part of the extremely safe Conservative seat of Dorking. Consequently, local political activity is minimal and there is visible evidence only of the Conservative and Liberal parties; with one exception all the new migrants who had joined political organisations were members of the Conservative party. The exception was 'a member of the Liberal party for local elections and the Conservative party for general elections'. She was probably not too disappointed to find that even in the important county-council elections of April 1973 the Horsleys (which incorporated the Clandons) and Shalford were the only two Conservative seats in West Surrey where no opposition had bothered to appear. Moreover, the Horsley Conservative Association (which had 1,460 members in March 1967) had pioneered a subscription scheme that became a model for the rest of Britain. Indeed, the general local assumption was that if there were any Labour-Party supporters then they were quietly hidden on the council estates.

A vestige of traditionalism is the way in which the Liberal party may still collect some general-election votes; one active East Clandon conservative was quite patronising:

> There are not many Labour supporters here although there are some Liberals because the last landowner was Liberal.

I canvassed for the Conservatives on the West Clandon council estate but most people won't touch it; one of the nicest people there is a Labour supporter.

A large Conservative parliamentary majority with only a few local dissidents has effectively produced a more than superficially conservative area. Yet in the past this Conservative dominance produced from inside the apparent uniformity mavericks who were willing to challenge accepted doctrines; some Surrey councils have deviated from Conservative principles on several issues, including comprehensive education and the sale of council houses.[33] Now it seems that, as commuters have increasingly taken over council politics from local squires, those Tories who were more reluctant to toe the party line have become excluded. Conservatism is increasingly apparent.

But the four parishes are only part of a county which is often thought to have the highest social status in England. Traditional jokes and caricatures all suggest Surrey as the location of the 'great white Stockbroker Belt', but the jokes are not in vain. When *The Economist* analysed the distribution of stockbrokers in 1965,[34] some 21 per cent of them lived in Surrey, far more than in any other county and usually concentrated around the railways. But if Surrey is railway-commuter country it also has one of the highest rates of car-ownership in Britain; in 1971 it had 1 car for every 3·6 people—a rate exceeded nowhere.

If stockbrokers are perhaps not now quite so dominant in Surrey the number of people listed in *Who's Who* that reside in Surrey suggests that Surrey's claims to high status are not shrinking. Again, more live in Surrey than in any other county and only Sussex runs it close. Each parish except East Clandon has some residents listed in *Who's Who*: each parish except East Horsley has some sort of stately home. To this can be added the massive amount of preserved land (Green Belt and 'areas of outstanding natural beauty') and the largest number of public or private schools in any county. The Beatles may not now be seen in Weybridge, but Virginia Water, once defined by Dury as 'the climax of dormitory settlement',[35] continues to expand amongst the golf courses and the pine trees. The conclusions can point only in one direction, a direction in some way epitomised by one English film director returning from the USA to make a film about the middle-class British: 'No-one has really examined them properly. The working class are boring now. I'm intrigued by the people who live in Farnham and Grayshott and Camberley. They're the real backbone.'[36] Away from western Surrey, for a time, 'Selsdon man' became the archetype of the conservative middle class. If that mantle sits heavily on the county, a few pockets, such as the Horsleys and Clandons, can claim even more conservatism and even higher social class than almost all the rest of Surrey.

CHAPTER 4

Migration and housing: élites and council tenants

In the largest cities like London it is said that the average income rises by steps of £100 or £200 a year with each railway station along the suburban lines as you go out from the centre, finishing up at Epsom, where the millionaires live conveniently near the race course.

J.E. Goldthorpe, *Introduction to Sociology*

The character of migration is the key to the changing social and economic structure of the four parishes. The migrants visually reflect changing economic circumstances and their movement shapes much of the district's social life; in the Horsleys and Clandons nearly 500 households have moved into (and within) the four parishes in 1968-70. No interviewee had been there more than two years. Societies exist simply to welcome new migrants and provide the first means of integration.

> During the last year my usual lament about church members leaving the village in the 'general post' which goes on nowadays, has not been heard quite so frequently, because there have not been many changes. However, it seems that it was only a pause in the pattern of life and I hear now of several church families who are about to depart, whom we shall miss a lot. Still, we have also welcomed some newcomers and I hope we have made them feel part of the 'family'. This is always a bit of a problem in a place like East Horsley; it can take so long for people to get to know

one another and whatever efforts we make to speed the process up have only limited success.[1]

In each of the parishes, with the exception of West Clandon, the new households are characteristically younger than the households already there, whilst a large decrease in retired persons is balanced by a considerable increase in the number of children less than 15 years of age. This is scarcely surprising; however, few of the new family heads or their wives are less than 30 years old and in each of the villages there is a conspicuous 'neck' in the population distribution pyramid. Adolescents leave between the ages of 15 and 20 and could only return to a home of their own a decade later; the economics of housing suggests that this 'neck' will be maintained and even lengthened. In other metropolitan villages the pattern is almost identical.[2] Despite the growing population of central Surrey a significant proportion of the population is of a pensionable age and there is an extremely high proportion aged over 44. Only in West Horsley, where houses are cheapest, is it less than 40 per cent (Table 4.1). Moreover, the elderly nature of the population is also reflected in the sex ratio, with women tending to outlive men. The cost of obtaining a house means that new migrants, whilst younger than the existing population, are still older than in many comparable areas.

Table 4.1 Age and population structure, 1961-71

		East Clandon	West Clandon	East Horsley	West Horsley
1. % population aged under 15	(1961)	27	24	19	25
	(1971)	28	22	21	24
2. % population aged over 44	(1961)	40	41	48	39
	(1971)	40	46	45	39
3. % pensionable (males over 64, females over 59)	(1961)	15	16	17	15
	(1971)	16	20	18	15
4. Sex ratio	(1961)	0·91	1·11	1·18	1·12
	(1971)	1·06	1·09	1·13	1·10

Comparison of the social composition of the migrants and the existing population (Table 4.2) gives possibly the single most important indicator of the character of social change.

Migration and housing: élites and council tenants

Even were the data to be slightly inaccurate (because of the 10 per cent sample in 1966) the changes are so substantial that the conclusions and implications are both striking and clear.

Table 4.2 Migration (1968–70) and social class

		East Clandon	West Clandon	East Horsley	West Horsley	All
Social class 1	1966	—	4	19	9	32
	migrants	9	24	76	50	159
Social class 2	1966	1	15	61	17	94
	migrants	2	12	110	77	201
Social class 3	1966	3	10	30	47	90
	migrants	1	3	25	32	61
Social class 4	1966	2	8	8	15	33
	migrants	4	3	8	11	26
Social class 5	1966	—	3	—	1	4
	migrants	3	1	2	7	13
Unclassified	1966	—	1	8	3	12
	migrants	—	—	5	3	8

The most interesting feature is the upward migration shift in relation to the existing social classes (and the small proportion of migrants in classes 3 and 4). Thus 75 per cent of all migrants were in social classes 1 and 2 compared with only 47 per cent of established residents: this is an extremely marked shift. This shift occurs in all four parishes and is repeated throughout the rural district, where between 1961 and 1966 the only two occupation groups that showed a decrease were farmers and foresters, and labourers, whilst those with the greatest increases were, in the main, white-collar occupations: clerical workers, administrators and managers and professional workers. These trends, too, are typical of other metropolitan villages, yet nowhere is the scale of this shift to the upper social classes as striking as in central Surrey. The rise and migration of the 'senior salariat' is making its impact on the most exclusive parts of south-east England.

Local moves and the origin of new migrants

Within the parishes, too, the population distribution is

Migration and housing: élites and council tenants

changing: households move to smaller or larger houses or to houses with studios or horse-paddocks. None of these is recorded in the Census classifications but the electoral registers show how the parishes differ in character. For example, in East Clandon they show that, of the 199 people listed in 1969, 85 (43 per cent) were there in 1959 and 56 (28 per cent) in 1949, whilst of the 214 adults there in 1959, 112 (53 per cent) were there in 1949. More than a quarter of the population in the parish has been there for at least twenty years; the majority is now elderly one-person households. However, some have moved within the village. Because the parish is so small it is possible to observe that several females (and males) have married and remained in the village, whilst several of the village farms, which own tied cottages, have farm workers living there who had previously lived in the tied cottages of other village farms. There is also a small amount of migration from village to council estate, whilst the surnames of residents in the estate show a much closer relationship with the village than could be deduced from the migration data alone. Finally, St Thomas's Cottages, built to house retired farm workers, have almost entirely provided for farm workers from the village. Internal migration is extremely complex and very closely related to employment—or former employment—within the village.

For a small village East Clandon has quite a complicated housing system. For the other parishes of central Surrey it is possible to calculate the proportion of those there in 1949 still in the same parish in 1969. The percentage of households there in both years was 12 per cent in East Horsley, 18 per cent in West Horsley (both North and South) and 15 per cent in West Clandon. None of these approaches the more stable population of East Clandon but even there stability is decreasing. Moreover, compared with many other estate villages, even East Clandon has a mobile population; indeed, compared with some metropolitan villages in Worcestershire and Hertfordshire it has a highly mobile population.[3] A stable population is not a characteristic of the Surrey Green Belt.

Low population stability is almost entirely related to the small extent of council estates and the absence of pre-twentieth-century housing. With very few exceptions the streets of council houses contain almost all those households that have lived in their own parish for the twenty-year period and are also almost the only place where local accents can be heard. The highest proportion of permanent residents is in Snelgate Cottages, East Clandon, where 16 of the 27 households have lived throughout the period, whilst many of the others have merely come from tied and condemned cottages in the same parish. The council-house tenants are now the true villagers.

Despite migration within and between the Horsleys and Clandons the bulk of migration is over longer distances. Overall, there is still a general outward movement from Greater London, especially from the inner and outer suburbs of the south-west. Moreover, the Census shows that this movement is part of a wave sweeping over Surrey: beyond the county boundaries Sussex, Hampshire and Berkshire have all recorded high net migration from Guildford Rural District. In some ways, just like suburbs, metropolitan villages are merely stepping stones to more distant pastures.

Overall, nearly half the migrant households into central Surrey came from somewhere else in the county (Table 4.3). Furthermore, as many as 72 per cent of all the households went from local authorities between the four parishes and the centre of London. The single exception to this strikingly sectoral pattern of migration is a small stream of migrants from Staines and Sunbury; more than half of those stressing medical reasons for migration came from these low-lying, unattractive towns. Nevertheless, perhaps the outstanding feature of the areas of destination is that by arbitrarily defining towns as places with populations of more than 10,000 it is found that some 80 per cent of all migrants have come from urban areas, representing a substantial urban-rural population shift.

The low percentage of migrants from central London boroughs suggests that for many households the move to central Surrey may be a second stage in the move from the central city. Indeed, one East Horsley estate agent posited a general cycle that seemed to apply to many new migrants. A household starts off after marriage in Sutton, Cheam or

Migration and housing: élites and council tenants

Table 4.3 Migrant origins and destinations

Origin	All parishes	Destination East Horsley	West Horsley	East Clandon	West Clandon
GLC					
Kensington and Chelsea	10	2	6	2	—
Kingston	22	12	10	—	—
Richmond	13	6	5	—	2
Sutton	12	9	2	—	1
Others	56	25	29	—	2
English counties	93	46	40	2	5
Wales/Scotland/Ireland	7	6	1	—	—
Abroad	36	23	10	1	2
Surrey					
Epsom and Ewell	13	4	4	2	1
Esher	27	8	14	1	4
Leatherhead	15	6	6	2	1
Walton and Weybridge	13	8	3	—	2
Woking	15	4	6	1	4
Other Surrey	37	21	11	1	4
Guildford District					
East Clandon	1	—	—	—	1
West Clandon	8	3	1	—	4
East Horsley	32	23	6	2	1
West Horsley	22	3	15	3	1
Guildford	21	9	5	2	5
Effingham	11	5	6	—	—
Ripley	5	—	5	—	—
Others	23	10	7	2	4
Unknown	2	1	1	—	—
Total	494	234	193	21	44

Croydon; children arrive and the family moves towards the countryside, possibly to arrive at Oxshott or Esher. Expectations rise and they purchase a house for £30,000–£35,000 in East or West Horsley. If the house is in West Horsley they eventually move to East Horsley; if the house is in East Horsley they move to a larger house. Finally the children leave home, the head of household retires and they move to a smaller house in East Horsley. The cycle has a great deal of validity, especially since very few households voluntarily move away from the four parishes except at retirement. Most movement out of the area resulted from job transfer; social mobility is the only decisive factor encouraging movement away, and significant numbers, especially those going abroad, let out their houses so that eventually they can return. Central Surrey is not an easy place to leave.

Reasons and explanations

There is a fundamental difference between reasons for leaving the previous area and reasons for coming to the Horsleys and Clandons. Overall, the total number of reasons given for out-migration was 535 and for in-migration 804; possible reasons for out-migration seem to have faded away, as the advantages of, if not the reasons for, migration into central Surrey are constantly visible. The real reasons for migration can never be totally differentiated from post-migration justifications; indeed, they may never have been logically formulated. Several households had simply seen the house and decided to move even though they had never really been looking for a larger house or a better area. Nevertheless, the main reasons for moving are summarised in Table 4.4.

Table 4.4 Migration decisions

	East Horsley	West Horsley	East Clandon	West Clandon	All
Out					
Changed employment location	63	61	4	9	137
Large/small/special house required	36	38	2	15	91
Dislike area	27	18	2	5	52
Retirement	12	8	–	3	23
Own home	26	19	5	2	52
Other	27	15	1	4	47
No reason/Don't know	35	21	5	5	66
	226	180	19	43	468
In					
Changed employment location	16	14	4	1	35
House/land available	27	15	2	15	59
House value/cost	7	10	1	1	19
Large/small/special house available	17	12	–	5	34
Country area	63	53	8	7	131
Character of local area	21	11	1	2	35
Friends/relatives	19	7	–	1	27
Transport facilities/location	38	34	–	7	79
Council allocation	9	11	2	3	25
Other	6	6	1	1	14
No reason/Don't know	4	6	–	–	10
	227	179	19	43	468

Migration and housing: élites and council tenants

The single most important reason why households left their previous address was because of their changed employment location. In many cases these moves represented promotion within a company and a high proportion of the remainder were 'organization men', moved round by their company to familiarise themselves with company problems, policy and organisation in a different area. Perhaps 25 per cent of all migrants were 'spiralists',[4] moving steadily upwards through their organisation with most of the upward moves demanding a spatial move and, in this case, with many having reached the top of their organisations and returning to work at home base in London. It is the ethos of this highly mobile group that characterises the local area; the village is a by-product of the husband's career.

The second largest group of out-migrants comprised those who had left their previous address because it was considered too large, too small or the wrong kind; several moves were into houses with studios, whilst bungalows exercised a particular attraction for older migrants. A similar group was those who left to move into their own home; most were newly married but many were from shared or rented accommodation, several came from caravans and one gave up a rented houseboat on the Thames. Almost all of these moved very short distances.

Those who moved from an area they disliked represented 11 per cent of all the out-migrants; only 1 of these had not previously lived in Surrey or Greater London, but 2 actually moved out of West Horsley. The London boroughs of Sutton, Wandsworth and Harrow all produced 3 such migrant households, as did Epsom and Ewell, and Guildford and Woking in Surrey. However, although there are certainly unattractive areas in all these adjoining districts the local nature of the migration suggests that the real reason was the unattractiveness of more urban areas. Indeed, only 20 of the 52 households concerned explained why they disliked their previous area. The reasons then were quite familiar: traffic and noise, dirt and pollution, no play space for children, and black immigration.

Other reasons for out-migration were relatively unimportant; significantly, 66 households (14 per cent) could not think of any particular reason why they had left. This is representative of a particular type of migration; it was not always clear why many households had required larger houses, although it was always clear for households requiring smaller houses. Apart from the old Parker-Morris standards, which are relevant to particularly overcrowded housing, there are no criteria for adequate densities of occupancy. Rough calculations suggest that of the 43 households for which some data exist (out of 51 households moving into larger houses) at least 28 had more than one bedroom per head. Hence, although many were obviously expecting to add to their family, their demands on increased space could scarcely be described as pressing. Moreover, some of both households wanting larger or smaller houses appeared to have moved into accommodation that was little different in size. Obviously, this was only apparent for some of the small group that had moved within the four parishes; what was more apparent for those households that had stated this, was that they had moved to a 'better' part of the four parishes, measured in terms of average rateable values of different streets. Additionally, many of the households (38) moved from their previous accommodation only because they disliked that area and moved into the four parishes only because they preferred that area. For this group, too, there was no particular catalyst to migration but only a desire to move into an area that was rather 'better' and had a little more status; the four parishes contain many examples of what might be called 'upward spatial mobility'. When this group is added to that of the spiralists it is apparent that for a large number of migrants this area represents a particularly suitable residential location to match the process of social mobility. A large proportion of the new arrivals in central Surrey had no particular objection to the last house area—they simply found the Horsleys and Clandons more pleasant and more convenient.

Overwhelmingly the most important reasons for in-migration are the rural nature of central Surrey coupled with the particular characteristics of the four parishes; together these account for 35 per cent of the main reasons for migration. However, it is impossible to consider transport location separately since local transport facilities alone account for a further 6 per cent of all in-migration. Availability of transport facilities only represents a small percentage of the main reasons for migration because in itself it is not a sufficient explanation for the move. Its role as a subsidiary reason is much more obvious: most migrants wanted a rural area (which they interpreted in different ways) within commuting distance of their employment. A high proportion of their work journeys involved visits to central London (Table 4.5); most of these migrants and many others were highly dependent on railway accessibility, although others travelling within Surrey were dependent on their cars. Not all location decisions are reached with reference only to the needs of the head of the household; ease of transport to both Greater London and a local workplace (especially Guildford) for other members of the household, often considerably influenced a simpler transport decision. In this context the parishes are ideal locations.

That more than half of the migrant household heads should travel to work in central London is indicative of the status attached to many of their jobs there, and is precisely why this area figures so prominently as part of the 'stockbroker belt'. However, for both new migrants and permanent residents, less than a third of all workplaces are within the rural district, which excludes Guildford (Table 4.6); East Horsley has the smallest proportion of local workers but, again, the contrasts between residents and migrants are substantial. Only 19 per cent of newcomers worked in the rural district, compared with 29 per cent of the total population. From a little more than 400 identifiable occupations of the migrants in all the parishes there were 18 brokers (10 in East Horsley and 5 in West Horsley), 8 bankers (4 each in East and West Horsley), 32 Senior Civil Servants (18 in East Horsley), at least 12 oil executives (11 in East Horsley) and 16 accountants (9 in East Horsley, 4 in West Horsley) in the sample. Engineers were at least as important as brokers and solicitors; surveyors, architects and other more specialised professions, such as surgeons and actuaries, were well represented. Perhaps, more significantly, this professional group excludes 'academics'; there was a thin scatter of teachers but only one technical college lecturer and one

Table 4.5 Workplace location: migrants

Workplace	East Horsley	West Horsley	East Clandon	West Clandon	All	Other Workers
East Horsley	19	4	—	—	23	23
West Horsley	2	25	1	—	28	9
East Clandon	—	1	3	—	4	—
West Clandon	—	—	2	1	3	3
Other Guildford Rural District	7	4	—	3	14	6
Esher	6	5	—	—	11	6
Guildford	10	10	—	7	27	33
Leatherhead	5	7	1	—	13	9
Walton and Weybridge	3	7	—	1	11	1
Other Surrey	14	10	1	2	27	6
Camden	12	5	—	1	18	1
City	20	13	3	8	44	2
Kingston	20	10	1	2	33	2
Wandsworth	6	4	—	—	10	—
Westminster	40	15	2	6	63	6
Other London boroughs	22	29	3	2	56	11
London (unspecified)	14	6	0	2	22	11
Others and unspecified	4	4	1	1	10	3
None or retired	22	21	1	7	51	—
Total	226	180	19	43	468	132

Table 4.6 Workplace location: total population

	East Horsley	West Horsley	East Clandon	West Clandon	All
Within RD	43	31	3	17	94
Outside RD	117	84	2	23	226
	160	115	5	40	320

Source: 1971 Census, E.D. Returns (10% sample).

university lecturer in the whole sample. Much the largest single group, however, was managers, directors and managing directors; more than a third of the sample fitted easily into this category and many others were on the fringes. But numbers are inadequate to indicate the sheer weight of the professional and managerial expertise concentrated in a small group of parishes. One—only a little untypical— example shows the kind of people attracted into the four parishes during the brief survey period. A new resident in Old Manor Farm, East Clandon, was Freddie Laker, owner of Laker Airways, two travel agencies (including Lord Brothers), a 75-acre stud farm close to Epsom, and some 1,000 acres of farm land based on Woolgar's Farm, West Horsley. His wealth and power may be exceptional but they are only more visible than with other local residents. Rather more than a veneer of affluence characterises this part of the Surrey countryside.

Overall, the strong correspondence of persons disliking the previous area and persons liking this particular area points to the large numbers who moved because of the relative attractiveness of the four parishes. At least 10 per cent of all migrants have moved primarily, and often solely, because they dislike one area and prefer another. Ordinarily, the fact that the Horsleys and Clandons are pleasant places to live in is an insufficient reason to explain migration; for this 10 per cent it was both necessary and sufficient. For them the move was not frivolous, but neither was it essential. Indeed, the move to better-quality accommodation represents a significant investment decision. It is a useful means of capital formation.

For the group of migrants that chose to move because of the characteristics of central Surrey, there are striking inter-parish differences. Nine out of 19 migrants into East Clandon stressed the area as the main reason for migration, while none stressed transport; for West Clandon it was only 9 out of 49 and, in between, East Horsley was fractionally above West Horsley. Significantly, the northern part of West Horsley, and Effingham Junction, in the Horsleys, have the lowest proportions that stress the particular local area; these two areas are simply not such attractive residential areas. Many households, especially in West Clandon and East Horsley, but very rarely in West Horsley, waited for a considerable period of time before moving to the area and eventually moved when the particular kind of house that they required came on to the market. Generally, only the group with changed employment location was likely to be looking for a house within a limited period, and was therefore obliged to choose one that was available rather than one that might have been preferred; the majority of the remainder was able to wait until a suitable opportunity arose.

Other reasons for moving to central Surrey are much less important. Only 7 per cent moved into the area because of local employment opportunities and 6 per cent came to be closer to friends or relatives; this is a high figure but even more striking is the fact that more than half was for friends. For many other moves friends and relatives have been extremely influential in fostering a liking for this particular area. Several of those who stated other reasons for migration knew the area well because of friends there before their move. In the local press many people wanting houses in the area specify particular parishes; selling is rarely difficult.

Finally, 19 households (4 per cent) moved into this area primarily because they considered the housing was of better value than in other areas in which they had looked. Although this is only a small proportion of the total it is certainly only the tip of an iceberg since many households have looked in wide areas and all are constrained to purchase a particular sort of house within their particular means. Although 45 households (6 per cent) considered this to be to some extent an important factor it is likely to be the one factor above all (because of the financial implications) that is least likely to be mentioned in a questionnaire survey. Nevertheless this is an exceptionally important group simply because they admit that there were economic restrictions preventing the choice of what they really wanted.

Choosing a house

It is interesting to examine the ways in which households went about finding a new home; despite the assumptions that the search process ought to be logical, hampered only by limited time and limited information, many decisions proved to be a result of very casual trips to central Surrey. Many 'just happened to see the house while driving past'; others chose almost the first they saw, especially if they only had a few days to look around. Yet even amongst those who didn't bother or didn't have time a very high proportion was subsequently entirely satisfied with the choice.

The major influence of transport in stimulating choice of house is reflected in the way decisions were made. Although no household stressed the cost of transport as opposed to accessibility and frequency, many had looked in circles or sectors of variable radii around the place of work. Thus around London various households had operated within radii of 20 miles, 25 miles, 30 miles and 40 miles. For some this was related to journey time: 'a 40-minute ring from Waterloo', and 'less than 50 minutes from Waterloo'; and to journey destination: 'anywhere nice along the Waterloo line', '30 to 60 minutes south of London Airport', 'an hour from Ealing'. London was not the only destination for work journeys and an extraordinary variety of circles, or part circles, about various places, usually workplaces, finally resulted in location in one of the four parishes. The full range of stated radii, without duplication and excluding those who specified particular areas, was as follows: East Horsley (2 miles, 10 miles), West Clandon (3), Effingham (5-10), New Malden (10), Dorking (10), Guildford (5, 6, 8, 10), Surbiton (12), Thames Ditton (12), Weybridge (10), Hinchley Wood (9), Kingston (10 miles, 30 minutes by car), Hersham (20), Leatherhead (4-5), Cobham (3-4), Twickenham (16-17), Woking (10) and Ealing (60 minutes by car). The most striking characteristic of this large group is the logical way in which many households bought maps and timetables and drew lines and circles on their maps to assist their decisions; all considered the chore well rewarded.

For several households distance was not as important as the particular quality of the area. Many sought houses in areas which they had known earlier, where relatives or friends lived or that they had passed through and liked. More general zones were searched by households looking in areas like 'west of London', 'somewhere up the A3', or 'started in Essex, then moved south of the river and looked as far out as Haslemere'.

Migration and housing: élites and council tenants

Other households had smaller regions to search in, usually where transport became important—for example, 'the Cobham-Leatherhead district', 'the rural bits between Leatherhead and Ashtead and Cobham', and 'the Godalming-Guildford-Leatherhead triangle'. Finally, there were very small areas, often only parts of a single parish, that were waited for by several short-distance migrants.

However, there was one further group: those searching particular areas and who could not find a house there or, more particularly, a house that they could afford. Several of their statements indicate the constraints of the housing market on optimal choice. Various households wanted to be: 'in the Horsley area but there were only two houses in our price range', 'around the Horsleys since it costs too much nearer Kingston', 'as near Weybridge as possible' and 'around Leatherhead but prices were more expensive nearer Leatherhead'. Others started searching in particular areas and moved when they could not find suitable accommodation. The household of a West Horsley steel erector, working near Slough and moving from Battersea, had 'looked in a wide area of Surrey, starting in Kingston and moving out since it was cheaper'. Another household looking for a larger house 'started in Merrow [a suburb of Guildford] and moved farther afield since it was too expensive there', whilst a third wanted to be near London and was surprised to find a house in West Horsley that was not too expensive. A separate group was those people who were not looking in particular areas, but who were looking in broad rings at a particular distance from London. Several households, all of whom worked in central London, were looking in such rings, as between Leatherhead and Woking, Weybridge and Coulsdon, Croydon and Walton, and Sevenoaks and Guildford. They may also have favoured rural areas but the size of the rings suggests that they in some way correlated distance with a particular price range. Finally, one household 'started off in Walton and Weybridge and looked as far out as here [West Horsley]; this was the only place where it was possible to get a 100 per cent mortgage on a new house.'

There is no accurate information on the relationship between house prices and distance from the City. It is generally assumed that prices tend to decline with the distance but this is certainly not always so and particularly favoured areas stand out as islands of high prices; the variations within Surrey are as great as those between Surrey and suburban London. Bowers suggested that prices of houses in villages between Guildford and Dorking within the past decade were £500 less than equivalent houses in either town;[5] this seems no longer true. In 1970 Surrey Homes built the same house at different prices in different locations: Guildford (£12,950), Reigate (£14,900), East Horsley (£16,000) and Burwood Park, Walton (£19,500). Local estate agents show convincingly that specific locations, especially East Clandon, significantly alter the price of housing. Although prices do tend to decrease with distance from central London much more important are the often very great fluctuations dependent on local situations. A small number of households therefore could not find accommodation in areas that they preferred and would not otherwise have chosen to live in the four parishes; however, what proportion of even this small group, or indeed of the total, had unrealistic expectations of the area in which they might live is unknown. The proportion of 'reluctant commuters'[6] in the four parishes is extremely small, much smaller than the proportions described in other metropolitan villages; the basic explanation is that within the four parishes there were very few new houses and almost no new estates completed during the survey period. This is one of the islands of high prices to which people are not reluctant to go. Because of the protective influence of Green-Belt legislation on the particular housing stock of the four parishes the 'reluctant commuters', supposedly typical of many metropolitan villages, are almost absent.

Tied houses

So far it has largely been assumed that new residents of the Horsleys and Clandons were free to choose their own residence, but this is not always so. Two groups of residents are restricted either to tied houses or to within the council sector. In the first case they must live more or less where their new job is and, in the second, where the council provides accommodation (although they can usually influence this decision).

In the four parishes 37 households moved into tied accommodation; these two groups are almost identical and East Clandon has a disproportionately high total. East Horsley has 16, West Horsley 15, East Clandon 5 and West Clandon 1. However, only 6 of these previously lived in the four parishes and the expected local nature of migration into tied accommodation is not apparent; indeed, only 17 of the 37 lived in Surrey before their move. The reasons for this are the particular occupations of the migrants in the group: the major categories are farm workers (7), shopkeepers (owners or managers) (6), housekeepers/cooks (3), police (3), publicans (3), farmers (2) and the army (2). Several of these are specialist occupations, and hence there is little reason for migrants to have previously lived locally, whilst for the single most important category, farm workers, the small number of local agricultural workers means that vacancies in this group are unlikely to be filled by local workers. Indeed, the high wages paid, because of the specialised agricultural work available, means that local opportunities are attractive to skilled workers in less profitable areas. None of the 7 agricultural workers had previously lived in any of the four parishes; 3 came from Sussex and 1 from Dorset. Thus although the four parishes are in a rural district, less than a quarter of the tied accommodation is related to agriculture and even within this group the migrants have come long distances—a very different situation from what might be casually expected.

Council houses

If access to the tied-housing market is subject to a bewildering range of clauses and sub-clauses related to the occupation and status of the new workers, then in some ways access to the council-housing sector is much more straightforward. Guildford Rural District Council, which until 1973 controlled all the council housing in the four parishes, had a lengthy set of rules enabling them to regulate carefully movement into and within this sector. Moreover, all local authorities have virtual autonomy in the selection of tenants for their houses. There is no statutory income limit or residential qualification that authorities have to observe. Indeed, the only statutory provision merely requires them to give 'reasonable preference to persons who are occupying insanitary or overcrowded conditions'.[7] Anyone may apply for inclusion on a local-authority housing list, although where the authority considers their present situation adequate they may wait indefinitely on the list according to the availability of houses and the allocation priorities of that council. Thus the significance of the list is not its absolute size but the situation of the households on it; nevertheless, the Guildford Rural District Council has always faced a lengthy waiting list. From the end of the Second World War the waiting list declined from 1,700 to about 1,100 in 1948 but at the end of 1968 the list was recorded at 1,307[8] and was still rising steadily in 1973 when the organisation changed. Access to a stock of only 2,600 housing units was therefore always fairly difficult.

Within the rural district an essential for consideration for housing allocation was the residential qualification—or what Guildford Rural District Council called 'claim on the district'. The council's residential qualification was for two years either living or working in the area, but exceptions were made for urgent cases of hardship or for 'key workers' (especially council workers). Accompanying the basic local residential qualification were two other associated qualifications that no single person under the age of 50 would be accepted on to the list and that a maximum annual wage must not be exceeded. This second criterion was introduced in 1957 at £700; in 1958 it was raised to £800, in 1964 to £1,000 and it was £1,250 between 1967 and 1971. In this area, with a wage of between £1,250 and £2,000, it was quite impossible to purchase any accommodation, and hence the limit was not very useful in terms of removing owner-occupiers from the list although it was useful for ensuring some priority for the poorest paid. Consequently the income limit was completely abandoned in 1971.

In addition to the basic residential qualification, which can be waived in cases of hardship, all local authorities have a selection scheme for the choice of tenants. Underlying each individual scheme is a chronological-order system whereby, other things being equal, applicants will be dealt with in order of application to the local authority. The basis of many selection schemes is a points scheme which, with varying degrees of complexity, is almost universal. The scheme used by Guildford Rural District Council was extremely complex, running to five closely typed foolscap papers. For elderly persons over 60 years of age there were five basic categories, one of which was claim on the district. The other four were health, eviction or insecurity of tenure, unsuitable accommodation and isolation. The maximum number of points available in each category was health 16, eviction 20 or insecurity 15, unsuitable accommodation 12, isolation 20 and claim on district 5. Health points were only awarded when the Medical Officer of Health had assessed the case, whilst the small number of points given for 'claim on the district' indicates its use only to differentiate between applicants of equal need.

The scheme for applicants under 60 years of age was based on the same categories but weighed the points rather differently. Overcrowding tended to be more important because of an increased probability of children; isolation and insecurity were less important. Tied accommodation is therefore more significant for elderly residents, especially when they wish to retire.

When the district council took over from the rural district council the rural points scheme was superseded by the district scheme. Like its predecessor it was highly confidential, especially so with regard to possible future council tenants since it was feared that they might abuse the system; however, an 'anonymous source' gave a copy of the list to the *Surrey Advertiser* and in 1974 it was published in detail[9] and can be summarised as follows:

> The scheme is broken down into various point-earning categories. The category which receives the highest individual maximum—16—deals with people whose present housing conditions are affecting their health, or physical disability, and the points are awarded by the Community

Physician. But the applicant is given only one point for each year he or she is on the housing list, up to a maximum of 10.

Points are allocated as follows: If a separate bedroom is needed for each occupant in the present house but they find they are sharing, 10 points are given for each extra bedroom needed. If a living room is shared with two other families eight points are awarded; if it is shared by one other family five points, and if there is no living room at all the applicant will get 10 points. For having no kitchen or sharing it plus a cooker 10 points are given and if there is no cooker, sink with hot and cold water, larder or refrigerator one point is allowed for each item needed— 10 points is the maximum.

For no bathroom five points are awarded; for a shared bathroom two and if there is no hot or cold water, bath or washbasin two points are given for each item. A maximum of five points is allowed. Where there is no lavatory five points are allotted; for a shared lavatory three points and an outside w.c. will get two points and five more if the applicant is elderly.

If the applicant has lived in the district for 15 years or more he or she gets a maximum of two points. Parents or children separated because they have nowhere to live, or children in care, receive 10 points. Elderly people living alone with a footpath entrance will get 10 points and two people with a footpath entrance get five. Housing with difficult entrances gets from one to five points. If the elderly person finds it difficult to climb stairs but needs to in his or her present home, or if the house is too large to manage they will get five points. If a house is overcrowded five points are awarded for each half person over the limit. If an applicant living in a tied house is within three months of retiring he will be pointed as if he had nowhere to live at all.

Compared with the old rural scheme this is a more bureaucratic and more urban-orientated scheme with a much greater emphasis on unsuitable accommodation and health rather than the eviction and insecurity of tenure more familiar in rural areas. Isolation is no longer a factor, and it is more important to become established on the housing list (for which 10 points are possible) than actually to have lived in the district for more than 15 years (for which only 2 points can be scored). So far no rural dwellers have moved to town, or *vice versa*, but it is impossible to predict how the merger will eventually operate.

The major difficulty of all points schemes is that they are extremely complex and it is very difficult to combine detail with fairness; they must be continually revised in order not to become outdated and, because of the complexity and confidentiality of such schemes, there is some confusion by prospective tenants over the basis for allocation of points. In 1966 part of one letter written to the housing officer read as follows: 'I now have a second child which is also a boy. . .I do hope that this will gain more points on your housing list.' Although, in this case, the gaining of points was inevitable, it is possible that some prospective tenants will try to cheat the system. It is also unfortunately true that persistent households will be housed most quickly and the assistance of councillors or even MPs will certainly speed the application along. A further difficulty is that several of the criteria are scarcely measurable; the degree of friction that results from overcrowding is simply not quantifiable although ideally it would not need to be quantifiable. Inevitably, despite this kind of qualification system, almost all applicants tend to consider that the principle 'first come, first served' is justified and this can be a problem for housing authorities that wish to discriminate positively in favour of applicants in the worst conditions of hardship.

Most local authorities, including Guildford, pay home visits to applicants; these may be used to gain information and give advice but they may also be used to assess housing standards and 'suitability' for different kinds of council housing. The justification for this is that some tenants will not take care of a new house or cannot pay high rents; local authorities seem loath to recognise the potential improvement in living conditions that can follow the transfer of a family to better accommodation. Consequently, many authorities pursue a somewhat moralistic approach; the

Migration and housing: élites and council tenants

Guildford records contain many references to 'clean', 'dirty' and 'nicely spoken' families and other even more personal details. Because of the vagaries of individual officers and the unavailability of the waiting list, it is impossible to assess the importance of this approach for the allocation of houses and the location of these houses in particular estates. Councils will tend to favour a potentially good (that is solvent, tractable, clean and quiet) tenant to enable efficient council-house management. Furthermore, this efficiency is increased by the segregation of different kinds of tenant in different estates or different parts of the same estate. Nevertheless, much of the existing social segregation is merely a result of historical accident, dependent on the structure of the waiting list at the time the first houses were built on a particular estate.

The rent structure is indicative of the status of the different estates (Table 4.7). The highest rents for 3-bedroomed

Table 4.7 Council-house basic rents (in shillings), March 1970

	Bedrooms			
	1	2	3	4
East Horsley				
Old Lane	—	69	—	—
Wellington Cottages	—	—	65	—
Kingston Avenue	—	74	93	—
West Horsley				
Mount Pleasant	50	51	90	—
Fulkes Cottages	—	69	72	—
Farleys Close	—	69	64	75
Nightingale Crescent	—	—	91	—
Northcote Close	—	71	—	—
Woodside	—	69	86	93
West Clandon				
Glebe Cottages	—	—	63/83	—
Meadowlands	49	69	86	94
East Clandon				
Snelgate Cottages	—	—	61	—

Source: Guildford Rural District Council housing records, 1970.

Migration and housing: élites and council tenants

houses are in Kingston Avenue and Nightingale Crescent, followed by Mount Pleasant, whilst the lowest rents are in Snelgate Cottages, Wellington Cottages and Farleys Close; for 2-bedroomed houses there is less difference. The oldest estates with the lowest rents, like Snelgate Cottages, do tend to have a class composition concentrated in the lower echelons (Table 4.8), whilst on a newer estate like Nightingale Cresent the classes are much higher up the social scale. At the time of the research the council allocated households to the particular estates in the parishes that they considered them appropriate for in terms of, for example, ability to pay rent and 'dirtiness'. No records of social distress are maintained as a statutory obligation in the council's housing records, but there are references to divorces, separations, eviction notices and, less regularly, mental-hospital treatment, court cases and gaol

Table 4.8 Council-house class structure, 1970

	Social class						
	1	2	3	4	5	Unknown	
Snelgate Cottages *E.C.*	—	1	2	2	3	4	12
Meadowlands	1	5	23	19	12	29	89
Glebe Cottages	—	2	4	5	5	6	22
West Clandon	1	7	27	24	17	35	111
Wellington Cottages	-	—	2	6	3	1	12
Kingston Avenue	—	3	12	10	2	18	45
Old Lane	—	—	2	2	—	4	8
East Horsley	—	3	16	18	5	23	65
Woodside	—	—	5	4	2	1	12
Northcote Close	—	—	—	—	—	8	8
Farleys Close	—	—	10	2	4	16	32
Nightingale Crescent	—	9	27	9	—	3	48
Fulkes Cottages	—	—	4	7	3	6	20
Mount Pleasant	—	—	5	8	4	11	28
Other WH	—	—	3	—	—	—	3
West Horsley	—	9	54	30	13	45	151
Total	1	20	99	74	38	107	339

Source: Guildford Rural District Council housing records, 1970, Classification of Occupations, London, HMSO, 1960.

sentences. This information is more confidential and diffuse, less readily available and less systematically collected, but it is quite clear that these particular problems are concentrated on a restricted number of estates and especially on the older estates. The extent to which this is cause or effect is problematical. In terms of the social status of individual estates, as reflected in the tenants' views and the views of owner-occupiers outside, social distress tends to confirm the divisions suggested by social class. Moreover, in style the pre-war council estates are more obviously council houses to an extent that the post-war houses are not; this again tends to maintain the higher status of the newer estates. Nightingale Crescent in particular probably merges most successfully with the adjoining owner-occupied housing, has the highest rateable values of any council-house street and a social-class composition most biased towards the higher classes. Elsewhere, as Tucker states bluntly:[10]

> An acrimonious hierarchy establishes itself among council tenants and is strengthened day by day. They are segregated from each other by income, social standing, job; by class in fact. People with low domestic standards may be concentrated (or allowed to concentrate) in particular estates and corners of estates so that other tenants will not be offended; and it is frequently these areas which create among private owners and tenants the impression of what local authority housing is like.

Residential qualifications inhibit mobility into the council-house sector but within that sector it is possible to be quite mobile. Transfers between different kinds of council accommodation can be made in two different ways. The council itself often moves households into more appropriately sized accommodation: thus Kingston Avenue, East Horsley, having a large number of flats, therefore contains small households and elderly people. Others are moved to accommodation for which they can more easily pay the rent. Normally a suggestion to the occupant, followed by a suggestion to a younger relative if this fails, is sufficient to produce a move; in a few cases it is more difficult. Those who most oppose a move are generally old people who have lived in their present parish for many years and for whom the alternative accommodation might be in a different, inaccessible parish. A letter from a woman in East Clandon rejecting an offer of a flat in Wood Street, Worplesdon, where her brother lived, in exchange for her 3-bedroomed house, might be regarded as fairly typical of this category:

> I am coming up to 72 and when you pull your roots up at that age there don't seem to be nothing left. I don't suppose I have a lot of years left and if I went away they would be miserable years we (*sic*) don't know what is in our path so please bear with me.

On the other hand, others who have refused to move (in one case recorded on the record card as 'should imagine she would have to be removed kicking and screaming') are ultimately found suitable accommodation and may be more satisfied by being on an estate with several other elderly people in similar situations.

The second kind of transfer is arranged by the tenants themselves, subject to the council's approval; tenants sometimes wish to move either to different parts of the rural district, perhaps to be nearer their job or relatives, or to different parts of Britain for a new job or to retire. Since only two local authorities in England consider there to be enough of this kind of potential migrant to justify the effort of maintaining a register of their needs they must arrange such a move themselves. This is usually done through the prospective workplace and by housing office, shop-window and newspaper advertisements, all of which are generally known to be methods of exchange and therefore effective in achieving the necessary contact between prospective migrants. Occasionally the moves become even more complex and three- and four-way exchanges have occurred in the rural district. However, since there are relatively few households that want to transfer, it is fairly unusual for there to be many successful exchanges; exchange is a very frustrating form of migration.

Although exchanges across local-authority boundaries

Migration and housing: élites and council tenants

account for no more than 10 per cent of all moves in a single year their interest lies in the fact that they are the only long-distance moves in the council-housing sector. Indeed, only in the immediate aftermath of the Second World War, when many ex-servicemen and women married spouses in different parts of the country, was there a greater proportion of long-distance moves. The organisation of local-authority housing is such that the market is extremely local and most households move very short distances to their council houses.

Table 4.9 Council-house migration: all tenants

Previous residence	East Clandon	West Clandon	East Horsley	West Horsley	Total
Same parish	0	44	13	58	115 (34%)
Rest of rural district	6	54	44	73	177 (52%)
Outside rural district	0	5	5	15	25 (7%)
Before 1938/Unknown	6	8	3	5	22 (7%)
	12	111	65	151	339

The last place of residence of all present council-house tenants is recorded in Table 4.9. Migration distances in the council-house sector are extremely short; at least 86 per cent of all tenants moved within the rural district and only about 7 per cent came from outside it. Not a single migrant came from outside the South East; 14 came from other parts of Surrey (including 7 from Guildford), 7 were from Greater London, 3 from Hampshire and 1 from Kent. Even the minor disruption of the Second World War scarcely altered the basic pattern. Moreover, each parish, and even each housing estate, has a catchment area which is specifically local; only 15 of the 292 tenants who definitely came from within the rural district came from parishes east of Guildford. Altogether more than half of all tenants were accommodated either in their 'home' parish or one next to it. The general availability of a range of accommodation in each parish aids this kind of stability, yet this kind of ripple-like migration pattern stands in striking contrast to the waves of owner-occupiers migrating into the larger, detached houses situated between the council estates.

Movements into the council-house sector from other kinds of local housing are entirely from accommodation which has been inadequate in some way, either because of insecurity (tied or other kinds of rented accommodation), unsuitability, or through sharing of accommodation. Caravans are a constant source of in-migrants to council estates; although there are no official caravan sites in the four parishes there are several in the rural district and a few individual caravans in the four parishes. Until 1961 they were sufficiently important for there to be a Moveable Dwellings Committee of the Guildford Rural District Council. This was then included within the General Purposes Committee as the whole caravan housing stock declined in numbers and improved in organisation and quality. It is impossible to enumerate reasons for migration into council houses accurately because they are inadequately recorded in the housing records, because they are usually a combination of several factors and because the initial reason may change substantially during the course of application; several of the present tenants waited between ten and twenty years for a house.

Nevertheless from a detailed inspection of the housing records and an examination of the letters to and from applicants it is possible to make certain qualitative judgments. First, the worst rural houses of the post-war years have almost all been cleared and conditions before re-housing are less inadequate now; hence overcrowding is now a much more significant factor than a totally unsuitable home. Second, the number of tied houses is declining with the decline in agricultural employment, and re-housing from tied accommodation is less frequent. Third, and perhaps most important of all, communications between the housing office and tenants are increasingly less formal and bureaucratic and hence the local housing situation is more clearly understood by applicants.

Both the awfulness of earlier housing conditions and the previous inability of the housing office to engage in a useful dialogue are indicated in the following letters written to and from the office in 1951, respectively handwritten and typed. Neither the conditions nor the formality is likely to be repeated.

Dear Miss ——
Just a line to ask you if you can get us any thing in the way house or bungalow I know you have some nearly ready because my hubbys sister has got one and she said she would very much like me to be her neyber but I told her that is impossible because you got all the tenants for then havit you, my hubby. . .has lived in send all his life and he would like to go back to send to get a far better job with more money, I cant live on 3 pounds a week I have to pay over a pound for coal to boil my clothes we have no boiler no bathroom no gas I only wish you could do something for us soon I wouldnt mind the rent how would you to go to work in the morning with no tea if its only a two room flat we could take it just to get away from here

. . .there is no bath room and no light of any sort only oil lamp and no gas we have to cook by fire and I heard it was a very old house and the boss said he could never afford to put light or gas in my hubby has to go without a drink because we dont it boiled in time.

This hot weather is making the rats come to through the garden we got a tin bucket for a lavotry its very damp in the winter any food goes green.

[Their single room was merely curtained off from the landlord.]

Dear Madam,
Housing Application Ref. No. p. 160 (please always quote)

Following receipt of your second letter giving reference No. I have now traced your application. This should always be quoted whenever you write to this office in order to avoid confusion with others of the same name.

Your application has now been reinstated on the list and it will be considered among the others when suitable accommodation becomes available.

Yours faithfully,
———————
Chief Asst. Housing Officer

Out of the total sample of 468 households, completed questionnaires covered only 29 council households, a reflection both of the relative local unimportance of the council-house sector and the low level of mobility into that sector. The reasons why this small group moved are set out in Table 4.10. The basic reasons are quite straightforward

Table 4.10 Council-house migration: new tenants

Left previous accommodation		Came to present accommodation	
Smaller/larger house	9	Smaller/larger house	9
Own home	5	Housing availability	11
Overcrowding	4	With relatives	2
Tied house	2	Changed employment location	2
Changed employment location	2	Nearer work	2
Nearer work	2	Country area	1
Poor area	1	Personal reasons	1
Personal reasons	3	Unknown	1
Unknown	1		

but there are slight variations from the apparent administrative possibilities. Personal reasons have some part to play and some households move to share with relatives; moreover, 8 per cent of all council households have lodgers whose migratory behaviour tends to be somewhat unpredictable. Thus the rigorous administrative structure of the local-authority housing masks a significant amount of arranged exchange migration for personal, and even trivial, reasons.

The most obvious reflection of the differences in housing within the four parishes is seen in the class composition of the council-house tenants, as it compares with either the whole of central Surrey (of which it represents less than a third) or with the new migrants (all but 66 of whom have moved into owner-occupied accommodation).[11] Most dramatically, although the two higher social classes include almost half the population of central Surrey, they include no more than 9 per cent of the council-house occupants but a massive 75 per cent of all the new migrants (Table 4.11). Council-house migrants are quite distinct from those elsewhere. Once again it is clear how migration is emphatically changing the class structure of central Surrey; moreover, in less than two years there were more migrant households entering central Surrey than there are council households permanently resident

Migration and housing: élites and council tenants

Table 4.11 Central Surrey: social-class composition

Social class	Council-house tenants		Central Surrey (1966)		All migrants		Council-house migrants	
	number	%	number*	%	number	%	number	%
1	1	0	32	13	159	33	0	0
2	20	9	94	37	201	42	1	4
3	99	43	90	36	81	17	8	33
4	74	32	33	13	26	5	7	29
5	38	16	4	2	13	3	8	33
Unknown	107	—	12	—	8	—	5	—
Total	339		265		488		29	

* 10% sample.

there. As the social composition of the council houses continues to remain almost unchanged the changes in privately owned houses continue to accentuate the growing distance between the two housing systems. Segregated spatially the two systems are structurally apart.

Parish housing structure

Owner-occupied housing and council housing made up 83 per cent of the housing stock of the four parishes in 1961 and by 1971 this was 89 per cent (Table 4.12). A small proportion is rented unfurnished, and this proportion is slowly declining, whilst the remainder still includes a small and very rapidly declining proportion of tied accommodation which is now almost non-existent, whereas in 1961 it represented 7 per cent (about 170 homes) of the total housing stock. Compared, therefore, with the national situation central Surrey is quite different; almost everybody either owns their own home or rents it from the council. This is a very basic dichotomy within each of the four parishes, although to a much lesser extent in East Clandon where more traditional forms of tenure are maintained still. Moreover the dichotomy is accentuated since unfurnished rented accommodation is very similar to owner-occupied housing, and tied houses are similar to council houses. Nationally this twofold division is blurred as a much greater range of housing situations presents a smoother gradation between different types.

Migration and housing: élites and council tenants

Table 4.12 Housing stock, 1971

	East Clandon	West Clandon	East Horsley	West Horsley	All parishes	England and Wales
Owner occupiers	43	57	84	73	76	50
Rented—council	13	31	6	15	13	28
Rented—furnished	3	1	3	2	2	5
Rented—unfurnished	42	10	7	10	9	17
Not stated (includes 'tied')	1	0	0	1	0	0

Source: 1971 Census, E.D. Returns (10% sample).
Note: All figures are rounded percentages and hence do not necessarily total 100 per cent.

The privileged position of central Surrey is quite clear in the massive percentage of owner-occupied housing. Not that central Surrey is totally unique in this respect; both within and beyond the Green Belt there is a scatter of high-status areas. Whitehand called these areas 'the cocktail belt' of Greater London, regarding it as 'the extreme manifestation of the social segregation of England'.[12] In this respect London, as the capital city, is unique, but although the Horsleys and Clandons are highly segregated they are only particularly advanced examples of processes going on at the fringe of all large west European cities.

Local houses are extremely expensive: in 1968 the average house price in the parishes was £10,827 compared with the London and South East regional figure of £5,786 and in 1970 the respective prices were £12,952 and £6,250. Since then prices have rocketed and the local variation has become even greater. (In 1976 the respective prices were £33,368 and £12,918, now nearly three times the regional average.) In the adjoining parish of Send, a cottage was sold in 1969 for £5,000 and in 1971 sold again, without improvement, for £12,750. Consequently, house prices are so high that there is no prospect of movement from the council-house or tied-accommodation sectors into the owner-occupier category. The owner-occupied sector is quite distinct from the other two inferior sectors.

Access to owner-occupied housing is usually by way of a loan from a building society willing to offer about two-and-a-half times the potential purchaser's salary. For even the cheapest house in the four parishes the income and deposit required by a first-time purchaser are now quite staggering and are almost certain to deter all but the most affluent. Moreover, many building societies have restrictive clauses; some demand that mortgage repayments be completed on retirement, others deter single young women and almost all discriminate in favour of professional persons. The usual conditions under which mortgages are granted act as a most conservative filter on access to local housing; with the very high house prices of central Surrey the filter is particularly effective. Those without savings, high incomes, regular professional employment and with any kind of social need have almost no chance of passing through the meshes. Thus both building societies, and to a lesser extent estate agents, have the power to allocate housing resources in the private sector whilst, in the public sector, the same role is played directly by the local authority. Moreover, there is a much more complex variety of operational rules within the public sector. Both groups of what have been called 'gatekeepers' are biased in favour of the more affluent applicants in their respective sectors, and the private sector is much more able to accommodate spatial mobility than the public sector, which allows only a very limited number of exchanges. In both cases the individual preferences of households are substantially constrained by institutional procedures; unconsciously, institutions shape rural life much more effectively than the conscious decisions of individual families.

In most circumstances the major distinctions within the housing market are between the private and public sectors and between the rented and owned sectors. Here these four groups intersect almost exactly; almost all private housing is owned and most of the rented housing is in the public sector. Nevertheless the two major groups are not alone. There is not one dichotomised housing market but a series of micromarkets between each of which movement is possible. First, there is the 'tied'-accommodation sector in which accommodation is allocated with a job and is given up when that job is left. In 1966 this represented about 7 per cent of the local stock but fell to less than 1 per cent in 1971; few of these were agricultural workers and many had white-collar employment where job security and consequently housing security are greater. Those losing their accommodation in this sector usually find it impossible to enter any of the other sectors easily. In the first post-war decade it was virtually impossible for a displaced agricultural labourer to obtain a council house; now the number of such people is much smaller and the possibility is rather greater if only because the circumstances arise less often. Second, there is the rented sector, which in this area is simply an extension of the owner-occupied sector since mobility between the two sectors is relatively straightforward and the social composition of the two groups is similar. Third, there is the council-house sector. In this sector there is very limited mobility; external migration is largely related to change of employment and internal migration is related to over- or under-occupation. Neither is very common. Movement out of the council-housing sector is virtually non-existent and certainly does not occur within central Surrey. Furthermore house prices (and rents) are likely to become so high at the same time as tied accommodation disappears that there will be a tiny and diminishing group of people able to make a 'claim on the district' whilst actually living in the area. Finally, there is the owner-occupied sector into which access is restricted to those with relatively high incomes. A further distinction between the last two sectors is in their organisation. The local-authority sector is administered from Guildford and supply and demand are almost entirely confined to town and the rural district around it; the owner-occupied sector has its supply locally based (in terms of distribution of houses and the advertisement of those houses in the local media) but demand, whilst being concentrated in a southwest sector out of London, has strong national and even international components.

In the early 1950s some council houses were sold in the rural district, including more than 200 in East and West Horsley alone; thus four houses in Woodside, West Horsley, were sold in 1953 for £2,350 each. The council placed various restrictions on the future use and resale of the houses, which were intended only for those in housing need. Subsequent squeezes on the purchase of private housing and the growth in the council-house waiting list from its mid-1950s trough persuaded the council to change its policy and in 1958 sales again ceased.[13] During the 1960s the council once more became interested in selling council houses and, despite some opposition within the council, it was again decided in 1971 that some houses would be sold. At that time some 488 of the 2,500 tenants expressed an interest but less than a year later only 183 tenants (representing some 7 per cent of the housing stock) confirmed this interest. By then it was known that the rural district council would soon disappear so that their interest was not then rewarded because the Guildford Borough Council had not then decided to sell council houses. In August 1976 the new district council also decided to sell off some council houses (at a time when the waiting list included more than 2,700 applicants), advertising some 3-bedroomed houses, in the town only, for between £12,600 and £13,200, a price compatible with the lowest prices for local private housing. For the first time it seemed that council houses would become available to their tenants in an experimental move that might subsequently be extended to the villages of central Surrey.

The changed policy of selling council houses will create an inferior owner-occupied sector in the sense that sales are subsequently restricted by particular local-authority conditions. It may also result in greater pressure on the diminished council stock creating an increased demand for new building in this sector and therefore a demand for building land. However, since a very small percentage of local-authority housing (about 5 per cent) is re-let there is unlikely to be a substantial loss of public-authority housing. It is in this competition for land that the two sectors already conflict and by transferring housing in this direction between sectors (making the not unreasonable assumption that present demands are more or less maintained) competition is likely to be intensified beyond the point where the council cannot afford to buy land for house construction. Indeed, since 1973 there has been almost no new building.

The characteristic social composition of the existing housing sectors in central Surrey has resulted in the existence of three partly homogeneous kinds of housing class: the owner-occupiers, the council tenants and a tiny and more anomalous group of 'tied' tenants. It is the growing division between the first and second group which characterises many of the social relationships within the Horsleys and Clandons.

CHAPTER 5

Country life

Perhaps in no other country is it possible by subtle delimitations, subdivisions, cul-de-sacs, golf links, bits of common land, pubs, gardens, unadopted roads, preservation societies and a thousand customs grafted onto an already uniquely made landscape, still to observe a distinction, sometimes in quite un-rural looking areas, between a town and country consciousness.

Paul Jennings, The Living Village

No migrants ever come to central Surrey because they are attracted by the range of social amenities there; yet, if the migrants are still a long way from American suburbia in belonging and taking part, it is quite clear that for many the attractions of the villages do include the local societies. Each village has a hall and a range of social organisations and beyond the villages there are regional facilities; even those who are not members are quite conscious that taking part is just a little expected of them and most have intentions of doing more than handing over their subscription to the Conservative Party.

Indeed, the range of opportunities is formidable, especially in East Horsley: if it does not represent all that a new migrant desires it certainly includes almost all that he or she might reasonably expect to exist. Even the list in Table 5.1 is not complete; it is certainly short of children's organisations, youth organisations (some of which tend to appear and

Table 5.1 Social organisations, 1971

East Clandon	West Clandon	East Horsley	West Horsley
EC Women's Institute	WC Badminton Club	Horsley Choral Society	WH Evening Floral Circle
	WC British Legion	Horsley Society of Arts	
	WC Football Club	Horsley Youth Theatre	WH British Legion
	WC Women's Institute	EH Floral Decoration Society	WH Old People's Welfare Committee
	WC Youth Club	EH Young Farmers' Club	WH Good Companions Club (old people)
	WC Young Wives' Club	Old Lane Gardening Association	WH Women's Institute (afternoon/evening)
	Clandon Seniors' Club	EH Young Wives	WHIPS (drama)
	WC Horticultural Society	Horsley Women's Liberal Association	Horsley Cricket Club
	WC Floral Group	Howard Women's Club (The Friday Nighters)	Horsley United AFC
	WC Tennis Club	St John's Ambulance Brigade	WH Badminton Club
	WC Conservative Association	Horsley Shelter Group	WH Horticultural Society
Clandon Society		Horsley Under 30s Club	
		EH Women's Institute (afternoon/evening)	
		Woodlands Senior Club	
		Good Neighbour Organisation	
		Nomad Players	
		Horsley Sports and Social Club (Pennymead) (including social, hockey, tennis, E.H. Cricket Club)	
		Horsley Conservative Association	
		Horsley Music Circle	
		Horsley Bridge Club	
		Horsley Red Cross Society	
		Horsley Liberal Party	
		Horsley Countryside Preservation Society	
		Ockham Road Protection Association	
		Horsley Association	
		Five Villages Association	

disappear at rather brief intervals) and possibly other organisations catering for very small minorities. Most of the present associations are quite recent but some have existed since the inter-war years. Nevertheless fashions change; in East Horsley in 1936 there was the British Legion, the Mothers' Union, the Parochial Church Council, the Choral Society, the Sports Club, the Scouts and Rangers and the inevitable Women's Institute,[1] but by 1956 there had already been substantial changes, the societies then being the Parochial Church Council, the Choral Society, the Red Cross, the British Legion, the Young People's Club, the East and West Horsley Gardening Society, the Boy Scouts, the Girl Guides, the WI, the Young Conservatives, the Young Farmers' Club, the St John's Ambulance Brigade, the Nomad Players (drama), the Floral Decoration Society, a camera club and a dancing club.[2] Even before the Second World War they were already quite unlike the village organisations that Orwin thought typical of post-war Oxfordshire villages: WI, young farmers' club, village produce association, pig club and flower show.[3] It is rather difficult to imagine a pig club in East Horsley.

The number of present-day organisations is roughly proportional to the parish population sizes but is much greater than in villages with a more traditional agricultural organisation. Moreover, there are more societies in each parish now than at any other time. Local life thrives now as it has never done before; for example, in West Horsley alone the number of bookings of the village hall rose from 685 in 1966-7 to 1,050 in 1973-4. The only really important political party is the Conservative Party; there is no trace of Labour Party existence, even in the council estates within the parishes, although the Liberal Party is fairly strong and well organised in the Horsleys. None of the council estates has tenants' associations, and the Clandon Ratepayers' Association that existed in 1930 has long since disappeared. Sporting amenities are variable. East Horsley, despite its size, does not have a football pitch; Horsley United play in West Horsley and are primarily manned and supported from there, although East Horsley does have hockey, tennis and cricket clubs, all at the expensive Horsley Sports and Social Club. West Horsley also has a cricket club, with a vastly inferior pitch and fixture list, and two tennis courts, operated and maintained by the parish council, rather than a club joined through private subscription. Very few of the social organisations appeal to more than a limited proportion of the local population and only the WI, the British Legion and the various old people's clubs draw in a variety of social groups. Moreover, apart from a few sports clubs, the majority of organisations cater almost solely for the middle class. This is most noticeable and least surprising for such small societies as the Horsley Music Circle but extends even as far as the horticultural societies— elsewhere usually a traditional working-class activity. Indeed, the president of the West Clandon Horticultural Society, which has existed since the Second World War, complained that: 'we can't get much out of the Meadowlands estate... they are a law to themselves.'

Many societies that have been existing for some time are increasingly being organised for and run by the most recent newcomers rather than either the village 'gentry' or working-class villagers. This is scarcely a unique phenomenon and has been recognised in a number of instances. Peake observed as early as 1922:[4]

> The advent into many villages of families from outside, usually of the professional or business classes...has had some effect on the social life of the areas into which they have come. Accustomed to the more sociable life of the towns and having ample leisure, they frequently set about organising amusements in the villages in which they have settled.

The change is important especially when it is coupled with a real decline in the number of working-class organisations. Furthermore, just as in Worcestershire,[5] the concentration of officer positions at one end of the social scale discourages members at the other end. It is a long time—about half a century—since the East Horsley Working Men's Club was in operation, and the street parties that greeted the Coronation and similar events are things of the past. Now another group of societies is declining; the Howard Youth Club (Effingham Junction) and the East Horsley Adventurers Youth Club both

Country life

closed in 1969, whilst the West Clandon Youth Club, which had 100 members in 1962, closed in 1970 from lack of support. A joint Effingham and Horsleys Youth Club was revived in 1974 but by then the Horsley Under 30s Club had gone under. There are simply insufficient young people in central Surrey.

Not all the societies are of equal importance in any sense. In many ways the preservation societies (see Chapter 6) are the most influential both in terms of size of membership and ability to change the local environment. By comparison, societies such as the Newlands Corner Riding Club and the Horsley Bridge Club are unremarked outside a tiny group of enthusiasts. Socially, much the most important are the Women's Institutes and in small parishes throughout Britain these are often the only existing social organisation; in East Clandon this is so, whilst in both Horsleys the population size is large enough to justify a separate afternoon and evening group. Furthermore the East Horsley WI has been in existence in the parish since 1919 and the others almost as long.

Migrants were questioned to find out which societies they took part in or had joined; the results are not entirely satisfactory since it was quite clear that for many migrants the churches were significant foci of social life—but there are few formal church associations. Moreover there is a difference between joining and taking part; although there were at least 28 members of the Conservative Association the number of activists, in any sense, was probably much less. Nevertheless the most important organisations, in terms of membership, exist in all three larger parishes and membership of these societies and the remaining minority societies can be aggregated and summarised (Table 5.2). Overall membership is roughly proportional to the social class composition of the parishes. However, the WIs, horticultural societies and floral groups have a slightly greater proportion of social class 2. Participation in 'other' organisations is more biased in favour of lower social classes, reflecting the inclusion in this group of many associations which have small memberships amongst new migrants, such as the seniors' clubs and the British Legion, precisely because there are few migrants who find these societies interesting to them. Of existing societies the

Country life

Table 5.2 Social-class composition of voluntary associations

	Social class					
	1	2	3	4	5	Total
Women's Institutes	13	25	5	1	–	44
Preservation societies	17	12	3	–	–	32
Horticultural societies	4	10	1	–	–	15
Floral groups	6	16	–	–	–	22
Young wives' clubs	6	7	–	–	–	13
Sports clubs	28	23	3	1	–	55
Conservative Associations	16	12	–	–	–	28
Drama groups	16	12	2	–	–	30
Music/arts societies	7	1	2	–	–	10
Others	16	13	9	1	1	40

only ones that did not have any members amongst the new migrants were Clandon Seniors' Club, West Horsley Old People's Welfare Committee and Horsley United AFC; others with one household member only were the East Horsley Young Farmers' Club, the West Horsley British Legion and the Horsley Bridge Club. The character of organisation and participation continues to change.

Of greatest importance in the four parishes are the sports clubs and, most important of all, the Horsley Sports and Social Club. This club, at the centre of the most affluent part of the parish, provides excellent cricket, hockey and tennis facilities. Its introductory leaflet boldly states: 'For those who value village life the Sports Club is something with which they and their family can identify, support and enjoy.' In 1971 full membership for a family cost £20; for an individual it cost £7.50 for tennis, £5.50 for cricket, and £3.50 for hockey. However, only 22 of the 55 members of sports clubs are members of the Horsley club; the others include 14 members of Effingham Golf Club, 6 of Effingham Rugby Club and 6 of West Horsley Badminton Club. The Pahls found that the tennis club was one of the most commonly mentioned clubs that middle-class managers belonged to, and they concluded that Margaret Stacey was right when she observed that: 'Banbury people do not engage in sport as an exercise in competitive athleticism but as an occasion for social intercourse.'[6] So it is in East Horsley and the other parishes. However, unlike in many other villages, sport was scarcely a mediator between the classes; in Surrey each local sports club contains members from a limited range of social classes and the demise of the West Clandon football club in the early 1970s did not result in the players joining other sports clubs in the village.

Almost as important as the sports clubs were the drama groups of East and West Horsley. Drama groups are less easy to maintain in small parishes but in the Horsleys they are exceptional; they do not merely have Christmas shows but produce plays at regular intervals throughout the year.

For migrants the most important voluntary organisation, after the sports clubs, is the Women's Institute, the almost fundamental basis of traditional village life and the one specifically rural organisation amongst the important societies. Moreover it is the only institution that exists independently in each parish and, with an entirely female membership, quite rivals the attraction of the sports clubs for new residents. The programme of activities remains typical of more rural institutes; the image of country orientation and good housekeeping gives it a particularly distinctive character. Membership, even amongst newer migrants, is more balanced in terms of social-class composition and, at the same time, its image finds some opposition: a manager's wife in East Horsley reported, 'I'm not a WI sort of person.' In comparison with other associations, and particularly with the sports clubs, WI members were significantly older. However, the WI is not just numerically important; its ethos is closely related to the supposed ethos of village life: unsophisticated, traditional and little changing.

In reality the Women's Institute too is changing; an urban flavour is gradually coming to characterise its activities. In a brief period of 1970 the East Horsley WI had a series of talks on 'Fashion and design', 'Safety in flying', 'Heraldry', 'Old silver and glass', 'Dutch art' and 'Traditional English roast', incorporating a demonstration of the art of cutting sides of beef, lamb and pork. There was also a film strip on Karamoja, an experimental farm in East Africa, and a discussion of the annual meeting at the Albert Hall in London. Interspersed with these talks were a coffee and wine morning, organised to provide cash for redecorating the hall, and there was the inevitable series of bazaars and bring-and-buy sales. Church pageants and WI fetes give the Horsleys and Clandons a distinctiveness that suburbs lack, yet for many people it is only in the columns of the *Surrey Advertiser* that they learn of these distinctive activities. In this quite typical period there was nothing that actually reflected rural life, yet the topics presumably reflected the interests of the members. No longer are those interests rural. The original idea that the Women's Institutes would 'improve and develop the conditions of village life' became obscured by the popular conception of 'big hats and jam-making'. Even so although the local Women's Institutes organise the Meals-on-Wheels service and in 1972 were hard at work planting crocuses in verges and daffodils around trees, their interests have moved away, as their members have, from the rural and parochial to the urban and international. In 1974 when the economic crisis fostered some interest in do-it-yourself activities, including crocheting and vegetable gardens, it was merely a temporary phenomenon. The WIs reflect their members' interests; few find country life particularly interesting.

The next most important group are the preservation societies; despite their relatively low membership the old-established members are unusually active and give the societies a distinctiveness and power quite unlike any of the more recreational associations. (Their role is considered in detail in Chapter 6.) The group for which overwhelming support is not reflected in membership totals is the Conservative Association; nevertheless with only 28 households (of predictable social-class composition) actively supporting the Conservatives compared with only 1 household supporting the Liberal Party the gulf is probably representative of the political beliefs of the migrants. Also important are the floral groups, the music and arts societies and the horticultural societies, each of which is supported by fairly large numbers of new migrants. The Horsley Society of Arts, integrating many of these, had its tenth annual show in 1976. One of the fastest growing groups are the floral decorators. When the first of these, the Horsley Floral Decoration Group (now Society), was founded in 1953 the local horticultural society called it 'a new fangled idea which would never catch on'.

Country life

Since then the Horsley group has grown, others have followed, and twenty years after exhibitors were even entering the Chelsea Flower Show and, like the Women's Institutes, afternoon and evening groups had emerged. Monthly competitions and talks make this second exclusively women's society one of the most successful of all. Overall, there is a striking contrast between the associations of central Surrey and those of most other English villages; in Surrey both the bias towards the upper classes and the relative absence of agricultural or working-class orientated societies are quite striking.

Religion

Data on religious attendance are notoriously difficult to collect; indeed it is one of the few questions to have dropped out of the Census. Historically the church was to a great extent the hub of parish and village life and participation in its activities was only loosely correlated with actual religious belief. Now, although the church plays a role in parish life, especially in a small parish such as East Clandon where it is almost the only existing institution or voluntary social organisation, it no longer exerts the leadership and moral authority that it had in the last century. Present membership is based more on personal conviction than social convenience. Moreover, although the parish church was historically the Church of England other denominations have partly removed its former rural monopoly. Allegiance to the parish church is no longer expected behaviour (although several respondents apologised for their absence from church) and this might be expected to be especially true of migrant households; hence the data in this section are almost certainly unrepresentative of the total population of central Surrey. This is one particular form of behaviour that is substantially influenced by migration.

Of 460 households for which data exist, 192 claimed that at least one member had attended church within the previous three months. Most noticeably almost all went to church in their own parish although some visited Guildford, usually because of its cathedral. East Clandon, where the church is very obviously the physical and to a lesser extent the social centre of the parish, had the highest participation rates

"Dates from 1089. Norman arcade, early English chancel, perpendicular additions—I forget the vicar's name."

Country life

(Table 5.3). Attendance is lowest in East Horsley, especially in Effingham Junction, possibly because the church there is only a daughter church or possibly because it is little more than a Nissen hut. The social composition of church attendance in central Surrey, being biased towards the two higher classes, is similar to that found elsewhere.[7] The tradition of occasional conformity continues to retain greater power in the countryside than in the cities.

Table 5.3 Church attendance

Social class	East Clandon	West Clandon	West Horsley	East Horsley	All	%
1	5/9	11/24	32/51	28/74	76/158	48
2	2/2	7/12	32/75	40/112	81/201	40
3	0/1	0/3	15/33	6/24	21/61	34
4	3/4	0/3	1/11	4/8	8/26	31
5	2/3	1/1	3/8	0/2	6/14	43

The churches themselves in some ways impose a social life on their most regular attenders; there is church cleaning, flower provision, magazine delivery and regular worship to inculcate a sense of community life and, predictably, it is the regular church attenders who are most enthusiastic about the community spirit of local life. The church magazines, too, foster this view, incorporating notes on the history of the parishes and even comments on the rural observance of Shrove Tuesday. It is still a struggle; when the East Horsley Parochial Church Council proposed a 'Harvest Supper' in 1971 the proposal was met with such little enthusiasm that the idea was abandoned. Even then much less than a quarter of the population are regular churchgoers; some of the rest may absorb their attitude to community but most are isolated and separate from it.

The churches have also generated their own social organisations: even East Clandon has a parochial church council, whilst groups like the Horsley Under 30s and the St Martin's Youth Club are direct spin-offs from the Church of England. In East Horsley the church is directly responsible for the Good Neighbour Scheme—each road in the parish has a road steward who puts through the door of each new arrival a booklet called 'Where and When' containing a letter of welcome, what goes on in the parish (including the times of services at the Catholic and Evangelic churches) and whom to contact. Subsequently the road stewards make personal calls and usually arrange introductory coffee parties; later, three or four times a year, a sherry party is arranged in the WI hall for recent newcomers to meet a wider circle of residents. (The road stewards also send flowers to the sick and cards to the newly born.) This widely appreciated service seems much the most important role of the church in the parish.

Recreation

Relatively few recreational activities are, however, institutionalised; the local societies are obviously not the limit to social life. Apart from other societies in Guildford (or London) a range of informal activities exists, from walking on the Downs to giving dinner parties, and from chatting over the hedge to discussing the balance of payments in the 'Duke of Wellington'. It is obviously quite impossible either to count up the number of times such activities occur or to evaluate their role in making life more enjoyable. Each has different values for different people; each household has its own social network within and beyond the parish. Nevertheless in the particular combination of possibilities and potentialities central Surrey is unique; the use that migrants make of the new environment gives a clue to the balance between urban and rural life styles and between newly acquired patterns of activity and ways of living retained from their previous environment. Necessarily few of these changes are easily measured; the changes themselves are sometimes quite superficial but a few trends are distinctive.

Some of the more formal leisure activities pursued by new migrants can be tabulated. Thus Table 5.4 records the proportion of households that had any member going to the cinema, the theatre, the public house or to London (for any kind of entertainment) in the previous three months. Variations are most obvious between social-class groups. The theatre was attended most by the highest social class, who actually attended the theatre more than the cinema; they were also the most regular users of London's facilities. Few areas of England are distinguished like this by greater proportions of residents visiting the theatre rather than the cinema. The lowest social class took little part in these recreational activities apart from visits to public houses; this may well be related to a relative lack of mobility, since pubs are the only amenities actually in the four parishes. Moreover, pubs are the only local social amenity formerly divided into two: a working-class section and a middle-class section. The destination of trips to the cinema and theatre conformed to an expected pattern: Guildford was overwhelmingly the most important focus of cinema trips but for the theatre London was just ahead of Guildford and Leatherhead. Regular theatre visits were reported as far afield as Windsor, Stratford and Chichester. Theatre-going is a relatively leisured activity and much more of a social occasion—it characterises a particular local style of life.

Table 5.4 Recreation: all parishes

Social class	Cinema (%)	Theatre (%)	Public house (%)	London (%)
1	27	48	47	39
2	37	33	55	32
3	36	30	52	28
4	35	12	50	31
5	7	0	50	7
All	33	36	52	32

Less than a third of households had visited London for recreation within the past three months. Significantly, there was a decline in visiting down through the social classes but both Clandons recorded higher proportions than the Horsleys. One West Horsley postman's wife had visited London for the first time the night prior to the survey and a garage erector's wife in West Clandon had not visited London since she was 6 years old. East Clandon proved to be the only parish where one local man (whose presence as a migrant in the survey had resulted from a move between different tied houses in the village) had never visited London. Not quite so traditionally his response to the question 'Why not?' was 'Why should I bother? I can see it all on TV.' Perhaps symbolic of East Clandon's supposed style of life was the tale, doubtless apocryphal, of the East Clandon villager who had only recently returned from the coast to report: 'There were acres of water there and I heard tell there were acres more of it around the other side.' Older households, too, are less likely to visit London. Thus, despite the proximity of the parishes to London, for shopping and recreation central Surrey is surprisingly independent of Greater London.

Changing public-house life indicates one of the social changes resulting from migration. In 1950 Pons described the three public houses in the village of Little Munden, Hertfordshire, as all having part-time publicans, and bar profits which did little to supplement their wages. Each of them complained that people drank less than before the war and all had saloon bars that were commonly unlit and unused.[8] This is unlikely to have been so true at the time in the rather more affluent central Surrey; if it were, the contrast is now even more enormous. Despite the unique equality in levels of attendance by social classes the number of drinkers in the three lower social classes is so small that it has been the public bar that has tended to remain unused, especially at lunch time. In 1969 one of West Clandon's two pubs became the first in the four parishes to join a national trend in removing its public bar, installing wall-to-wall carpeting and saloon-bar prices throughout, and consequently also removing much of its former clientele; the other pub re-orientated completely so that drinking became very much secondary to dining. In East Horsley, two years later, the Horsley Hotel, which at one time had been the Railway Hotel, became The Horsley, similarly ejecting the public bar and bringing in expensive dining and the steak-house section. In the 1960s only the publican in the Queens Head, East Clandon, had a second occupation (the inn is unique in being away from a through road). Now this, too, and all but one of the eight pubs in central Surrey have removed their public bars; wining and dining have almost completely replaced the traditional public house.

Rather like church attendance public-house visiting is a very local affair. In each parish more than half the residents

Country life

"Sweet or dry Martini?"

mentioned pubs only in that parish. Very few of the other pubs visited were in towns. More important than all of these were the parishes of Albury and Shere, immediately south of the Downs, where before the more recent local changes it was possible to eat out as well as drink. Indeed it is entirely because of this facility that public-house visiting is so high among the upper social classes. Otherwise it is still something that is not quite the thing to do; older-established residents are not so frequently seen in the Surrey pubs. For many of the two lowest social classes, most of whom only visited pubs in their own parish, this was their only participation in any kind of social activity at all and it had nothing to do with the period lounges and charcoal grills.

It is not only in central Surrey that the public houses are changing; in other Surrey villages 'the villagers'' public houses are being expropriated by the newcomers, and other middle-class people who arrive by car, and are being converted into restaurants (scampi and chips and chicken in a basket) and cocktail lounges. Researchers from the University of Surrey found two doors in one such pub: one marked 'villagers' led to a stark and bare bar; the other, marked 'Inglenook', to subdued red lights, food, wine and spirits and the signs of expense-account money flowing rather freely. Elsewhere, where pubs had been converted into a single bar, 'villagers can often be observed sitting quietly in a corner while the atmosphere of the Costa Brava imitation of an English pub flows around them'.[9] The price of progress is rarely evenly shared.

By linking all the local activities into one composite Table (Table 5.5) it is possible to indicate the proportion of households whose members take some interest in all or none of the three possibilities considered here. Despite the limited value of this kind of analysis and its arbitrary conclusions and exclusions the results are interesting. Participation in three or more activities falls steadily from high to low social classes

Table 5.5 Local participation: public house, church and social organisations

(a) *Attendance at all three*

Social class	East Clandon	West Clandon	West Horsley	East Horsley	All
1	3	16	25	10	54/158 (34%)
2	2	4	33	9	48/201 (24%)
3			12	1	13/61 (21%)
4					0/26 (0%)
5			1		1/14 (7%)
	5/19 (26%)	20/43 (47%)	71/178 (40%)	20/220 (9%)	116/460 (25%)

(b) *Attendance at none*

1	2	1	5	16	24/158 (15%)
2		1	14	32	47/201 (23%)
3		2	6	7	15/61 (25%)
4		2	4	5	11/26 (42%)
5			3		3/14 (21%)
	2/19 (11%)	6/43 (14%)	32/178 (18%)	60/220 (27%)	100/460 (22%)

and the converse for no participation at all is nearly true. The spatial variations are less distinct; West Clandon and West Horsley have high proportions of participants in all three activities and East Horsley has very low proportions. Table 5.5 gives some indication of the social class and spatial location of those households that are most 'integrated', in this respect, into local social organisation.

Perhaps the most obvious limitation to local participation

is the nature of the existing social organisations. Social organisations where participation has been mainly by the working class have continued to decline in strength; this decline has reduced the number of opportunities for council households to meet others from outside their own estate, especially because of the peripheral location of several estates. The only organisations that effectively cater for the council tenants are a limited number of sports clubs, the Seniors' Clubs and the British Legion; but there isn't even a bowling green in the whole area. However, in the limited period after migration many tenants are home centred enough to ignore some of the social and economic limitations of the small size of estates.

The existing social organisations in the parishes are unlikely to attract working-class people, in part because of their *raison d'être* and in part because of their ability to attract middle-class people. As Pahl put it: 'By and large the working class are not deprived of any activity by the middle-class immigrants, despite many activities taking place in which they are not represented: they just do not want to join things.'[10]

Although the fundamental gulf in participation levels is between council households and owner-occupiers there are other variations too. The most obvious division is sexual: the largest organisations are exclusively for women and, as is generally true, commuters are less likely to participate than those who do not leave the parish and the commuters are usually men. Old people are less likely to participate, prevented by darkness, low levels of mobility and the irrelevance of many existing institutions. To some extent the same is also true of young people. For women a major reason for joining any organisation is simply to participate in some activity, 'to meet other women'. The area south of the Guildford-Leatherhead road has very much lower rates of participation than any other parts of the parishes; distance is compounded with a more obvious orientation to the road network leading out of the parish centres. Participation was lowest in East Horsley, which is the only one of the three larger villages with a real central area—a shopping centre, where it was relatively easy to meet fellow residents. Residents in more peripheral areas, especially in West Clandon, thought that if there were a village shopping centre or a village green there would be a much greater sense of community. However, social participation is independent of 'sense of community' and is related more closely to the social structure of the parish than to its spatial structure.

Some new migrants hoped that a more rural area would provide the organisations that they had found lacking in urban areas. Each parish has many more social organisations than would be found in any suburb of comparable size. Few were therefore disappointed in this respect. An East Clandon architect's wife thought the village was 'very pretty in summer but now I hate it. Nothing happens here.' Perhaps significantly, like many other wives, she was still learning to drive. A few others, however, were content to have withdrawn from a more time-consuming social life elsewhere. One housewife, a member of four local organisations, claimed that she 'had not joined much since it took up too much of her time in Stoneleigh'. Another had scaled down her social life by joining 'only charities like the Red Cross and the Conservatives'! The high level of local mobility generates a style of life that can exist despite this; as Willmott and Young suggest,[11] there are institutional forms that are entirely appropriate to households where members need social support and friendship quickly when they move in but will not give them a strong sense of loss when they move away. Several of the organisations in central Surrey, and especially the Good Neighbours, can be described like this; moreover many exist in a similar form in many other English villages. New ties can always be remade even if they become increasingly superficial.

A number of respondents felt that they would have participated more had they lived in the parish longer or could spend less time on their house or garden. Despite the obvious justification that new households wanted to mould a new house and garden to their own needs and ideals, a secondary explanation was occasionally suggested: that several households had spent so much to come to the area that they were subsequently unable 'to make ends meet'. The secondary explanation is not unlikely: households that have just bought an expensive house, a major form of conspicuous consumption, and use their car to a greater extent, are likely to find themselves relatively short of capital. Where households are 'reluctant commuters' this is even more likely to be true.

A further influence on participation is location; a particular part of the parish is one factor but the specific house is even more important. Migrants are fairly evenly distributed throughout the parishes with two major exceptions: Hooke Road (East Horsley) and Overbrook (West Horsley), both new streets completed during the survey period, in each of which all the residents were migrants. The correlation between this and high levels of both formal and informal social participation of households in both streets is quite plain. Each street is very friendly since 'there are lots of newcomers'. Elsewhere migrants are more isolated from each other, information diffuses to them and between them less readily, and their neighbours are likely to have their own social networks and to be more aloof. The difference between the residents in these two streets and the migrants elsewhere is most impressive in terms of informal social participation. Almost all households in each street claimed friends there and many had informal links with them for child-minding, shopping, drinking coffee and so on. Almost all claimed to enjoy living in the area and to have settled in successfully. (These were the only two areas where my interviewing progress could be charted and, at the end of each, the last households were all well aware of why I was there.) The two groups were also noticeably more enthusiastic about the parish and their own part of it than in any other streets. In addition to proximity and simultaneous movement into the street the structure of housing finance meant that many of these households were very similar in age, number of children and occupation; all this aided integration. By contrast a 25-year-old accountant's wife in East Clandon observed: 'newcomers don't fit in since until the agricultural people went it was only rich elderly people here'. In the new streets it is the street itself which constitutes community; the parish is of more peripheral significance especially in the earliest period after migration.

Country life

Villagers

Since a major reason for social participation is to become integrated into local life and to build up a network of friends for informal social participation, to some extent membership of formal social organisations is irrelevant. Questions were therefore asked on the way in which newcomers to the parish fit in and to what extent migrants considered themselves to be villagers (Tables 5.6, 5.7).

Table 5.6 Do you think of yourself as a villager?

	No		Yes		Don't know	
	N	%	N	%	N	%
East Horsley	149	65	45	21	32	14
West Horsley	118	66	49	27	13	7
West Clandon	28	65	10	23	5	12
East Clandon	8	42	8	42	3	16
All	303	65	112	24	53	11

Table 5.7 Do you think of yourself as a villager?

Social class	No		Yes	
	N	%	N	%
1	105	75	36	25
2	129	73	47	27
3	37	71	15	29
4	13	62	8	38
5	6	50	6	50

Most households considered themselves to be villagers or not primarily according to whether they felt that the area in which they lived was a village and secondarily on the basis of a combination of how long they had lived in the area and the extent to which they participated in local activities. Typical of this kind of reasoning was that of an East Clandon landscape gardener's wife: 'we've been here a year and know lots of people. We feel a part of them.' Again most households (but certainly not all) valued the ethos of villager: 'At heart we're villagers but we haven't been here long enough to deserve that.' Some considered themselves villagers but doubted if established residents would agree. One West Clandon wife stated: 'I won't be a villager until I join the activities, but I don't know if the village people are still in these things.' A minority had a more aloof approach: 'A villager is someone who joins in: a nosey parker. Most people aren't...'; 'I'm not a villager since I don't like the gossip that villagers thrive on.' Others had a determinedly rustic view of village life, which they were keen to avoid: 'Villager conjures up a toothless old wreck by the village pub. No thank you' (accountant's wife); 'certainly not, sounds country bumpkinish...like some old dear in a shawl' (doctor's wife); 'someone very parochial, not going anywhere', and 'the sturdy types are the villagers'. Overall three-quarters of the migrants did not consider themselves to be villagers and this proportion was marginally higher for the upper social classes. Scarcely surprisingly migrants were most likely to think of themselves as villagers in East Clandon and least likely in East Horsley, although the Table disguises the fact that in the north of West Horsley only 23 per cent thought themselves villagers whilst in the south it was 31 per cent.

A high proportion of households felt that their parish could not be described as a village. This argument was put forward most often by those households who took little or no part in local social organisation. The correlation between being a villager and a high level of social participation is quite marked; the wife of one London commuter observed: 'I'm a villager but my husband isn't since he doesn't join in', whilst one household who were particularly interested in sport suggested that 'in the summer we're more villagers'. A typical reaction was 'you can't have a village this close to London', but reasons varied as to why it wasn't a village and what a village was. The most frequently cited reason ran along the lines 'You can't have a stockbroker suburb and call it a village', or 'too pseudo-stockbrokerish to be a village', to 'this is "glorified suburbia" full of people playing at living in the country' (forester). Partly, therefore, it was not a village because the wrong sort of people were there and the right sort of people were not there: 'I had an Agatha Christie view of the village with a squire and a parson' (company director); 'There's no village atmosphere, no cross-section of population and we don't all know the vicar' (banker's wife). There was 'no local economic activity' and 'no craftsmen', or it was not 'a working village'. For some the parish was simply too large; for most this gave it the characteristics of a suburb or a small town and for several it was part of London: 'a bit of London outside London; most people have come from London at some time.' Almost without exception those respondents who proffered opinions on where real villages might be found said 'the West Country' (including Devon, Cornwall, Somerset and Gloucestershire); the bucolic image of the village is clearly deeply rooted in popular mythology and still maintained locally.[12] One migrant complained that the rural image was slipping away: 'you can't hear a cock crow nowadays.' A measure of just how far it had slipped away in some areas was the view of a driver's wife in West Horsley who was pleased that this was 'more of a farming village than the other side of East Horsley; there must still be cows somewhere.' Indeed there were. Independent of what they thought their parish was some migrants thought that because of their own life style they could not be villagers: a Colonel's wife was 'too sophisticated to be a villager', another was a 'post-Londoner' whilst a publicity consultant suggested that he was not a villager but 'a cosmopolitan sophisticate with tender overtones'. Conversely a number of migrants had come from other villages and many of these, especially those in the lower social classes, considered themselves to be villagers but not in this area. Several respondents described themselves as cosmopolitans, making their own informal recognition of the distinction that Merton first drew in the USA between cosmopolitans and locals.[13] This large group was in the village but not of it. Finally, a company representative in Effingham Junction observed, somewhat sadly: 'We're suburbanites; we ruin what's left of the village atmosphere.'

The physical shape and size of the village was occasionally important; East Clandon, with its small size and definite centre (plus its old buildings) was visibly a village for most people whereas for some households West Clandon was too spreadeagled and with no real centre (the historic centre in the south being a considerable distance from the railway station and the central point of the village). Because they weren't physically a part of the village the small number of households separated from the more built-up part of the village, and especially those on farms, rarely thought of themselves as villagers. Viewpoints were often dependent on where the migrants had lived previously; migrants from large towns tended to see the parishes as much more village-like than those who were familiar with 'West Country' villages. Some, who had moved locally, observed how the villages had grown; all thought that there had been some decline in 'villageness' because of this.

Households that had lived in a particular parish longer than average were more likely to think of themselves as villagers; those who worked locally and especially those who had retired, and therefore spent much of the day in the village, were the most likely to think of themselves as villagers. Most households conceded that they would not become villagers overnight although a number deduced that 'since we live in a village we must be villagers'. They were in it and they intended to be of it. Different lengths of time were suggested in which it might be possible to become a villager. It was generally considered that it was relatively easy to fit into East Horsley since the rate of migration was greater there but conversely that this was the least village-like area on other criteria. Several respondents, including a council-house widow who had been in West Horsley for twenty-five years, considered that one had to have been born there. In another group of Surrey villages some residents said, almost bitterly, that even twenty years' residence was not enough to make a villager out of someone born even in a neighbouring parish.[14] The overall range of those who put a time limit on their having become villagers ran from 'two years just about makes us villagers', balanced against another respondent who had also been there two years and who pointed out that 'roots don't come this quickly', to 'our family originally came in 1745'. Perceptions of themselves as villagers were therefore extremely varied. There is an obvious parallel between Park's definition of the city as 'a state of mind'[15] and the perceptions of village indicated here.

Response to the question of whether they were villagers was obviously partly linked to the migrants' associations with local people and the extent to which they felt they fitted in with them. East Clandon is the parish with the most obvious group of established residents who are significantly different, in terms of socio-economic structure, from the new migrants. Consequently it is primarily in East Clandon that there is friction between these groups. A gardener who had moved from West Horsley identified himself with the established villagers: 'We don't have much to do with the newcomers... don't like people coming in and buying up houses.' A company manager's wife was less aware of the friction: 'villagers resent us doing up the houses and therefore monopolising the village eventually—but we still manage to get on' whilst a chartered accountant in one of only two new houses in the centre of the parish stated baldly, and correctly, 'our house has spoiled East Clandon'.

The extent to which old-established lower-social-class residents were both unnoticed and, especially in the case of East Horsley, simply absent is reflected in many responses which considered relationships only between that household and the fairly immediate neighbours. Additionally, and again to a greater extent in East Horsley, many households inverted the question to refer to how even more recent migrants fitted in with them. The highly transient nature of the East Horsley population resulted in a rather different response to that given elsewhere. Statements such as 'Are any people around here local?', 'Most local people are not local really' and 'There aren't really any local people as such; real locals are few and far between. The rest are the *nouveaux riches*', all of which were made in West Clandon, would not be phrased in this way in East Horsley. There the local people were simply other people who had lived in East Horsley longer, and they were seen, as indeed they invariably were, to be little different from the newcomers themselves.

Less commonly, in the absence of an established village population, the local population was seen by owner-occupiers as those people in the council-housing estates, but often there were not many of them either and they do not figure in higher-class conceptions of the village. Their segregation inhibited contact and encouraged rumours about what went on there: 'the council-house kids come and beat up ours. I was very surprised in an area like this' (teacher, West Clandon). Most of the council estates were very small and often distinctly separated from the rest of the parish, behind the shops in East Horsley or outside the village in East Clandon. Outside East Clandon there are very few established residents in the lower social classes not living in council estates. Thus the established residents have often moved or been moved away from direct contact with newcomers and, outside East Clandon, have had a much longer time to get used to an influx of migrants. Spatially and socially isolated from the middle-class migrants, they are almost always out of sight out of mind; social distance is accentuated by spatial distance.

Few owner-occupiers have any social or economic relationship with the council-house tenants or with other older-established lower-class groups. The only real link of owner-occupiers and council-house tenants is through the latter's role as gardeners or cleaners for the former. A West Horsley housewife thought: 'Presumably our daily is a local, otherwise I don't know many.' In all the parishes, and especially East Horsley where the ratio of owners to tenants is very high and where the largest council estate has many retired people, postcards in shop windows and several responses indicate the shortage of local domestic labour, some of which came from as far away as Weybridge. Reactions to the local housing situation were often phrased in terms of this relationship; thus, despite the obvious *non sequitur*, a common statement was: 'we can't get a cleaner/gardener, therefore there must be insufficient housing locally.' Again, especially in East Horsley, the problem of a housing shortage was seen as the demands of people similar to themselves not now living in the local area. Typical replies included: 'God, yes; if anything too many', 'I've got my house and that's it', 'There must be [a housing shortage] : people keep buying up houses and converting them', 'We wouldn't like to see any more; we spent a lot of money to come to reasonably rural surroundings.' Others, if unaware of local need, were prepared

Country life

to concede that it might exist, but nevertheless that there should be no more housing locally, or, as one respondent rationalised it: 'This just doesn't seem the place for a council estate.' Only a handful had actually observed any need, however they defined it.

Friends and conformists

Migrants were naturally much more familiar with their immediate neighbours and consequently were most successfully integrated on the new streets. From Overbrook, for example, came the following statements: 'This is a very friendly area; you start from the Overbrook clique and work outwards', 'Overbrook is a community in itself', 'We don't know any local people but on Overbrook it's OK', 'They're a great lot of people here, especially in Overbrook.' Nevertheless there were problems there because of (rather than despite) this; one or two households, who had come to the area primarily for a slower and more peaceful life, resented the more frenetic neighbouring, which came close to Whyte's *Organization Man*[16] at leisure, especially in the case of Overbrook in an 'open-plan' estate. They were consequently unable and/or unwilling to keep up and so were attempting to move out. As in the Oxfordshire village of Berinsfield, intimacy may lead to friction as often as it leads to friendliness.'[17]

Elsewhere response was mixed yet frequently the need to conform was stressed. Primarily, as numerous respondents stated, 'You have to go half way', yet for households considered eccentric to local norms a greater effort might be required; thus, 'It's a very one-class society. If you don't conform to the social pattern you might be unhappy. One woman had deadly bright pink clothes but conformed in a year to the normal pattern' (LSE sociology graduate, West Horsley). Unfortunately she did not specify the normal pattern: a certain conservative sobriety might be inferred. Furthermore there was a general consensus that those who did not conform moved elsewhere. Conformity could be viewed in different ways: 'It's difficult to fit in unless you work for a big organisation; people must be a certain type.

You don't find many academics here' (civil servant, East Horsley); on the other hand a West Horsley steel erector's wife, not in a council house, felt 'a bit out of place here. They're all very posh down here; some are very serious minded.' It was therefore obviously easier for some kinds of people: 'It depends on who you are. Elderly civil servants get on OK but young policemen don't' (young policeman, East Horsley). However, some considered that there were 'so many different types here so one is bound to meet some kindred spirits' or 'you usually find your interests shared by someone else', or 'you get some very class-conscious people round here but they all fit into their own cliques'. Both of these respondents came from professions locally well represented. Others were more aware of a difficulty: 'the London set may include you in if you have any money' (teacher, West Horsley). Finally, the wife of a Baltic Exchange broker observed, 'we know several people; it seems to attract my husband's sort of people' (West Horsley), whilst a 32-year-old accountant's wife 'fitted in well with people of our vintage' (East Horsley). In every kind of street respondents were very keen on homogeneity; unusual neighbours were not welcomed. People are undoubtedly happiest in a community consisting of people of like interests and in such a community group interests can thrive best.

Other reasons explain the ease with which migrants fit in, notably the fairly regular turnover of population in the area and the orientation of social organisations to their needs; but then few would admit to not fitting in well since at least some of the responsibility for this might be thought to be their own. Many pointed to the friendliness of their own particular area (variably defined, but most often one or two streets at the most) and the unfriendliness of other areas, especially those of higher social-class composition. A pilot's wife in West Horsley had 'no desire to know richer people further away. We fit in well here.' Indeed, a fairly common response in West Horsley (South) was the ease with which it was possible to get on there rather than in 'the more snobby East Horsley'. Occasionally this was shared in East Horsley; a secretary stated: 'I prefer West Horsley; it's more rural, more of a community...here, there's too much keeping up with the Joneses, all living beyond their income and means.' Obviously few could really have experienced that, yet the feeling was common. Needless to say some others in West Horsley who did not echo such a statement had aspirations towards living there. The continual reference to East Horsley coupled with parallel desires to move there clearly indicate a certain degree of 'sour grapes'. In the same way claims that 'people are snooty: wrapped up in their own bridge, cocktail or coffee parties' or that the Horsleys are 'a bit cliquey, coffee-morningyfied and one-upmanship is common' may also represent frustrated desires to conform. 'Keeping up with the Joneses' is far from a cliché. The myth that people in the north are more friendly than in the south was both attacked and defended but, at this level, it is clearly crucial exactly where one's house is placed, where one lived previously, how socially mobile one has been and so on. As one housewife put it: 'it depends on the position of the house in certain parts of West Clandon plus individual personalities.' Critical to the ease of settling in were relations with immediate neighbours and these appeared often quite unpredictable; the non-working wife of a West Horsley doctor who had been there six months stated: 'Everybody is very friendly here... but we don't yet know the names of our next-door neighbours.' Another statement indicates the way in which apparently minor details may be important: 'It's not very friendly round here; everybody travels by cars. We might see our neighbours once a fortnight.' Nevertheless in most areas informal social organisations exist to enable newcomers to fit in; the Good Neighbours are almost certain to call, whilst several streets organise welcoming parties to break some of the ice.

Clearly, respondents had particular perceptions of their own parish and how it differed from other parishes. Surrey parishes generally tended to suffer when their sense of community was compared with the apparently traditional villages of the West Country; but this comparison could also be made locally: 'There's no insular feeling in West Horsley, like in Ripley where everybody is somebody's cousin.' Shere and Abinger Hammer were both mentioned as more like villages, but distance is certainly highly correlated with enchantment. So, too, respondents had particular conceptions of the sort of people who lived locally, not all of which were complimentary: 'middle-aged women with sheepskin coats who would walk over you as soon as look at you.' There were also conceptions of the cars they drove; Tod's contention that 'it's not all rum and Rovers in the metropolitan villages'[18] is not the popular image that exists in East Horsley: 'you only see the back end of a Jag or a Rover' (economist's wife). Perhaps the most surprising insight came from an East Horsley cook who stated: 'This is a spiralist area.'

Nevertheless most new owner-occupiers outside East Clandon saw their own parishes as being composed largely of people similar to themselves; again most recognised that this was increasingly so: 'The villagers are dying out' or 'There aren't many of the Mrs Mop type left' (East Clandon chartered accountant). Those who did not see it in that way were particularly likely to characterise the parish as containing two polar extremes; a retired engineer in West Horsley stated: 'there are two classes here: farm labourers and women domestics, and the rest.' The image of the two-class village was most strongly maintained amongst the council households; outside the council estates people seemed always to be 'stockbrokers and people of that kidney'. A widow in a West Clandon council house commented: 'I can see no possibility of change in this area until people change and social barriers are removed.' A lorry driver's wife commented of West Clandon: 'too much private property with not much in between; too big a gap.' In West Clandon this is particularly true yet in the other parishes the social divisions are also reflected in housing divisions and current house prices are widening these divisions. Those in intermediate positions, such as policemen, publicans and shopkeepers, tend to live in particular kinds of tied houses. For many of these their social position is least enviable of all.

Ways of life

The majority of evidence on changed ways of life following the move to central Surrey shows conclusively that life has scarcely changed at all. Most changes in behaviour were planned and most were a result of life-cycle changes such as marriage, retirement, birth of children and so on. The most frequently reported changes that have taken place are not caused by a move to the suburb but are the reasons for moving there in the first place. The sort of breakdown in family ties that Young and Willmott observed in the London suburb of Greenleigh[19] is not apparent here since relatives were often a considerable distance away from the previous residence also. In many cases family and home-centredness have increased; this is usually a definite choice as households have spent considerable lengths of time renovating their house or garden. In others, and especially the council households, this has not been a formal choice but is a result of a decline in family or friendship links. For all groups the television initially plays a more important role.

Much more important is the continuation of a similar pattern of life but in a more aesthetic environment. Thus shopping is likely to be quieter and slower; the view from the window is liable to be more beautiful, the walk to school safer and traffic problems slighter. Conventional tasks are more pleasant. At the same time, and for the same reasons, walking becomes more popular and the pace of life slows a little. This represents the only real change in way of life. There can be few specifically rural life styles remaining in these parishes; this is the nearest that new migrants can come to adopting them. None works on the land who did not do so previously; there are no allotments for migrants and a larger garden is a much more acceptable substitute. Perhaps the least likely topic of conversation in the Duke of Wellington pub is local agriculture. It would be wrong to suppose, however, that former city dwellers merely diffused their own habits and failed to adopt country habits; the sad reality is that inadvertently their values are transmitted into the countryside as a local population becomes conscious of relative deprivation, whilst there are few country values that, with the best will in the world, can be adopted. It is only the superficialities of peace and tranquillity that are sought after and sometimes found.

Bonham-Carter suggests that new migrants in villages 'are seeking a quality of living so often absent in the town—a

Country life

feeling of permanence, some element of solitude and self reliance, contact with soil and green fields, and the chance to live as a person at your own pace—in a word, a sense of identity'.[20] Although this kind of ideal was only present for a minority there is a strong feeling that the 'good life' is easier to find in this sort of area; it is a place where children ought to be able to roam through fields of buttercups and lovingly bring home jam jars of tadpoles. Not surprisingly response varies according to previous location; for most of the migrants who have come from more rural areas the style of life in central Surrey approximates to suburban or small-town life: 'the pace of life is faster after Suffolk.' Several found that central Surrey was less rural and more suburban than they had expected. Conversely in one household that had moved from Greater London to a house without mains electricity, water or drainage, the main change in life style was reported to be washing less! Residential satisfaction is closely related to previous place of residence. If for some it was friendlier and for others unfriendlier than they had expected, for most it was not an unfamiliar environment and local social and spatial organisation offered few surprises. Indeed it was for some of the council tenants, despite their short-distance moves, that the differences between this area and the last were most striking. A Ripley man, moving three miles to West Horsley, had never visited the area previously, whilst a migrant from Chilworth was extremely disappointed with the landscape north of the Downs because of its absence of copses. For individuals whose spatial and social networks have been confined within a small area for quite a long time even relatively short moves represent significant changes.

The most obvious change was in response to local transport. In the majority of cases public transport was less satisfactory than in the previous place of residence; a director claimed that the whole family's social life, and especially that of his teenage children, had been 'seriously disrupted by the lack of public transport'. For some households, especially in the southern fringes, dependence on the car was greatly increased: 'Now we live in the car, otherwise we're the same.' For others: 'you have to start off by car to get anywhere.' Many wives were learning to drive and a number of households had bought a second car since moving to the area. Even some of those who claimed to enjoy an increase in walking observed that they had to drive to the start of their walk! Nevertheless increased walking was the most commonly claimed benefit of a move to this area, even if more than one household 'thought there would be more places where you could walk' or play in a rural area. The Green Belt is not the recreational area it is sometimes claimed to be. Overall the fairly slight changes in life style point to the fairly slight influence of this particular location on life style. Yet were the owner-occupiers, whose life style is most closely linked to more distant urban centres, not able to get to the city easily this might not be so—but then they would not have been living there.

Not all residents welcomed the slowing down; one wife who had worked prior to her move claimed to have become 'cabbagey'. A minority of wives had taken up jobs to keep them occupied. Those who had no access to a car or could not drive were particularly conscious of this quietness, which brought forward the standard joke from an East Horsley advertising executive: 'I've heard about the Peyton Place of East Horsley but I can't find it.' Given the number of times that phrases like 'gin-and-sin belt' emerge, perhaps it is no longer a joke for some. For those who felt that their way of life had altered there were two identifiable sorts of change, both of which were noted by an insurance broker in East Horsley: 'We've conformed by learning bridge—a retrograde step—but have begun to participate in a community—an improvement.' It is unlikely that many new residents would admit to conforming but it was clearly expected of them. Perhaps significantly one Overbrook respondent had become 'more stereotyped and always worried about what the neighbours might think'. Again the specific location of housing is crucial. A West Clandon household observed that they were 'more remote from the neighbours here. We can just go and eat in the garden without feeling we have to get dressed up like in Merrow.' Some were only too ready to claim that they had become part of a community or even a village, although their way of life had not changed in any obvious way. Certain values are generally rated higher than others. A few groups had rather more specific changes in their way of life: older people, as a group much less mobile, felt more cut off, one claiming that her friends were now 'all on the phone'; another was an 'urbanite in exile'. Young people were unanimous in their objection to the quietness of local life and the absence of relevant social organisations. Where they, too, were immobile their objections were greater. Finally for those migrants who had come from abroad the changes were basic; a household that had come from Malawi was learning to live without a house boy and (oil executive) 'You can't even compare East Horsley with Venezuela.'

The idea of conformity in suburbia produced, at one time, a mass of literature mainly from North America, which accepted that there was always some degree of conformity there, culminating in one attempt to depict 'suburbanism as a way of life'.[21] Regardless of the causes, the suburb is generally seen to be the locus of a particular range of characteristics such as do-it-yourself activities, status symbols, a middle-class way of life, a central role for the family and child-rearing, a high degree of social activity, conformity and conservatism.[22] In a few parts of the four parishes—notably central East Horsley and the north of West Horsley, which are the two areas with regular street layouts of relatively high-density residential development—many of the owner-occupiers would be likely to agree that these were also characteristics of the area in which they lived; in this respect parts of the four parishes approximated to suburbs and the suburbs were those of Greater London. Moreover, the residents were able to impose suburban values on the area in two ways: several households enthusiastically pointed out the way in which individual households had conformed or moved away whilst they themselves interacted with similar people; and, in addition, the parishes themselves are to some extent known to have some of the characteristics of a suburb and hence those who do not aspire to these life styles are unlikely to wish to move there. Moreover, the expense of local housing is such that reluctant commuters are rare.

The essence of the suburb seems to be that not only does it permit all the components of the 'suburban myth', several of which are certainly present and encouraged there, but it enables most households to live the sort of life they want rather than necessarily conform to a particular sort of life style. In the metropolitan villages of central Surrey this also appears true although the greater variety of house types, residential densities and social composition ensure that the metropolitan villages are several stages removed from the more obvious conformity of many suburbs. Nevertheless this kind of area is most likely to suit the needs of a particular social group within a social class at one stage of the life cycle; almost as in suburbs, 'the prices of houses act as a social sieve, with graduated meshes as it were, through which drop each homogeneous segment of the population round the edge of towns'.[23] Yet central-Surrey prices, although high, are variable within parishes. The zoning is on a much smaller scale than this kind of statement supposes. Consequently homogeneity, even between migrants, does not yet exist. Central Surrey, although in several ways suburban, is far from the homogeneous conformist suburbia so beloved of American sociologists.

Residential satisfaction

Perception of the local environment is related to a wide range of variables: particular spatial location, transport availability, previous residence, social-class composition of the household and, perhaps above all, the previous expectations of that environment. 'The environment in which men live is an order of things remembered and expected as well as of things actually perceived.'[24] Even more importantly, perception is also shaped by what the migrant will read about this new kind of area; it then matters little what American academics write about the conformity of New York suburbia but rather more what the local vicar writes:[25]

> In a village deep in the country one sees something of the old pattern of life, when people stayed put and there was an innate sense of belonging. In most parts of England this has all changed and today even the few who do remain long in a place are surrounded by a shifting population and a changing neighbourhood. Perhaps the young welcome

the excitement of this, but I know the old and many of the middle aged feel deeply, if not always consciously, of the loss of that 'primitive' sense of belonging.

Nor does it matter if journalists from popular newspapers take away from brief visits slight exaggerations of a rather unpleasant kind of middle-class culture, such as that entitled 'Honesty, Loyalty and Decency on the Up Line to Effingham', for the *Daily Mirror* is not widely read locally:[26]

> Effingham Junction serves the parish of Effingham and the fringes of Bookham and East Horsley. The villages are joined by the main Leatherhead to Guildford road and by their commuter residents' common aspirations among which are: to send their children to the best schools the mortgage will allow; to entice roses from a garden within sight of a common; to walk a collie or a labrador to the village and to buy Radox, South African sherry and fish fingers in bulk; to play a little golf, cricket or bridge; to acquire a second car and a second mower (one for the difficult patches) and also an oak door, a deep freeze, a double sink, two coloured telephones, a wine rack, an outside christmas tree and perhaps even a bidet; to hold parties of repute for the children, preferably with gas cylinders to blow up the balloons; to employ a twice-weekly woman or even an au pair (Portuguese rather than French: more efficient and cheaper). And to assist a good cause, preferably multiple sclerosis or Guide Dogs for the Blind; to drink real coffee with sugar crystals and Earl Grey tea, and to receive deliveries from Bentalls of Kingston (Motto: To strive and not to yield). People in and about Effingham achieve all of these things, some of them none of them. They are civil servants, accountants, surveyors, bank people; people in oil, advertising and computers.

But it does matter what is written in *Surrey Life* or the *Daily Telegraph*. The brief newspaper dialogue that follows could so easily have come from Surrey rather than Hertfordshire and it is very probable that many of the new migrants, however inaccurately, derived some satisfaction from the

Country life

second instalment.

For the first 22 years of my life I lived in the small Hertfordshire village of Hinxworth. During the past 20 years or so many changes have taken place in this village which have vastly altered its character. When I was a child most of the people living in the village were 'natives' or came from neighbouring villages. The men practically all worked on the land, living in cottages in the village or in the six existing council houses. Just after the second war, eight new council houses were built and these were all allocated to local people, but after this, any vacant cottage or row of cottages were bought up, modernised and converted into large (and often beautiful) houses by 'foreigners', i.e. upper-class town dwellers. Add to this some new private building, all of the large 'executive' style, and you have the new pattern: most of the 'native' villagers living in council houses and affluent 'foreigners' living in the old part of the village. We moved away from the village 10 years ago because there were no council houses available at that time, and the only type of house we could afford was on a new town estate. This pattern has been followed by practically all my generation and I can foresee the time when there will be no really local people left in the village. I feel that in this way many small villages are being wiped off the map just as surely as if a bulldozer had been driven over them.[27]

I should like to express my regret at the attitude of your correspondent in her letter last Sunday. As a 'foreigner' (i.e. one who has recently moved from town into a village house), I should like to point out that one becomes local by residence and interest and not necessarily by trade or profession; or indeed by virtue of living in a council house. Interest is not lessened because one may happen to drive or ride to one's place of work instead of ploughing the neighbouring fields. If village life is to flourish, then new people, new ideas and new patterns of life must be brought into them. Different faces in the village High Street should be welcomed, different paint on the front door admired.

Country life

On the eve of entry into the European Community I feel we should make a start nearer home by accepting the oddities of our immediate neighbours who do use the same language and share the same heritage.[28]

These quotations are not untypical of the kind of descriptions that have often been made; they are only distinctive in that they have been made in easily accessible and much read periodicals rather than in the obscure corners of academia. Their significance lies partly in their emphasis on conformity and partly in their ability to depict accurately, but according to different sets of values, the social changes going on in this kind of area. It is in the context of these kinds of statements that individual views are formed.

Even more important for local residents are local newspapers and periodicals. The weekly *Surrey Advertiser*, published in Guildford, is widely read in central Surrey and there is a special Horsley edition. Its emphasis is naturally on local and regional events which are more country orientated than the national press; there are always sections on agriculture and markets, and regular features on Surrey homes and history. Moreover, all the parish events are recorded in the classic tradition of the local press. It would be impossible to read the Horsleys and Clandons sections for long and not to develop the conviction, however erroneously, that there was an active community with a range of varied social activities. Similarly, the inevitable newspaper orientation towards Guildford is more apparent than real beyond the columns of the press.

Whilst the *Surrey Advertiser* reflects the pedestrian aspects of parish life, the church bazaars and the parish council, at a higher and more glossy level *Surrey Life* and *Surrey* create a different kind of illusion to be welcomed by a different group: the illusion that there is a continuing good life enjoyed by a prosperous upper middle class, that life is one of expensive property, rugby and cricket, finance, fishing, hunting and farming, stately homes, bridge and the theatre (which the two magazines regularly feature). But beyond the good life that these enshrine, incidentally providing a range of choices available only to a very small leisured class, is the attitude to country life. Industry does not intrude into the pages, unless it is the quaint relics of a water-driven mill; and *Surrey* has run a whole series on such traditional craftsmen as blacksmiths, thatchers and wheelwrights, showing how their skills live on locally. A further emphasis on wild life, picturesque villages, local history and folklore further emphasises the rural nature of the county. At least in their pages tradition has not ended, and the tradition is that of a rural gentry.

In different ways the local press provides rose-coloured spectacles through which the environment can be viewed and, since both views are to some extent true, these particular perceptions are often maintained by migrants long after arrival. In some ways those who were least familiar with the area and made least use of it were those who enthused most eloquently about the benefits of rural village life. Those who had tried to hunt or walk were not quite so sure; attitudes to the area reflect the occasional abrupt contrast between journalism and reality.

It would, however, be unreasonable to think that many households, having moved voluntarily into the area, would admit to being unhappy and few were in any way disappointed. A large proportion of responses to the question, 'What do you think of this area?' ran along the lines of 'Very beautiful. We love it', 'Best area in the world', 'Never lived in a better place', and 'East Clandon is the prototype of a nineteenth-century village: delightful'. Demurring responses ran along three different lines. The first were those who found it 'very pretty in summer; now I hate it' and 'very pleasant in summer, tedious in winter'. The second group was those who found it 'very pleasant, but expensive'; their numbers were greatest in West Horsley (North). An economist in a rented flat in East Horsley commented, 'very nice but very wealthy; even the trees drip wealth. . .we would love to live here'. The third group consisted of those who found 'the area is O.K. but you can't change the people'. For many, the local environment was not the physical environment but the social environment. They would have agreed with the anonymous lady who said, 'What's environment? Just the polythene bag around the kipper. Give me the kipper. The people make a place what it is.'[29] Almost without exception the households found the physical environment satisfactory; it was the social environment that was less attractive, but even then only for a small minority. Several of these disappointments are reflected by the 63-year-old widow who had moved from north London to West Horsley to 'recapture childhood'. She was, however, disillusioned: it was lovely but too quiet and not very friendly, transport was poor and her friends thought it too far to come.

Attitudes like these are not those of households that had been allocated to council houses in the area; their dissatisfaction runs along similar lines but is mentioned by almost half the newcomers rather than a mere 1 in 20 owner-occupiers. No more than four were completely enthusiastic: 'very nice; all pretty friendly', 'smashing, great; happy with the community', 'nice and quiet'. Others had reservations: 'like it; very friendly round here but no time to be close', 'very nice; sorry to say we don't know next person but one yet' (after 18 months). Almost all differentiated firmly between place and people: 'Don't like it: too many rich people; should have more council estates', 'Don't like the village; old residents don't want you since they're all in private houses', 'Gorgeous place but a living tomb: oppressing in winter', 'Don't like it, too snobbish', 'Everyone is aloof, just a dog-loving dormitory. Would like a multi-racial society here'. The last suggestion would not have found much support with the tenant on the other side of the street who was more content with the 'nice area, free of coloured people and undesirable tenants'. A lorry driver's wife summed up what would be the view of many other council residents: 'not terribly keen...too much private property with not much in between; would like more shops but they wouldn't allow it'. Thus despite the euphoria which might be expected to follow a move to a council house, particularly after a wait of some years, many residents had soon discovered some of the social and economic limitations of life in this beautiful semi-rural area.

The Horsleys and Clandons suit those with a particular set of aspirations, which might include a semi-rural or rural environment, a sense of community (whether one participated or not) but also ready access to urban centres. For many of those who were happy in their new home their life styles were virtually unchanged. It was enough that the potential for change existed and that tradition seemed to be not far removed, the scenery was greener and there was a hint of a real community. Access to it was always possible if desired. For those whose place of residence was chosen for them there was more to complain about; the community that did exist excluded them, and their own desires were frustrated by the absence of power. The traditional life styles that the owner-occupiers sought to preserve or resurrect, belatedly and in vain, were irrelevant and in conflict with their own needs.

Apparent from a lack of desire for change and the high level of residential satisfaction on the part of the owner-occupiers is what Pahl calls 'the essential ordinariness of English domestic life',[30] which is elaborated elsewhere: 'the emerging style of the "new middle class" in Britain is not the self-conscious status-seeking typical of the American literature but rather a contented domesticity centred round shopping trips on Saturday and annual camping holidays with the children.'[31] Lives are well organised and run along well-charted lines; diversions are unwelcome. But if domestic life is, in some sense, ordinary, it is extremely satisfying to all but a minority of central-Surrey residents. That minority is primarily the council-house occupiers.

Despite high levels of residential satisfaction several households had considered moving away from the area or from the particular house; not all wanted to go, especially those whom their company had once again uprooted: 'It's breaking our hearts to go.' Family splits are sometimes almost inevitable: 'My husband intends to retire to Scotland. People are supposed to be more friendly there but I think it's cold and misty.' It would be interesting to know which myths eventually prevailed for this family. A significant proportion of households observed that despite their own satisfaction they would probably move because it was their habit or because regular change prevented 'mental stagnation', but most went to where their firms promoted them. The husband's career is the basis of the residential life style. Continued residence in privileged suburbs and villages demands

Country life

continued success. The West Horsley publican's comment that 'This is the frustrated area: people are continually looking for something better', has more than an element of truth. The 'seven-year itch' is certainly applicable to residential mobility. Once again a large number of those who thought they might move was intending to go to the 'West Country'; the myth is retained. But at least there are few who intend to abandon country life so soon; only one household definitely intended to return to a city.

Despite the trends towards conformity and the inadvertent superimposition of urban life styles on an unwilling countryside each parish retains a little of its historical uniqueness and independence. If the Young Farmers' Club and the Women's Institute are less and less the traditional face of country life most of the new urban and nationally orientated social organisations, and even the political parties, have not escaped some mellowing by their location. The irony is that the one group that would welcome even more superimposition of urban life styles is quite powerless to achieve it.

CHAPTER 6

Participation and planning: preservation and people

In the Norfolk village of Horning, the owner of an 18th-century thatched barn has been asked to demolish it because it is out of keeping with neighbouring 20th-century bungalows.

New Statesman

Gradually, but in fits and starts, the idea that planning is the preserve of the professional and that the completed plan is presented to the public as a *fait accompli* has waned. Participation by the public, and even co-operation in goal formulation and plan formulation, have increasingly been generally viewed as 'good things'. Yet there have been consistent and considerable problems: How should any kind of co-operation exist? What are the best forms of joint decision-making? Who should formulate the goals and for whom are they formulated? The major (and also many minor) problems of town and country planning, concerning, for example, land values, compulsory acquisition and cost-benefit analysis, can be highly technical yet participation demands that a public with, in this sense, restricted education and limited political sophistication be at least partly involved.

The official machinery for objections and appeals (in reaction to the plan as a *fait accompli*) is a quasi-judicial process which is limited to a restricted range of interested parties. The statutory provisions of local enquiries are not concerned primarily with the encouragement of public participation in planning, and participation is constrained by particular formal channels. Yet this is only the final objection to formulated plans; channels for participation in plan formation are extremely hazy. Some of the recommendations of the innovatory Skeffington Report were obvious and mundane: 'people should be kept informed throughout the preparation of a structure or local plan for their area', and 'people should be encouraged to participate in the preparation of plans by helping with surveys and other activities as well as by making comments'.[1] Yet this report, which is still the only official contribution to the role of participation in planning, evades two of the major issues: first, should there be any official or semi-official channels within which participation and planning can co-exist, and second, what are the political implications of participation?

The former has never been satisfactorily resolved and is a subject of continued debate; it represents a classic problem in the micro-politics of interest groups, consultative committees and users' committees, which merges easily into the second problem: is participation a job for the local political activist or the local 'consumer'? Are local interests formulated, or able to be formulated, along formal political lines or are they the concern of formal or informal voluntary bodies? The role and evolution of local participation, both formal and informal, in the planning of central Surrey, the effectiveness and means of its articulation, the representativeness and significance of the views put forward and, much more tentatively, the values of the participants in the planning process and the costs and benefits of planning are examined here. Skeffington rightly observes that 'Not everyone's wishes can be met. But the fact that some people may ultimately be hurt only strengthens the need for them to know of proposals early, to understand them and to be involved in shaping them'.[2] The questions considered here are who are these 'some people' and are they the people best able to benefit from, understand and shape proposals?

Amenity societies

The historic lack of any channels of participation meant that negative obstructive opposition was the only form of participation in the planning process; scarcely surprisingly this kind of participation was found earliest in the present century in two significant areas: the more beautiful parts of the Home Counties—like central Surrey—that early on felt the pressures of the expanding metropolis, and the most beautiful parts of England, such as the Lake District, where any kind of development was felt to be detrimental and where an extreme local reaction was that the environment should be preserved eternally entirely as it was.

The task of documenting and dating the emergence of the local and national protest movements and interest groups that are concerned with general planning problems is fraught with difficulty even if there were adequate definitions of a minimum level of local organisation and the kind of planning problems that are of interest. The country's first civic society was probably the Sidmouth Improvement Committee, still in existence today, which was formed in 1846 'for securing to the public the existing walks on the cliffs and Salscombe Hill'.[3] In 1865 John Stuart Mill, T.H. Huxley and others founded the first national society, The Commons, Open Spaces and Footpaths Preservation Society, specifically to fight enclosures, in the course of which they were able to preserve Hampstead Heath and Epping Forest. A decade later William Morris founded The Society for the Protection of Ancient Buildings, and in 1895 Octavia Hill founded the National Trust. In 1901 the first major action, *Commons Preservation Society* v *Lord Avebury* (concerning Stonehenge) was fought in the Law Courts whilst in 1932 the first militant action was a campaign for National Parks which involved mass trespassing. The two societies that are currently most closely involved in the preservation of amenities—the Council for the Protection (formerly 'Preservation') of Rural England, and the Civic Trust—were founded much later, in 1926 and 1957 respectively. The Civic Trust estimates that there were about 100 local amenity societies in 1939; these were rapidly augmented in the 1940s and 1950s, especially in the south east, and when the Trust was formed in 1957 there were about 200. A 1968 estimate suggested 600 such societies and a 1971 estimate suggested 'well over 700';[4] the rate of expansion continues to increase.

Participation and planning: preservation and people

It was not until 1919 that the Government made any attempt to deal with the statutory business of amenity, however defined. The department concerned, the Ministry of Housing, was given too many responsibilities and lacked cohesion and organisation since its power was inadequate for radical change. Thus physical planning and the control of land use were submerged in the post-war chaos of reconstruction when development ran riot. Although the first Town Planning Act had been passed in 1909 there was no statutory control of development in the countryside before the Town and Country Planning Act (1932) and the Restriction of Ribbon Development Act (1935). In the circumstances, it was not surprising that until the Second World War few local areas had become sufficiently organised to look after even their own interests. The earliest reference traced to local amenity interest within the four parishes was in 1928 (see Chapter 2) and again in April 1930 when at a Ministry of Housing Public Enquiry into the development of a housing estate at Wix Hill, West Horsley, a local landowner, Mr Clough Williams-Ellis (later to become the famous architect-planner of Portmeirion), speaking both in his private capacity and as a representative of the CPRE, objected in principle to development and in practice to the scale and density of development (which the Enquiry eventually rejected). He was, however, a single influential individual and the present local societies did not emerge until the 1950s, whereas the nearby Leatherhead and District Countryside Preservation Society was founded in 1929 (but never concerned itself with the affairs of the Horsleys). In the following year the Clandon Ratepayers' Association (on which there are no other data) was complaining of overcrowding on rush-hour trains from Waterloo, but generally the inter-war period in central Surrey was a time when protest over planning came from, and through, the parish councils.

The quintessential nature of early protest was its middle-class origin and membership—or, as Barr put it, 'typically middle-aged and middle class, guarding their comforts of quiet and privacy and beauty'.[5] In the nature of things beautiful, easily accessible places have tended to become early outliers of middle-class residential (or recreational) development, or even of special scientific interest; thus societies are most liable to emerge where these are threatened in some way by some kind of development. Current national interest in the environment and especially pollution has fostered a host of national societies and journals and these have had a spin-off at local level in the creation and consolidation of local interest groups.

Surrey, both because of the long-standing local interest in conservation and because of the extent of that interest over the county, has more than its share of societies and has an organisational system that is more efficient and better developed than in any other county and which exhibits a fairly clear hierarchical structure from national to street level. At the top of the hierarchy are national organisations such as the CPRE and the Civic Trust. The CPRE, for example, has more than fifty national constituent bodies (such as the Town and Country Planning Association, the NFU and the Civic Trust) and, although maintaining close touch with these bodies, the majority of its active work is done through its county branches and through local affiliated societies. The local societies are expected to fight their own battles but with assistance where the CPRE considers that an issue of principle or of national interest is involved. In Surrey the county branch of the CPRE is the Surrey Amenity Council.

Between the national and county bodies lies a rather curious regional society: the Green Belt Council for Greater London. It was formed by a number of amenity societies in 1954, 'to preserve the Metropolitan Green Belt, to resist all efforts to abolish it, to resist all encroachments upon it, and to advise as to the use of the land and assist in the planning of its use'.[6] Although its members are amenity societies, both regional and local, none of those in the four parishes is a member; the Green Belt Council plays a rather secretive role and 'do not propagate our aims because all we need to do is to fight planning applications for encroachment on the Green Belt and to argue with local authorities of different kinds who do not give it the protection it should have.'[7] It publishes no recommendations on use of Green Belt land, nor any other publications or newsletters; representations are made entirely to the ministries and local authorities concerned.

Its role, as the only organisation that attempts to represent the whole of the Green Belt in any way, is obviously valuable, yet the cloak of secrecy that guards operations would seem to militate against success; certainly such secrecy deters any kind of public participation. Hampered by the lack of funds the Green Belt Council is a somewhat toothless watchdog.

The Surrey Amenity Council was first mooted in December 1950 when a meeting of representatives of six organisations with allied interests was held in Dorking at the invitation of the Dorking and Leith Hill District Preservation Society. In May 1951 a conference was held and attended by representatives from twenty amenity societies as a result of which the Association of Surrey Amenity Societies was formed, which in July 1956 became the Surrey Amenity Council. The SAC has grown steadily since its inception; where necessary it acts locally for the CPRE, the Civic Trust and other national bodies such as the Commons, Open Spaces and Footpaths Society. Its two main aims, which have remained constant since its creation, are, first, the maintenance and where possible the enhancement of the beauty of Surrey and, second, the assistance of member societies and the encouragement of the growth of local amenity societies throughout the county. Towards these aims the permanent functions of SAC are to provide a standing conference to discuss members' problems, to act on their behalf on county problems such as development plans, major roads and the Green Belt, and to act as a local society where there is none until such time as one can be formed.

At the end of 1972 the membership of the SAC consisted of some fifty-nine organisations. Forty-four of these were entirely local organisations, three were local branches of the National Trust and the remainder were county branches of regional and national associations (such as the Inland Waterways Association, Men of the Trees, the Ramblers Association and the River Thames Society). Among the local organisations were the Clandon Society and the Horsley Countryside Preservation Society. The last area still 'unprotected by any amenity society'[8] was the distant south-east corner of Surrey, but societies were finally established there in 1970. Other areas are more adequately served: in April 1971

Guildford alone had no less than twenty-eight amenity associations. The functions of the SAC are exemplified particularly in its role as a county committee of the CPRE; since it covers the whole of Surrey it is not generally able to take a specifically local interest in any matter but has to consider the benefits of any proposal with reference to the county as a whole. It is apparent, from the annual reports of the SAC, that its conferences produce statements like the well-meaning platitudes set out as its aims. The annual report tends to disguise the kinds of discussion and dispute that must have ensued where national and regional decisions unevenly benefited different parts of the county. However, it is only by taking on this mediating role that the SAC is able to function. So far in SAC there have been no disputes between constituent societies, and no decisions, even on the siting of major roads, have been taken that have alienated specific societies. Although a few societies have dropped out its simple general functions can be usefully maintained.

The Surrey Amenity Council has no individual members and operates through conferences to which individual constituent organisations send representatives. At the end of 1970, it consisted of a chairman, an honorary treasurer and three honorary secretaries, none of whom was paid for his services. The chairman was a knight, two of the secretaries retained high military titles and, in any sense, the whole council had a solid professional flavour. The essential constituents of the SAC are the local societies, and in the past decade central Surrey has been extremely efficiently served by the Horsley Countryside Preservation Society and the Clandon Society. The elder of these two is the Horsley Society founded in April 1956, following a disputed planning decision and a letter in the *Surrey Advertiser*. By the time its first *Newsletter* was printed in June 1956 it had 325 members.

In the first two years membership was small, as the benefits were less obvious, but it grew rapidly until 1961 when households in the two Horsley parishes made up a large proportion of the members (Table 6.1). In the ten years up to 1974 the membership grew only slightly, doing little more than keep pace with the general increase in population, despite a membership drive in 1964 when business reply cards were

179

Participation and planning: preservation and people

used. Yet this is an extremely large membership and even in 1961 the membership figure was the highest of any amenity society in England, urban or rural, apart from the London Society.

Table 6.1 Horsley Countryside Preservation Society

Date		Membership
June	1956	325
March	1957	543
April	1958	931
February	1959	c. 1,150
April	1960	c. 1,250
March	1961	c. 1,430
April	1964	c. 1,400
April	1965	1,490
May	1966	1,500
March	1968	c. 1,800
April	1969	over 1,800
April	1970	over 1,900
November	1973	c. 1,900
March	1974	c. 1,900

Source: Horsley Countryside Preservation Society *Newsletters*, irregular

The policy of the society at its inauguration in 1956 was set out as follows:[9]

a) *Building Development* The Society's aim is, in furtherance of the policy of the Green Belt and the Surrey County Development Plan, to oppose the development of building estates on farmland, woodland and scrubland, and the excessive break-up of private gardens for building. The Society is also committed to the prevention of 'clashing' building types as far as possible, stressing the importance of architectural good manners.

b) *Tree Preservation* The Society is opposed to the cutting down of healthy hedgerows and trees for road widening or building purposes, and the replacement of hedgerows by chain link or other incongruous fences.

c) *Footpaths and Bridleways* The Society aims to walk each of the highways shown on the definitive maps under the National Parks and Access to the Countryside Act

Participation and planning: preservation and people

1949, and to support every application for further ways to be included in the maps if there appear to be good grounds for doing so.
d) *Rural Manners* The Society is against untidiness in general; litter, rubbish dumps and the like will be the subject of any action that can be taken for their removal.
e) *Relations with Municipal Bodies* The Society aims to cooperate to the full with the Parish Councils of East and West Horsley, the Guildford R.D.C., and the Surrey County Council, but as an independent body reserves its right to differ and criticise wherever necessary, and to take such action as it deems desirable in the interests of the preservation of the amenities of the two parishes.

Subsequently the main aims of the society have been unchanged. These ideals epitomise the 'watchdog' nature of the society, especially in its stated concern with the less important minutiae of planning, such as tree preservation, rather than with larger issues such as airports and motorways. There is no lack of concern: it is simply that attitudes to developments of this kind are predictably negative and are shared by all other local interests.

The Clandon Society was formed in 1962 as the West Clandon Society for the 'preservation of the rural character of East and West Clandon and environs'.[10] In November 1963 residents of East Clandon became eligible for membership and the name of the society was altered. The Clandon Society has an official constitution in which the objects of the society are defined as follows:[11]

The objects of the Society shall be to promote and encourage:
(i) high standards of architecture and village planning in West/East Clandon;
(ii) public interest in the preservation of the history and character of the area and its surroundings;
(iii) the preservation, improvement and beautification of features of general public amenity; and
(iv) to pursue these ends by means of meetings, exhibitions, lectures, publicity and the promotion of social and other schemes of a charitable nature.

The objects are not so precisely defined as in the Horsley Countryside Preservation Society but in practice the two societies have had close informal links and operate in almost exactly the same manner. The growth in household membership (Table 6.2) indicates that the society has not achieved the steady rate of growth that the Horsley society has had and yet this membership represents a significant proportion of the villages and it has been at least as influential as the Horsley society.

Table 6.2 Clandon Society

Date	Membership
November 1963	77
February 1964	136
1965	183
July 1970	141 (120 in WC; 21 in EC)

Source: Clandon Society *Newsletters*, irregular

East Clandon has always had very few members of the Clandon Society. The small size of the village, its location away from a main road and its basic composition of pre-twentieth-century housing have made it less likely to have any kind of change; also, the society is rooted historically and geographically in West Clandon. At its November 1963 AGM there were seventy-three members from West Clandon and four from East Clandon, but even these numbers fell so that in 1967 there were no members in East Clandon. Subsequently, with the influx of new residents into the village, membership in East Clandon has grown. However, throughout the records of the Clandon Society there is not a single reference to planning in East Clandon.

The formal, and informal, activities of the two societies are almost identical. The major watchdog role of the societies is in the examination of the Guildford District Council Planning Register. Both in Clandon and in Horsley members of the executive committee examine the register in Guildford at least every three weeks so that immediate consideration can be given by the committee to any significant planning proposals. In this way planning proposals can be studied as soon as they become known to the public and can be opposed where this is felt to be necessary. Most of the specific activities of the societies are generated by this examination: an impressively systematic concern for the local environment. Moreover, since the societies began there has been a considerable increase in the number of applications for planning permission and, particularly in the past five years because of the consolidation of Green-Belt policy, there have been large numbers of applications for extensions to houses. This creeping urbanisation is particularly resented by the preservation societies. Some of the concern of the societies is with single local issues, and others with more general matters of principle; as far as possible these are linked to emphasise the general importance of any local opposition to change.

An early example indicates the care that is taken by the societies to present a solid case to the council. In this case the following objections were presented against Application No. 120093 (a proposal to build 78 houses, each with a garage, on 58 acres at Oakride Farm, Tythe Barns Lane, East Clandon), which is the largest planning proposal put before the council while the Clandon Society has been in existence. First, the proposed development was in the Green Belt; second, it was not infilling and was between 1 and 1½ miles from either Clandon village; third, it was not 'rounding-off'; fourth, there were no transport facilities and the proposed development was on a minor road in an area where commuter and rail facilities were already overstrained; fifth, there were no shopping services and hence any shopping-area development that might follow would destroy local amenities; finally, there were insufficient local schools (public or private) to meet an influx of population on this scale.[12] The proposal was eventually turned down by the council and there is no indication that the views of the Clandon Society were of any significance in this decision. Their views are significant primarily for developments of much smaller scale.

There are two basic planning situations for the amenity societies: major decisions in which the views of the amenity society are those of just one of a large number of interested parties, and minor decisions in which the amenity society is one of perhaps two or three interested parties. Major decisions, for example on motorway alignment and air-traffic routes, tend to be decisions that affect more than one local amenity society and, apart from straightforward opposition to any scheme at all, the local societies are in a position to be played off against each other where they adopt a simple 'anywhere but here' policy. Since a new motorway affects the amenities of all areas through which it passes (although these amenities are varied) a decision on location is less likely to be made on amenity grounds because of the high cost of departure from the most economic location. Local societies tend to be frustratingly impotent in influencing the more important decisions that are primarily their *raison d'être*, When the chairman of the Horsley Countryside Preservation Society reviewed the first eighteen years of the society's life he concluded that there had only been a single case where the society 'did not see eye to eye with the authorities',[13] which was in the early 1970s when both the rural district council and the county council wanted to develop a plot of land, of about nine acres in East Horsley, for flats for old people. A public enquiry was held at which the society argued that the land was outside the East Horsley built-up area and therefore did not constitute 'infilling' or 'rounding off'; moreover, the inspector who conducted the enquiry did not recognise any special local need justifying the development. However, ultimately the minister agreed to the proposals and the flats have now been completed. Increasingly, therefore, as pressure on the fringes of the Green Belt has become more intense it appears that the preservation societies may lose what little influence they have, as bigger battalions become involved in what have hitherto been relatively unimportant development decisions. There are, after all, no more than thirty pensioners in the new East Horsley home but the possibility of even small amounts of land becoming available for development has become an important planning issue.

It is the minor decisions, some of which can scarcely be rated as 'planning', yet many of which affect the quality of the landscape, that the amenity societies are most able to influence. In the past six years both societies have been concerned with five different aspects of planning: first, the preservation of rights of way (by walking over them at intervals and preventing their becoming bridle-ways); second, a general concern with amenity in the broadest sense (for example, overhanging trees, untidy village-hall grounds, railway-station re-decoration, condition of footpaths and style and size of new buildings); third, concern over speed limits and visibility at road junctions; fourth, tree-preservation orders; and, finally, the type and extent of street lighting. Thus the societies act as a pressure group, where relevant, to the parish council, the district council and the Surrey County Council but so far, never as consultative groups.

The relationship between parish council and preservation society is of some interest here. Formally, the powers of any parish council are extremely limited and of minimal importance; they include control of allotments, parochial charities, maintenance of public footpaths and bridle-ways, provision of parking places for motor cycles and bicycles and roadside shelters and seats. (Functions common to parishes and district councils include provision of bus shelters, litter control, provision of parks and recreation grounds, footpath lighting and acquisition of rights of way.) The functions of the parish council are very similar to the interests assumed by the preservation societies and an examination of the business of the local parish councils in the period from 1968 to 1971 indicates their parallel functioning. In this period decisions were taken by the councils on donations to local charities (and also the cricket club), size of footpaths and footpath lighting and (in the case of West Horsley) parish tennis-court management plus general problems of maintenance and preservation of amenity. The second main parish-council function is to put forward the council's views on local matters to the relevant higher authority, in this case, for example, on pollution of a parish pond, speed limits and requests for the designation of conservation areas. (West Horsley Parish Council also has a planning sub-committee which examines extracts from the council planning register and puts forward its views in exactly the same way as the preservation societies.) For the functions exercised solely by the parish councils the preservation societies act as pressure groups to the councils but, for the functions exercised by the district council and the Surrey county council, their role as pressure groups is essentially the same as the parish council. All the members of both Horsley parish councils and the representatives on the rural district council have been members of the preservation society.

Neither the council nor the preservation society view their parallel roles as entirely satisfactory. In May 1968, at a public meeting called by the East Horsley Parish Council, the Horsley Association was set up, its object being 'to further the interests of the people of Horsley, to work together with existing statutory and voluntary organisations, to facilitate liaison between them, and to help focus public attention on matters of local interest and importance'.[14] The parish council was involved because of its view that certain functions could be more easily carried out by a voluntary organisation rather than an official body. In Clandon opposition to considered inadequacies of the parish council with reference to planning are thinly disguised. As the Clandon Society *Newsletter* stated in May 1967: 'sadly, there is no longer any member of the Society resident in East Clandon. There being no opposition, the present members of the Council are automatically re-elected'; but the society was able to list members of the society who were standing for election to the West Clandon Parish Council. Indeed, the *Newsletter* provided detailed biographies of the five candidates who were society members but not even the names of their opponents. It was felt to be 'desirable that new candidates offer themselves for elections to provide fresh blood and new ideas'. Yet from these different kinds of manoeuvre more adequate roles have failed to emerge; the frustrations of decision-making at parish level are unresolved and several groups continue to have heavily overlapping and interlocking concerns and spheres of influence.

Although the parish council has real powers the limitations on these powers result in little local interest. The attendance at the AGMs of the preservation societies is consistently higher than at parish-council meetings (although the latter occur more often). Indeed, parish-council meetings are so sparsely attended that they are sometimes held in private houses. The 1972 annual parish assembly in East Horsley attracted a mere fourteen members of the public; the preservation societies can command more than twice that number. If Paul Jennings is right in stating that 'it is probably true that the parish council is the last expression of a rural community',[15] then central Surrey has little trace of a rural community. In many ways the preservation societies rather than the councils are, to a much greater extent, the custodians of the values of the existing population.

Despite the overlapping interests of parish councils and parish amenity societies there were still those who felt that some interests were inadequately represented. The basic *raison d'être* for the Horsley Association was that it should look after the *'general* interests of the residents, rather than the *particular* interests which were probably covered by other Associations'.[16] Nevertheless the original stimulus was the awful possibility of the A246 Leatherhead-Guildford road through the south of the parish being improved to motorway standards and it was thought that the Horsley Association might co-ordinate local opposition on this matter. It was to some extent, therefore, a forerunner of the Five Villages Association discussed later, whose formation removed this particular activity from the Horsley Association. Subsequently, the association has concerned itself with smaller issues; the most important of these have been the availability of parking places at the local shops and the extended use of Wisley Aerodrome.

Even then there is no evidence of effective action on its part; furthermore the association has a mere seventy-five members after more than three years, thus 'there appeared to have been very few subjects arising which affected the village as a whole. One can therefore say that we are a dormant body ready to take action when the need arises.'[17] So far the topics that have concerned the association have been minor matters that will fall into the laps of other societies, especially the Countryside Preservation Society, should they become more important.

There is one more level in the amenity-association hierarchy and that is the individual road. Again this is exemplified most completely in East Horsley where many roads, among them Glendene Avenue, Cobham Way, The Highlands, High Park Avenue, Norrels Drive and Woodland Drive, all have residents' associations. The only two of these that are not culs-de-sac, Glendene Avenue and Cobham Way, still retain gates at their eastern ends and regular ramps to reduce traffic speeds. Exclusiveness is physically maintained. All are private roads built on Chown's land and not maintained by the district council: hence the residents must organise their own repairs and maintain their roads, should they wish to do so. Glendene Avenue may be regarded as typical of an active road association. Initially the developers collected 6d per foot of frontage for annual upkeep after the completion of the first house in 1932, but nothing was collected after 1941 and hence the residents' association was formed in 1963 to carry out by then much needed maintenance work. All residents automatically become members and are charged a yearly subscription per house, from all twenty-six houses, based upon an estimate of the work that would be required in the year. This is likely to be about £10 per house. Formal rules were laid down in 1969; these were summarised as 'to preserve Glendene Avenue as a private country road, to maintain the surfaces, drains, etc., and to attend to such things incidental thereto as the Association shall from time to time consider to be of benefit'.[18] Thus the association takes a general interest in external affairs and has circularised its members and written to the local press on general parish policies that might affect the avenue. At the start of 1971, in conjunction with the Horsley Association, it was able to persuade the parish council to revise its policy on parking at the shopping centre; even a tiny association with very specific protection aims is able to achieve some measure of success. However, all the roads with associations are those roads in East Horsley with the largest detached houses in the parish. Their social composition is overwhelmingly weighted to the upper middle classes; their effectiveness tends to be related to this social composition.

Of those associations and groups discussed so far, even those concerned primarily with a single street, all perform essentially 'watchdog' roles where the implications of relevant institutional decisions at any level are examined. Each individual society therefore deals with a large number of varied planning decisions and reacts to them according to their considered merits or demerits. There is, however, a second kind of association: one that has developed especially to meet a particular proposal, invariably to oppose it and which, when a final decision has been taken, is likely to disappear. There are two such associations, the Five Villages Association, which covers the five parishes, including Effingham, between Leatherhead and Guildford, and the Ockham Road Protection Association, based primarily in East Horsley.

The Ockham Road Protection Association was formed at a public meeting in April 1965, called by the East Horsley Parish Council. In July 1963 the county council proposed widening the road (which is the main spinal road in East Horsley) initially to 24 feet and later to 33 feet, finally becoming a 50 feet wide highway. At some points it is now only 14 feet wide. The parish council registered a strong protest with both the rural district council and the county council and then called the parish meeting which passed unanimously the motion 'That this meeting, while recognising that selective widening of Ockham Road is necessary, resolves to form the Ockham Road Protection Association to take all possible steps to ensure that the rural character and outstanding beauty of the district should be preserved.' Just as the preservation societies emerged from the local belief that the parish councils were inadequate to control development so, too, the Ockham Road Protection Association was seen by its chairman as 'an unorthodox alternative to the Parish Council'. Membership of the association, which was not confined to households on the road, reached 500 before the end of the year, was 1,274 in May 1970 and in mid-1971 was around 1,500.

The basis of opposition was first that the particular nature of the road as a still semi-rural backbone, which partly gave East Horsley its character, would be spoilt; second, that existing traffic on the road was mainly locally generated and unlikely to increase significantly since large-scale development in the Green Belt is impossible; and, third, that the accident record of the road was good and a wider, faster road might only increase the accident rate. The association was not opposed to such improvements as footpath levelling and they also proposed improvements at one particular danger point.

Since priority for the main road was low within the rural district it was thought that piecemeal improvement of this kind at particular danger points would receive higher priority and might obviate the need for subsequent complete reconstruction. The county council rejected this idea but through constant discussions with the county council, aided by letters in the press, some modifications of the main plan were accepted by the council in 1970 to the extent that the maximum proposed highway width was reduced to 26 feet although the basic scheme was continued with. The influence of the association had been significant. It had taken up a position that the parish council felt it could not deal with adequately; it had opposed the basic county-council scheme but eventually had merely pressed for an amelioration of the major scheme. Nevertheless, a major highway had been considerably scaled down as a result of the activity and organisation of one amenity group.

The Five Villages Association arose specifically in response, and opposition, to proposals to build a trunk road, 'Route 37', of motorway standard through the five parishes. The history of the 5VA therefore coincides closely with the recent history of Route 37, whose origin is traceable to 1937 when the county council put forward plans to improve and re-align the A246 Leatherhead-Guildford road and bought up adjoining property where necessary. In December 1938 both East and West Horsley parish councils wrote directly to the Ministry of Transport objecting to the county council's decision to sterilise land for the purpose of building the road. In the Development Plans of 1958 and 1965 this new realignment appeared only as a principal traffic road rather than a major trunk road. Subsequently, a county-council feasibility plan indicated that the council intended to build in the mid-1970s a two-lane carriageway of motorway standards with a minimum width of 120 feet which, where necessary, would be carried on embankments. The main purpose of the road would be as a feeder to the South Orbital

(M25) Motorway, the outer ring road around London. Although the line for the road was more or less established in 1937, the county council has still not submitted a final preferred route to the Ministry of Transport.

The 5VA was officially launched at a meeting in West Horsley village hall on 24 April 1969. The earliest groundwork had been laid by the Horsley Countryside Preservation Society and set in motion by a Joint Sub-Committee of the Parish Councils. The basic position of the association was its opposition to Route 37, and its formal policies were:[19]

> a) the opposition to the construction of a road, described in the Surrey County Development Plan 1958 as 'Road No. 37' and now commonly known as 'Route 37', through the parishes of Effingham, East Horsley, West Horsley, East Clandon and West Clandon in Surrey, on whatever line through those parishes or any one of them such road may now or hereafter be proposed.
> b) where expedient or necessary the opposition to the improvement and/or diversion of the Class 1 road now numbered A.246 within the boundaries of those parishes or any of them.
> c) the protection, preservation and enhancement of the rural amenities and characteristics of those parts of the parishes subject to, or likely to be affected by, any proposals for the building of new, or the modification of any existing, road or roads.

This verbose, legalistic amplification scarcely disguises the sole aim. The association was formed as a straightforward opposition group to the road, on the obvious grounds that it would be of motorway standard and therefore detrimental to amenity and, second, because it was feared that the county council was engaging in secretive planning without any, even less an adequate, consultation with local elected bodies or voluntary organisations.

Before the inaugural meeting the joint sub-committee contacted other voluntary associations in the five parishes to gain support and their assistance in the distribution of literature; the associations that co-operated in the four parishes were:

in East Horsley the Horsley Countryside Preservation Society, Ockham Road Protection Association, East Horsley Parish Church Council, Horsley Association and the WI; in West Horsley the West Horsley Parish Church Council, the WI and the Old People's Welfare Association; in East Clandon the WI; in West Clandon the Clandon Society, the Clandon Seniors' Club, the WI and the British Legion. This list consists of almost all the associations in the four parishes that were not concerned solely with recreational activities, with one exception: the political associations. Despite the conspicuous existence of both the Liberal and Conservative parties in the four parishes they were not consulted at any stage since it was considered that the road was not a political issue. In view of the way that national political issues and divisions tend to be mutilated and unrecognisable at local level this was surprising but it would have been even more surprising if the support available from individual members of the parties had not been available. Indeed in the 1970 General Election all three candidates for the Dorking constituency stressed their opposition to the road. From this breadth of support a committee was formed, composed essentially of 'responsible people';[20] apart from the five parish councillors and the chairman, who had retired, there were four other members— a solicitor, a QC, a schoolmaster and a bank manager (who was the treasurer).

Immediately after the establishment of the 5VA and its committee, action was begun in three directions: first to raise a working fund for immediate expenses and to obtain financial guarantees to cover any expert advice required for the next public enquiry on the South Orbital (and for any potential Route 37 enquiry); second to collect a group of local experts in all fields of activity which would be useful to mount the campaign; and, third to demonstrate opposition by the presentation to the county council of a petition from the residents of the five parishes. The petition demonstrated a considerable degree of solidarity behind the association; in three months between the founding of 5VA in April and the presentation of the petition on 1 August 1969, some 4,924 signatures had been collected from an electoral strength of 7,890. With the help of the voluntary associations[21] each house in the five parishes had received a newssheet of the association with details of the proposals, a letter of indemnity (for those who wished to give financial assistance) and the petition sheet, which ran as follows:

> We, the undersigned residents of Effingham, East and West Horsley, East and West Clandon, are opposed to the building of a road up to motorway standards through the five villages. We recognise the need to find a solution to Surrey's traffic problems but call upon the authority to find an alternative solution which will not destroy the rural character and amenities of the villages.

In itself a motorway through the villages was clearly of little local benefit, but no more suitable location was suggested. Certainly in September 1968 the aim was simply to 'get the Route 37 out of the villages. It is wrong to put a motorway through built up areas. It must be possible to put it elsewhere'.[22] It was not until 1970 that an alternative was suggested: 'a better solution, if required, would be along the Tillingbourne valley.'[23] Yet the Tillingbourne Valley is south of the North Downs in an area generally regarded as more beautiful and certainly less built up than the five parishes. Nevertheless for such a petition it was not surprising that 62 per cent of the electorate had signed; there are now no regional breakdowns of response to the petition but the reported lack of response in Effingham Junction and, initially, in the north of West Horsley is an indication that distance from the prospective route was related to response.

After the early flourishes of the association in response to the apparently imminent arrival of a motorway the fervour died as official uncertainty over the location and timing grew apparent. The 5VA has been represented at subsequent official enquiries, such as that over the M25 motorway (South Orbital) around Greater London, which began in June 1971. In 1970 a new alignment had been proposed for the motorway, pushing it north instead of south of Leatherhead. Those affected in that area joined together to form an 'M25 Action Group' to campaign for the retention of the old southerly route. Inevitably this did not please the 5VA which joined forces with Bookham Residents Association and a number of other organisations, as far as Mays Green in the north west, to form the 'M25 Northern Support Group'. Thus the long public enquiry through the summer of 1971 became an expensive battle between the two groups of preservation societies with the ministry experts on the sidelines. In the end the long-awaited decision, published in September 1973, favoured the northern route with only very slight modifications. However, economic crisis has prevented work on this motorway, and hence also on the Route 37, and it is most unlikely that any construction will begin before the 1980s. The 5VA has been effectively put into 'cold storage' until the issues are once more revitalised; the economic climate suggests that the storage period will be lengthy.

It has already been noted that the Five Villages Association had a committee composed of 'responsible people' and that the Surrey Amenity Council executive was very firmly middle-class. The composition of the other societies and their committees can be briefly examined; in addition local support can be compared and contrasted with local opposition or lack of interest. The more recent letter heads of the Clandon Society *Newsletters* merely indicate that the president is the Earl of Onslow, the chairman a Lt.-Col. (retired) and that the honorary secretary holds an OBE. (The treasurer, who has no titles, is the only other individual listed.) There is no official indication of the present structure of the Horsley Committee other than that in a committee of ten the honorary secretary is a solicitor and one member is a doctor. However, when the initial ten-strong committee was established in 1956, the first *Newsletter* pointed out that 'on the Committee are architects, solicitors, an accountant, civil engineer and underwriter—a well-mixed bag of professions'. The addresses of committee members of the Ockham Road Protection Association and the Horsley Association suggested that the majority came from high-status areas and there were certainly two solicitors and two civil engineers. The members of individual road residents' associations clearly come from high-status streets.

Information on the individual membership of the societies, if little more comprehensive, is at least more conclusive in its indications of their social composition. The Clandon Society, despite a membership of some 140 out of 430 parish households, has not found a single interested person in 123 council households although there was at one point a council-house member who retired owing to the exigencies of shift work. The Horsley Society has a very similar composition with few, if any, members in council houses. The rationalisation for this tiny membership in council houses, given by the secretary of the Clandon Society, is that the residents of the estates 'are tenants of their houses and this may, understandably, have a bearing on the lack of response'.[24] Council-house reaction is phrased less formally—as one Kingston Avenue tenant observed: 'They're all right—they've got what they want.'

Conventionally similar societies elsewhere are thought to have the same sort of social-class composition as those of central Surrey. Jennings suggests that:[25]

> the preservationist movement *is* overwhelmingly middle-class and not all of its members have enough moral sensibility to feel faintly foolish at having to say in effect, 'I appreciate this beautiful place, having been born in it, or having moved to it because I am sensitive to this kind of thing; I/we thought of it first, why do you people want to come pouring in here and muck it up?'

This observation can be compared with the address of the president of the Horsley Countryside Preservation Society at its 1968 Annual General Meeting. He appeared to take as his main text 'better the devil you know than the devil you don't' and spoke at length of his disagreement with those who objected to the society as a group of individuals interested in preserving the value of their own properties and, in particular, with the views of one individual who had resigned from the society in 1964 after it had opposed an estate for 150 families in East Horsley on the grounds that he had enjoyed his stay in East Horsley and felt that others should have the same opportunity. (Route 37 was also opposed and compared with a third London airport.) Most recently, concern with the extension of already large houses has enabled the Horsley

"Another bloody farm labourer's cottage by the look of it."

Countryside Preservation Society to incorporate some measure of social justice into its objections to this practice; it claims that 'the larger houses and bungalows become, the less chance there is of accommodation for those with limited means and thus a possibility of imbalance in the community.'[26] Unfortunately the community seems to be already in a state of some imbalance.

Elsewhere it has been observed that it is the new, middle-class residents who are most vociferous in wishing to protect what is left of the countryside,[27] although in a different sort of area, more remote from urban influence, unskilled manual workers in the village of Wheatley, Oxfordshire, played a leading part both in the parish council and in formulating a local village plan.[28] The central-Surrey parish councils do contain some council-house occupants and almost all the councillors have lived for a period of more than a decade in the parish; nevertheless the parish council stands in a rather different position from the amenity societies in relation to the planning process. It appears that either the demands of the council-house tenants are unrelated to the desires of the amenity societies (a possibility which is examined subsequently) or that the middle class is most likely to protest in favour of conservation policies.[29]

Street lighting

One single specific issue was covered in the survey: the provision of street lighting, an issue that was continually raised in the same period in the parish councils, preservation societies and local newspapers, and although in itself apparently unimportant it epitomises many of the relationships between planning and the social and spatial structure of the four parishes. In 1968 there were only seven street lights in the four parishes, all in West Clandon where parish-council candidates had found in 1967 that there was a general feeling in the parish that street lights were necessary, especially 'among families with young children'. The parish council organised a vote on the matter and recorded 134 for and 36 against *some* street lighting, so a pilot scheme of subdued lighting was introduced. Subsequently the Clandon

Society stated that: 'Members' views were as follows: Many residents had come to live in Clandon to be within a village atmosphere and were opposed to street lighting as this would lead to suburbanisation. A modified form of lighting with lights too far apart might make roads more dangerous as motorists were not likely to see pedestrians between the lights....After full discussion it was agreed that the rural atmosphere of the village should be preserved, but that modified lighting might be of help to some of the older members of the Village.'[30] Parish-council meetings in East Clandon have always generally concluded, as they did in 1933, that 'there was no wish or need in their village for any lighting'. In West Horsley street lighting had been considered in the council and an informal parish meeting had been held at which the majority had opposed the scheme and the project been turned down.

In East Horsley, after a letter from an individual to the council complaining of the danger of walking from the station at night, the matter of street lighting was raised by the parish at its annual meeting in March 1969 and, since several people favoured some sort of scheme, the council set up a sub-committee to draw up and cost a plan for limited footpath lighting. At a later meeting to discuss this plan all the speakers but one were in favour of the submitted scheme for twenty-six lights at selected points along the two main roads, Ockham Road and Forest Road, and a vote of 136 to 10 was passed in favour of a resolution giving the council powers to provide lights. At this point, the Honorary Secretary of the Horsley Countryside Preservation Society, speaking in his capacity of parish councillor, and with the support of four other councillors, demanded that a poll be taken. This demand was accepted and the poll held on Saturday, 22 November 1969. Some 613 voted (21 per cent of the electorate), of whom 340 were in favour of the scheme and 272 against. Despite the increase in opposition the scheme was passed and was fully installed early in 1971. In West Horsley a poll was held in July 1971 on exactly the same lines as at East Horsley. Only 207 people voted (9 per cent of the electorate) and by a narrow majority of 13 a scheme which proposed twenty lights along the main roads of the parish was accepted. 'Safety was the main factor considered by those in favour of lighting, while those not in favour felt that safety could only be met if lighting was extended along minor roads and this would bring a suburban atmosphere to the village.'[31]

Survey results parallel the voting figures. Response to the question, 'Would you like to see street lighting here?' (or 'more street lighting' in the case of West Clandon), is indicated in Table 6.3. East Clandon and West Horsley emerge as the two parishes most strongly opposed to street lighting, whilst the introduction of street lighting to West Clandon has not produced a strong objection to further expansion. Many, however, qualified their 'Yes' with a plea for discreet lighting with its restriction to danger points. Those most strongly in favour were council tenants and the most strongly opposed were those unlikely to benefit, such as families without children, living in roads remote from the parish centre or the

Table 6.3 Desire for street lighting

	Yes	No	Don't know	Not asked
East Horsley	88	75	35	27
West Horsley	66	76	24	15
West Clandon	17	16	2	8
East Clandon	7	11	0	1
	178	178	61	51

railway station. For them street lighting would simply be an additional burden on the rates. The usual objections to street lighting were similar to those expressed by the Clandon Society, that it would ruin 'the village atmosphere' and that 'people know what it is like here and shouldn't come if they don't like it as it is'. It was also 'the thin end of the wedge' or 'the start of suburbia'. However, the example of West Clandon indicates that initial objections may disappear once the scheme has been established and has been proved to be discreet, so discreet in fact that many people felt that seven lights were neither here nor there, and many respondents in all the parishes had to be prompted to remember whether their parish had lights or not. Some were genuinely surprised to know that their parish did not have lighting. At the same time, low overall demand for any lights suggests that most respondents are not in favour of even minor change within their own parish if this is felt to be detrimental to the 'village atmosphere'.

Planning and change

More significant than the actual answers to questions about street lighting was the nature and phrasing of response, which indicated very clearly that in the vast majority of cases this topic and other topics of general planning interest, such as motorways, shops, housing estates and so on, had never been seriously considered. But then there is little reason why they should. Concern with planning has emerged only when an important issue—such as the Route 37 motorway—developed, but more significantly when a well-organised association was able to generate a local response. In these circumstances the response to planning is negative and 'planning' itself is looked upon with disfavour. Under planning, everyone becomes conservative. The lack of response to any concept of planning, either as preservation or especially as change, is a result of the general feeling that individuals are powerless — the direct opposite of the views fostered by the preservation societies. There is, therefore, something of a divide between the preservation societies, which are well-subscribed and with certain functional teeth, and the mass of newcomers into the area, who may be sympathetic to the societies to the extent of subscribing both to their aims and finances but who are apathetic to the possibilities of change.

Yet if their arguments are unrehearsed many individuals do have strong feelings about their local area and examination of their demands casts a very clear light on concepts of planning and the relationship of planning to real and articulated requirements. These demands were examined through an analysis of responses to the question: 'In what ways, if any, can this area be improved?' 'Improvement' was clearly not a value-free term. Many responses, such as the apparently contradictory 'Any improvement would be detrimental', indicate that any kind of change, in whatever shape or form, is seen by many as undesirable and by some as absolute anathema. However, only three-quarters of the respondents had any views on change; the 'Don't knows' in this case may reasonably be construed as almost entirely opposed to change and in almost all cases they were owner-occupiers. Of the owner-occupiers who did respond (on other than street lighting and main road widening) less than a quarter could, even in the loosest sense, be regarded as putting forward real suggestions for positive changes in the area and many of these were such minor and uncontroversial changes as smoother pavements and more adequate drainage.

Suggested improvements rarely represented significant changes. Levels of satisfaction were high; only one respondent in East Clandon even regretted the absence of such amenities as 'gas, mains drainage and sewerage'. More than three-quarters of all households wanted no changes.

Responses from the most conservative group included: 'Keep the people out' (East Horsley civil servant), 'Improvement would turn it into suburbia. This is one up on suburbia', 'need tight control on building; we came for peace', 'You can't improve on nature', 'You can't improve it...you can certainly spoil it', 'All change is for the worse', 'Stop infilling; it spoils the character', 'No improvements; we don't want to see it get spoilt', 'We've arrived here; I hope no one else does', most of which can be summarised in one response: 'I think it is a delightful spot and don't want to see it change.' All of these were owner-occupiers.

A rather less conservative group suggested changes that might improve the area. The most strongly advocated of these in East Horsley was a change in aircraft flight-paths since one of the approaches to London airport was directly over East Horsley. Clearly this would offend no one (at least *within* the local area); other changes that came into this category were improved public transport, speed limits, road repairs and improved tidiness. 'Rurality is not grubbiness.' Other suggestions, made more than once, that would certainly have altered the character of the area in a way that the most conservative groups might have considered detrimental were facilities for children (especially playgrounds), more shops, a bowling green, a clinic, a launderette and a swimming pool. Some of these suggestions were quite tentative: 'But where do you put recreational facilities?' and a number of households thought that as relative newcomers they were in no position to suggest improvements. Others thought along the lines of: 'Improvements are very unlikely; there's too much opposition.' Many of these suggestions came from council-house tenants—a group with more limited access to facilities outside the parishes and less able to escape from their immediate environment. They were much more likely to suggest fairly radical changes (radical as seen by the more conservative group) such as more shops, more houses and a meeting place for alternative social organisations. One of perhaps only two positive opponents to the Five Villages petition proclaimed that the road 'might bring some life in'.

The suggestion of several council households that there should be more council houses in the area stemmed rather more from the knowledge that increased numbers of council houses would provide an adequate threshold population for other social facilities, and hence more social contact, than from a concern to house local people who would otherwise have to leave the area. Exactly the same kind of response was found before the development of New Ash Green village in the Kent Green Belt, where local council-house residents welcomed the intrusion since they anticipated that it would result in better schools and shops, whilst those in the largest houses objected.[32] The latent conflict between the two groups is revealed in this way: as the function and form of the parishes increasingly reflect the wishes of higher-class residents working elsewhere, and often shopping and socialising elsewhere too, the less each parish can satisfy the needs of the council-house residents.

For the majority of owner-occupiers, especially those who are newcomers, the four parishes are not their final residential location. Changes may spoil their amenities and result in a real decline in the value of their property but, in the last resort, they are mobile and can move away. For the council-house tenants there is little possibility of a move. Detrimental change affects most severely those who are unable to escape; inadequate positive planning, in the provision of social services, for example, similarly affects the same group. Thus for them a pleasant environment is arrived at by little more than chance, a result of a council-house allocation decision that does not and cannot consider environmental requirements. A pleasant environment is a fortunate benefit, which may be allocated away again when the council household reaches a different stage in the life cycle. In the circumstances, concern with the physical environment is simply not a major concern of council-house tenants; concern with the home environment is more immediate and pressing. Orwin was not far from the truth in 1945 when he commented, somewhat patronisingly: 'There is little evidence of any reaction by the countryman to the beauty of the countryside...[they] are quite unmoved by the beauty around them....People prefer to occupy a speculating builder's bungalow rather than a house typical of the district and mellowed by time, even when reconditioned to bring it up to the standards of modern living.'[33]

As McDonald has observed 'it is now part of the conventional wisdom that life chances are subject to constraints of social class and geography',[34] yet there are also semi-political constraints. Different local authorities have different policies on education, housing and planning; access to these is varied and not necessarily related to either social or spatial structure. An underlying theme of this chapter is the inability of council-house tenants to formulate their grievances in a viable way or to become involved in any useful way in debate over local provision of amenities. The two major social institutions that can represent working-class protest are trade unions and tenants' associations, both of which are entirely absent from the four parishes. Only one council estate in the rural district, and none in the four parishes, has a tenants' association. Briefly, council-house residents have no power. Moreover, no group or even any individual is involved in wider issues fringing on economic planning or physical planning in the South East. The four parishes are essentially a residual to major decisions made elsewhere without local knowledge or participation. The wider issues of economic planning, which ultimately have the greatest impact on the local area, can have no local response. In this particular case the 'leapfrogging' of development beyond the Green Belt and the resultant 'filthy, dirty rim of housing estates'[35] suggest that for most owner-occupiers the present inability to participate is quite satisfactory.

The Green Belt is permanent and it crystallises the difference between owner-occupiers and council-house residents. The social problems existing in the four parishes, which include social and physical isolation, financial and youth problems, cannot be resolved locally and hence concentration of participation in planning at the local level will not assist. 'Community consciousness will remain predominantly a middle-class ideology, shared by the deferential and traditional working class.'[36] The middle-class mystique of the countryside may indeed hamper the quality of life for the council-house tenants. The arrival of a commuting middle-class population and their resources has led to a realisation of the existence of national class divisions and consequent resentment by the local group. A sense of deprivation was induced by the changing social conditions that brought into the parishes resources about which they had previously little knowledge. Information heightened dissatisfaction.

If conservatism is therefore unsurprising, perhaps the greatest irony is that apart from East Clandon, to which none of the newcomers 'belongs', none of the villages is of the kind that is really worth preserving. They have never fared well in the Surrey Best Kept Village competition, nor are they quite how Blythe claimed the Suffolk village of Akenfield to be: 'the kind of place in which an Englishman has always felt it his right and duty to be.'[37]

CHAPTER 7

The end of tradition

> I have been amazed to discover that town-bred people are destitute of knowledge which every cow or sheep possesses.
>
> Bertrand Russell, *On Education*

Until the Second World War the geography of central Surrey was steadily changing and the changes were physical. Woodland was cut and replanted, railways and roads constructed and national institutions and national figures gradually moved into the villages. The imposition of the Green Belt resulted in one abrupt change: no longer was physical change possible. The processes of externalisation continued but within the existing framework: an increase in commuting, a growing dependence on the railway for work journeys, the concentration of social and other services either in the largest village, East Horsley, or in an urban centre and, perhaps most important of all, an increasing polarisation in the social structure of the area. The four parishes have evolved from relatively self-contained communities to villages highly dependent on other areas for the provision of work and various services. Within the parishes these changes have been far from uniform; relatively little change is evident in East Clandon whilst East Horsley has a large, high-status residential area very dependent on central-London employment and so bears almost no resemblance to an agricultural community. In East Horsley above all, perhaps more so than in any

The end of tradition

other metropolitan village, change has produced an entirely new village social structure.

Large areas of Surrey protected by the Green Belt have remained almost unchanged since the Second World War. Despite considerable local and regional pressures for some land to be released for new housing almost none has been developed. Hence it has been a constant criticism of Green Belts 'that they have fostered elitism in that those who have been fortunate in living in the agreeable surroundings of the Green Belt have benefited more by the comparative lack of use of it, than have those for whom it was designed, namely the urban dwellers of the metropolitan areas'.[1] Moreover by the mid-1960s the rounding off and infilling of central-Surrey villages was virtually complete so that development control policy was quite unable to cope with the problem of reserving sites for genuine local needs. Peter Hall concluded in 1973 that 'the Green Belts have lost their old point and have not gained a new one. Their protection today is less a matter of planning policy than of planning politics: the rural counties want them to preserve their ratepayers' and voters' way of life and the Department of the Environment seems only too glad to concede the point so as to gain agreement to major growth elsewhere'.[2] Three years later the balance between planning policy and politics remained much the same yet rural counties such as Surrey could point to a new rationale: no longer is the Green Belt merely preserving the countryside, it is also preserving London from decay. For the city it is a lifebelt and for the country villages it is a green noose.

As agriculture has declined as a source of employment in Surrey so too has its visible impression in the landscape. Moreover no longer is it dominated by seasonal fluctuations; demands for harvest labour are fewer and can more easily be met by machinery than the flow of unskilled labour that now exists only in the Kent hop fields and a few vegetable-producing areas. Surrey's agricultural labour force is generally highly skilled—as familiar with the workings of expensive agricultural machinery as with their cars; it is not typical of England. The agricultural labourers whom George Bourne described so sympathetically are quite unrecognisable; the dream of rustics leaning on a country stile is rarely even a figment of imagination. The reality is a fairly well-paid skilled man, albeit probably living in a tied house, almost indistinguishable from other local workers and rarely meeting the migrant middle class. The 'marginal peasants' that Jones claims can still be found in the New Forest and other corners of southern England[3] are quite absent from Surrey. As machinery has replaced manpower the traditional artefacts of agriculture have gone too: tools like scythes, sickles and the complementary horse-drawn carts. It would now be much more difficult to find a working horse than a race horse. Small farms have become large farms and, as small fields are amalgamated into the larger fields that mechanisation demands, a little of the creeping 'Prairiefication' that dominates the English agricultural landscape is present here too. It is 'a tamed and civilised countryside'.[4] In all these ways agricultural organisation becomes decreasingly the product of local unskilled labour laboriously producing foods intended for nearby markets; orientation to the outside and the imposition of modern technology and accounting systems has removed almost all the vestiges of what might once have been traditional agriculture — in the main it is easier but less picturesque.

The decline of a local agricultural system is indicative of the other dominant pattern of change: the externalisation of village life. As agricultural workers travel between parishes for employment and move between counties for better jobs, so also do most other workers. Only a few council-house residents work in their respective parishes; many prefer the improved security and wages of urban factory employment. Symptomatic of improved opportunities elsewhere is the inability of local labour to supply the demands made from the rich households for gardeners and cleaners. Demand permanently exceeds supply. If changing employment opportunities are the main reason why most workers travel outside their own parish they have been, historically, the means of access to a variety of other opportunities; briefly they provided wider horizons. Moreover, they enabled a new kind of perception of the urban world. Between the wars the diffusion of knowledge of the world outside the village had already come from the radio and newspapers yet this was a privileged knowledge. Little of the events on the radio or in national or even local newspapers was relevant to the style of life of most villagers; as late as the inter-war years even events in the *Surrey Advertiser* could have meant very little to most rural workers. Grain prices, gentry marriages and estate development were essentially peripheral to the social and economic organisation of the poor. But, by then, the situation was changing. The proportion of the village population working locally was falling rapidly and a new and different kind of élite was moving in. This new population was already orientated to urban life and almost all remained so, especially for employment. The housing advertisements, plus those of London Transport and the Southern Region, had cajoled them into purchasing a combination of countryside and easy commuting. They were intent on having both.

At the same time that job opportunities in towns were becoming more important for the village poor, a new, richer and more urban group was moving into the villages. Very rapidly, especially between the wars, a more than superficial veneer of urban life was laid across the villages. Of course this varied from place to place: in East Horsley the acquisition was almost complete by the start of the Second World War. In East Clandon there was scarcely a hint of urban life; even the main road effectively bypassed the village and it remained a typical estate village until well after the Second World War. But even there life had changed. The estate's agriculture was mechanised and villagers had begun to seek work outside. Bus services improved whilst the range of goods in the village store contracted. Few of the changes were great but together they represented the increasing externalisation of village social and economic life. So few of the changes were radical yet in a period of less than a century they had resulted in a 'quiet revolution'[5] in village social and economic life.

The arrival of commuters to fill the new estates was significant, as much in the life style that they brought with them as in the gradual increase in numbers that eventually made them a majority. Economically they were divorced from the village; the pattern of their labour was completely unrelated to the agricultural cycle and the seasons. But at

The end of tradition

least until well after the Second World War many of their purchases of goods and services were made within the village. Only in the past decade when the price differential between rural and urban shops began to widen substantially has the transition to urban shopping been made. For the most wealthy households there is still no need to shop in town. But the most obvious difference is social. The few agricultural and improving societies that existed between the wars had for the new migrants no real purpose or claim on their attention. The post-war horticultural societies were orientated towards a rather different end of the agricultural spectrum. Moreover in the earliest periods of immigration they were thrust together on new estates; initially, social life could quite easily be restricted to a single street. These new streets laid the bases of conformity and, even had the village gone out of its way to incorporate them, they were segregated and usually happy to remain segregated. The parish church almost alone could successfully draw them; alone it could not integrate them into parish life.

In many parts of British cities particular social classes are becoming segregated into particular areas, especially as large council-housing estates are constructed in the city centre and at the city fringes. Official and unofficial attitudes to this segregation have vacillated. In the early 1950s attitudes in favour of segregation were so strong that in several places, including one particularly well-known part of Oxford, walls were even constructed between council houses and private housing estates. In the New Towns around London policy favoured a definite mixing yet the belief that profound changes in the social structure were unlikely to follow from simple social mixing on housing estates finally dominated. Planning policy no longer tends to favour integration. In rural areas, on a smaller scale, practice and policy are much the same. Nevertheless a common view is retained that social mixing is more usual and desirable in villages and that the sort of mixing that occurs there should be encouraged. Aneurin Bevan, at a symposium on planning in 1948, suggested that 'we have to try to recapture the glory of some of the old English villages...where the doctor could reside benignly with his patients in the same street'[6] and an anonymous reporter has commented that 'the right "village mix" may soon be as important as central heating'.[7] However, most of the social relationships within the mixture have always been deferential and often patronising but, with the decline of village economies and especially agriculture, coupled with the increasing scale of housing development and the emergence of council estates, economic and social links throughout even the smallest villages have become very tenuous: 'A change from hierarchical to segregated structures is one of the distinguishing features of the metropolitan fringe.'[8] Yet even the hierarchical structures of the nineteenth century scarcely masked the massive gulf between the village rich and the village poor; the economic differences have diminished but the social differences are as great as ever. The most significant process in twentieth-century rural life is the gradual induction of villages into a wider network; only the preservation societies protest and protect against this externalisation. Conformity is established both through the opposition to change by the amenity societies and in the sentiments of most new residents and the symbolism they attach to rural life. The repeated argument that 'people come knowing what it's like' can be contrasted with the knowledge that owner-occupiers choose to live in the villages that council-house occupiers are constrained to live in. The middle-class image of what a village ought to be like hinders the quality of life available to the villagers as a whole.

In every metropolitan village there is a growing polarisation and segregation of two main social groups, the council-house residents and the private-house residents, although nowhere is this division absolute. Everywhere there are tied cottagers, gypsies, publicans, private renters and many others who make social boundaries fuzzy and prevent neat dichotomies. Pahl fed the myth of the two-class village in his early work on the Hertfordshire village of 'Dormersdell'[9] but later amplified his own over-simplification to recognise eight distinct groups: large-property owners; salaried immigrants with some capital; spiralists; those with little income and capital; the retired; council-house tenants; tied cottagers and other tenants; and, finally, local tradesmen and owners of small businesses.[10] Although all of these groups can easily be recognised in

The end of tradition

central Surrey, too, some of them are now very insignificant. The traditional large-property owners have almost completely disappeared; large houses are losing their squirearchy and becoming institutions of various kinds. Both the retired, and those with little income and capital—the reluctant commuters—are increasingly rare since local house prices are much too expensive for them. Institutions can accommodate some of the recently retired. Tied cottagers are also dying out. Surrey is clearly a special case; the Green Belt's restrictions on building so close to London in an attractive environment have enabled the process of polarisation to go on for a long time and hence access to housing has long been critical. Those who cannot afford expensive housing and those who cannot meet council-house restrictions are effectively excluded. The division within the Horsleys and Clandons is not so much between social classes as between housing classes. More so here than in almost any other part of Britain housing is a scarce and desirable resource; indeed, 'being a member of one or other of these classes is of first importance in determining a man's associations, his interests, his life style and his position in the urban social structure'.[11] So, too, in the rural social structure but increasingly with the simplification that there is a polarisation towards only two housing classes. If most of the owner-occupiers do not recognise this division but see instead a variety of different kinds of middle class, it is especially apparent to the smaller number of council-house tenants; there the two-class image is strongly maintained. The dichotomy is a long way from being absolute but at the bottom of the heap it inevitably seems that way.

One East Horsley man, living with his wife in a rented flat, was fined £16 in 1969 for poaching rabbits although he told the court that he needed the rabbits for food. Gavin Weightman has subsequently described this event as the only recently recorded example of subsistence poaching.[12] On the other hand the few other examples of observed poverty (for example, diets of bread and dripping, lack of meat, no carpets or lino) came with one exception from the council-house sector. The poorer members of the community, lacking advanced education, financial resources and useful social contacts, are continuously made aware of the disparity between their situation and that of their more favoured neighbours. In probably the richest area in the whole of the Green Belt it is still possible to be poor.

Shelley once called poets 'unacknowledged legislators' and in earlier centuries poets influenced and sometimes were social, moral and political thinkers. Their concepts of the countryside were sufficiently strong to hold over to the present day; Wordsworth's 'nature poetry' conveys as convincingly as the pastoral idyll the idea that rural life is sweet and simple and that material well-being will only destroy it. But literary sensibility was not entirely of one mind. Although Crabbe was the only major English poet to attempt to convey the whole truth about rural life, for others the poetry of rural idyll was the poetry of nostalgia. Clare lamented that because of enclosure 'Helpstone' was not the same village as it was when he was a child, and even Goldsmith feared that he could not return to 'Auburn' because the old memories had been driven out, along with the villagers, to make room for a great house.[13] Underlying the main theme of pastoral idyll is a minor theme of unease: rural life was not quite as it should be. More recent new arrivals to the countryside have discovered the same differences.

Surprisingly, as the evidence suggests, the present counterparts of the early commuters have the same kind of view of rural life as their predecessors. It is an antiseptic view of the countryside, in which the Green Belt is very much a *'cordon sanitaire'*, a place where one can walk, play, enjoy fresh air and perhaps see farm animals, but not one where one can smell the animals, find mud outside the garden gate or see workers ejected from tied cottages. It is a vision that wants fields but not farm workers. Some of these expectations are not easy to maintain; there are very few places where animals can be seen and few enough where it is possible to walk or play. Nevertheless the green fields and the copses obviously do mean something. They enable a view of the countryside nurtured and possibly even natured by *Country Life* and its local counterparts. The view is easily sustained, by calendars, chocolate boxes, picture postcards and Best Kept Village competitions. Yet it is usually only an idyll. Beyond the chocolate box façades is a range of less attractive and very variable fillings. The idyll has become the myth and the myth is deep-rooted.

Moreover the new residents of central Surrey are literate people. Many have read their Jane Austen and can easily come to feel that they, too, are almost a part of the world she describes. They may even share some of her values: they, too, may treat the agricultural workers with the contempt of total neglect. Others may have gone no further than Agatha Christie, Miss Read or Maurice Wiggin. The result is likely to be the same. The literary world has a remarkably circumscribed view of contemporary village life— determined rusticity always seems to prevail. The location, and sometimes the name, of a place suggests the sort of people who are supposed to live there rather than those who actually do.

For the new arrival to central Surrey there are two compelling strands that can be considered traditional: the visible agricultural system and the semblance of related community life. The assumption that traditional aspects of English life are restricted to the countryside is not unreasonable but locally the assumption would be almost impossible to maintain. Mechanised agriculture serves a national market whilst local community life encompasses a minority of residents. However, if most new residents have scarcely needed systematically to adjust their life styles to a more rural setting, the setting has inevitably encouraged change even though the changes are trite: a little more walking in fresher air, safe walks to schools and greater participation in the place, both formal and informal. If these kinds of changes are ubiquitously considered to be beneficial they are partially offset by the absence of public-transport facilities and some dislocation involved in moving. Those new arrivals who experience disillusionment, or occasionally even dislike, of modern country life can assure themselves that they have at least made a rational economic decision. Even if they, like Osbert Lancaster, begin to think of their homes as 'Wimbledon transitional', 'Stockbroker's Tudor' or 'Bypass variegated' they know at least that solid, conventional, twentieth-century architecture in the Green Belt is almost certainly of lasting and increasing value.

The end of tradition

Overall the pace of life is slower and few new arrivals regret this, but the slower pace of life is the only index of change for most new residents; they cannot adopt a traditional country life style since even its semblance has long since gone. The repositories of tradition are now the Guildford reference library and Kingston Public Records Office rather than the oldest inhabitant. Village life has become suburban life and, for those who can afford the move, a pleasant rest from city life with just the merest hint of a lost country tradition. Metropolitan convenience can incorporate pastoral peace if not tradition; in doing so it becomes a new suburbia from which the simple life has gone. The village community is a memory of the past and a hope for the future. Country life is extremely ordinary.

Notes

Chapter 1 Rural England

1. E. Jones, Foreword to R. E. Pahl, *Urbs in Rure: The Metropolitan Fringe in Hertfordshire*, LSE Geographical Papers no. 2, 1965, p. 3.
2. *Ibid.*
3. W. Cobbett, *Rural Rides*, ed. G.D.H. Cole, London, Davies, 1930, p. 313. First published 1830.
4. H. Peake, *The English Village: The Origin and Decay of its Community*, London, Benn, 1922, p. 218.
5. C.S. Orwin, *Problems of the Countryside*, Cambridge University Press, 1945, pp. 65-6.
6. D. Defoe, *A Tour through England and Wales, 1724-26*, London, Everyman, 1928, p. 145.
7. Cited by H.J. Dyos, *Victorian Suburb*, Leicester University Press, 1961, p. 27.
8. Defoe, *op.cit.*, p. 146. Camden had also observed the gentlemen's houses in 1607 to the extent that Taylor suggests Surrey already had a 'dormitory aspect'. See E.G.R. Taylor, 'Camden's England', in H.C. Darby (ed.), *An Historical Geography of England Before A.D. 1800*, Cambridge University Press, 1963, p. 356.
9. I. Nairn and N. Pevsner, *Surrey: The Buildings of England*, Harmondsworth, Penguin, 1962, p. 44. They also stated that 'a history of medieval architecture could be written without once mentioning a surviving Surrey building; a history of the suburb or folly could almost be written without going outside the county' (*ibid.*).
10. B. Russell, *The Autobiography of Bertrand Russell, 1872-1914*, London, Allen & Unwin, 1967, p. 47.
11. S. Low, The Increase of the Suburbs, unpublished paper read to the British Association, August 1904.
12. Anonymous, *Westminster Review*, April 1866, p. 4.

Notes to pages 6–17

13 K.D. Fines, 'Landscape Evaluation: A Research Project in East Sussex', *Regional Studies*, 2(1), 1968, pp. 43-4. His scale runs from 32 to 0 but the highest score is 24·0 for a view of the Himalayas from its foothills. A score of 18·0 for a view of the Cuillins of Skye across Loch Coruisk is the highest score he gives in Britain.
14 B.E. Cracknell, *Portrait of Surrey*, London, Hale, 1970, p. 144.
15 *Census of Surrey*, London, HMSO, 1871, p. 57.
16 G. Bourne, *Change in the Village*, London, Duckworth, 1912, p. 17.
17 M. Davies, *Life in an English Village*, London, Fisher Unwin, 1909.
18 C.R. Jervis, 'Land Use and Rural Life in South-west Surrey: A Survey of the Human and Historical Geography of the Rural Districts of Guildford and Hambledon', unpublished MSc thesis, University of London, 1954, Ch. 19.
19 I.C. MacPherson, East Horsley 1956, unpublished Diploma in Town Planning thesis, University College, London, 1956.
20 R.E. Pahl, 'The Two-Class Village', *New Society*, 3, 27 February 1964, p. 9.
21 Cracknell, *op.cit.*, p. 75.
22 J. Barnard, 'Country Style', *New Statesman*, 86, 15 June 1973, p. 880.
23 The parishes are not ideal units: Effingham Junction, although a part of East Horsley parish, was in almost every respect separate from it, whilst part of Send was so much a part of West Clandon that the parish boundary ran down the middle of an important residential street there. The details of the survey, like much else, are described in J. Connell, Aspects of Housing and Migration in Central Surrey, unpublished PhD thesis, University of London, 1973.

Chapter 2 The past as prologue

1 L.D. Stamp and E.C. Willatts, *The Land of Britain: Surrey*, London, HMSO, 1943, p. 366.
2 J. Sheail, The Regional Distribution of Wealth in England as Indicated in the 1524-5 Lay Subsidy Returns, unpublished PhD Thesis, University of London, 1968, p. 327.
3 A.G. Parton, 'Crop Returns of 1801', *Surrey Archaeological Collections*, 64, 1967, p. 121.
4 *Census of Surrey*, London, HMSO, 1851, p. 17.
5 *Census of Surrey*, London, HMSO, 1861, p. 233.
6 W. Howitt, *The Rural Life of England*, London, Longman, 1840, p. 594.
7 A. Young, *A Six Weeks Tour through the Southern Counties of England and Wales*, 2nd edn, London, 1769, pp. 228-9.

Notes to pages 17–29

8 L. Simond, *Journal of a Tour and Residence in Great Britain During the Years 1810 and 1811*, London, 1815, p. 222.
9 J. Malcolm, *A Compendium of Modern Husbandry*, London, J. Malcolm, 1805; Sir Frederic Eden quotes similar wages in Epsom, of from 9/- to 10/6 per week, rising at harvest times (*The State of the Poor*, London, Davis, 1797, p. 693).
10 F.G. Huggett, *A Day in the Life of a Victorian Farm Worker*, London, Allen & Unwin, 1972, p. 83.
11 Royal Commission, *First Report from the Commissioners for the Employment of Children and Young Persons in Agriculture, 1867-1868*, London, HMSO, 1868.
12 G. Jekyll, *Old West Surrey*, London, Longman, 1904, p. 203.
13 G. Leveson-Gower, 'The Dialect of Surrey', in G. Clinch and S.W. Kershaw, *Bygone Surrey*, London, Simpkin & Marshall, 1895, p. 43.
14 Jekyll, *op.cit.*, p. 247.
15 G. Bourne, *Change in the Village*, London, Duckworth, 1912, p. 166.
16 P. Laslett, *The World We Have Lost*, London, Methuen, 1965, p. 203.
17 Bourne, *op.cit.*, pp. 53, 60.
18 *Surrey Advertiser*, 28 April 1972.
19 Jekyll, *op.cit.*
20 Only East Clandon and East Horsley record books were available. All the quotations in this section are directly from these.
21 E.W. Martin (*The Secret People*, London, Phoenix House, 1954, p. 175) describes how at the age of six, in 1867, Thomas Cook of Feltham, Middlesex, was scaring birds for 3d per day; a bit later he drove horses in the plough for the same wage. At eight he was hired out as a ploughboy and would plant cabbages at 9d per 1,000. The conditions in Surrey were probably very similar.
22 U.H.S. Snow, *A Hundred Years in Churt*, Woking, privately printed, 1969, p. 23.
23 *Ibid.* p. 24.
24 Bourne, *op.cit.*, p. 57.
25 Although in September 1918 some East Clandon children had gone blackberrying this seems more likely to have been just truancy.
26 Where harvest seasons were sharply demarcated, as for example in Farnham, the use of child labour almost certainly continued after the First World War.
27 See E.J. Hobsbawm and G. Rudé, *Captain Swing*, London, Lawrence & Wishart, 1969, p. xxiv.
28 The parish council minutes of West Clandon before 1930 have been lost but subsequent volumes and all the records of the other three parishes from 1894 to date are accessible.
29 West Clandon council minutes record that the parish council was having great trouble defining need in 1961 and as early as 1944

(actually during the war) they had requested permission from the Charity Commissioners to postpone payment until need became more urgent than it was.
30. In East Clandon in July 1900 the chairman was writing a letter to Byron Noel, Esq., who was then the Agent of Lord Lovelace in East Horsley. There seems to have been some local confusion on names of gentry!
31. Bourne, *op.cit.*, p. 64.
32. Hobsbawm and Rudé, *op.cit.*, p. 34.
33. M. Davies (*Life in an English Village*, London, Fisher Unwin, 1909, p. 107) comments on the rich variety of occupations in the Wiltshire village of Corsley, which then included one retired mole-catcher.
34. P.J. Perry, 'Working Class Isolation and Mobility in Rural Dorset, 1837-1936: A Study of Marriage Distances', *Transactions of the Institute of British Geographers*, 46, March, 1969, p. 134.
35. V.G. Pons, The Social Structure of a Hertfordshire Parish: A Study in Rural Community, unpublished PhD thesis, University of London, 1955, p. 163.
36. Churt, at least, had a lending library in 1892 (see Snow, *op. cit.*).
37. J.E. Morris, *Surrey*, London, 1926, pp. 82, 80.
38. G. Home, *The Charm of Surrey*, London, A. & C. Black, 1929. Moreover as late as 1970—in the same year that sodium lights arrived at West Clandon crossroads—E.R. Chamberlin wrote of West Clandon: 'A village lane runs northwards, sprinkled with cottages and gardens, a farmhouse and a school whose tiny walled playground gives onto open meadows so that the low wall seems a child's model of a city wall' (*Guildford: A Biography*, London, Macmillan, 1970, p. 33).
39. D. Moul and G. Thompson, *Picturesque Surrey*, London, 1902, p. 101.
40. E. Parker, *Highways and Byways in Surrey*, London, Macmillan, 1909, p. 119.
41. H. St J.H. Bashall, *The Oak Hamlet: Being an Account of the History and Associations of the Village of Ockham, Surrey*, London, Stock, 1900, p. 1.
42. Jekyll, *op.cit.*, p. 248.
43. J.W.R. Scott, *The Dying Peasant*, London, Williams & Norgate, 1926, p. 269.
44. *Ibid.*, p. 43.
45. *Ibid.*, pp. 49-50.
46. Only 22 per cent of the population then had television sets.
47. *Surrey Advertiser*, 6 June 1953, p. 4.
48. M. Wiggin, *Faces at the Window*, London, Nelson, 1972, pp. 175-6.
49. *Ibid.*, p. 178.
50. Bourne, *op.cit.*, p. 11.

Notes to pages 56–73

51 Lord Ernle, *English Farming, Past and Present*, 3rd edn, London, Longmans, Green, 1922.
52 See R. Williams, *The Country and the City*, London, Chatto & Windus, 1973, pp. 9–12; R. Parker, *The Common Stream*, London, Collins, 1975, pp. 230–1.
53 M.K. Ashby, *The Changing English Village. A History of Bledington, Gloucestershire in its Setting 1066-1914*, Kineton, The Roundwood Press, 1974, pp. 407–8.
54 D. Thomas, *London's Green Belt*, London, Faber & Faber, 1970, p. 72.
55 *Ibid.*, p. 76.
56 D.B.S. Fitch and R.P. Power, 'The Green Belt: Its Origins, Development and Uses', in J.E. Salmon (ed), *The Surrey Countryside*, Guildford, University of Surrey, 1975, p. 65.

Chapter 3 Contemporary countryside

1 P.G. Hall, *London 2000*, London, Faber & Faber, 1969.
2 The 1966 Census was carried out on the basis of a 10 per cent sample. Consequently, for small units, and especially for parishes such as East Clandon, the results are likely to be very distorted.
3 M. Frisch, *Andorra*, Frankfurt, Suhrkamp, 1962 (English translation, 1971).
4 General Register Office, *Occupation Tables*, London, HMSO, 1966, p. 9.
5 Cited by P. Ambrose, *The Quiet Revolution*, London, Chatto & Windus, 1974, p. 204.
6 G.P. Wibberley, *Agriculture and Urban Growth*, London, Michael Joseph, 1959.
7 G.F. Stoddart, Secretary to the Surrey NFU, personal communication, 29 March 1971.
8 M.J. Field, 'Mid-Surrey', *Agriculture*, 73, September 1966, p. 444.
9 O.B. Silver, 'Factors Influencing Land Utilisation in the Parishes of Effingham and Abinger, Surrey', unpublished external Diploma in Geography dissertation, London, 1969, p. 22.
10 J.E. Lousley, *Flora of Surrey*, Newton Abbot, David & Charles, 1976, p. 49.
11 *Ibid.*
12 Horsley Towers Estate sales catalogue, 9 November 1920.
13 Manor and Place Farms sales catalogue, 1925.
14 Burbridge Builders, *East Horsley, Surrey*, London, n.d., p. 20.
15 *Ibid.*
16 Cited by A.A. Jackson, *Semi-Detached London: Suburban Development, Life and Transport 1900-1939*, London, Allen & Unwin, 1973, p. 171.
17 *Ibid.*, pp. 177–8.
18 Hatchlands sales catalogue, 19 July 1888, p. 2.

219

19 *Ibid.*, p. 38.
20 *Surrey Advertiser*, 29 March, 1930.
21 J. Connell, Aspects of Housing and Migration in Central Surrey, unpublished PhD thesis, University of London, 1973, pp. 503-5.
22 H.P. White, *A Regional History of the Railways of Great Britain. Volume 2. Southern England*, Newton Abbot, David & Charles, 1964, p. 182.
23 *Ibid.*, p. 194.
24 West Clandon Parish Council, *Minutes*, October 1959.
25 R.F. Ashby, 'Books on the Move', *Surrey Life*, 1 March 1964, pp. 25-7.
26 Guildford Rural District Council, *Minutes*, 27 March 1964.
27 Glenesk House, Introductory Brochure, n.d. (1971).
28 *Surrey Advertiser*, 26 March 1971.
29 Connell, *op.cit.*, pp. 135-7.
30 P.R. Bean and A. Lockwood, *Rating Valuation Practice*, London, Stevens, 1969, p. 138.
31 A. Thorburn, *Planning Villages*, London, Estates Gazette, 1971.
32 D. Pitt and M. Shaw, *Surrey Villages*, London, Hale, 1971, p. 64.
33 A. and L. Tropp, 'Some Aspects of the Social Structure of Surrey', in J.E. Salmon (ed.) *The Surrey Countryside*, Guildford, University of Surrey, 1975, p. 217.
34 Anonymous, 'Stockbrokers and their Belts', *Economist*, 216, 28 August 1965, pp. 792-3.
35 G.H. Dury, *The British Isles*, London, Heinemann, 1961, p. 440.
36 Cited in J. Connell, 'Green Belt County', *New Society*, 17, 25 February 1971, p. 304.

Chapter 4 Migration and housing: élites and council tenants

1 Rev. E.C. Craft, *St. Martin's Parish Magazine*, East Horsley, April 1970.
2 J. Connell, 'The Metropolitan Village: Spatial and Social Processes in Discontinuous Suburbs', in J.H. Johnson (ed.), *Suburban Growth: Geographical Processes at the Edge of the City*, Chichester, Wiley, 1974, pp. 77-100.
3 J. Connell, Aspects of Housing and Migration in Central Surrey, unpublished PhD thesis, University of London, 1973, pp. 202-4.
4 The term 'spiralist' was first used by Watson in 1960 and he defined spiralism as: 'the progressive ascent of specialists of different skills through a series of higher positions in one or more hierarchical structures, and the concomitant residential mobility through a number of communities at one or more steps during the ascent.' See W. Watson, 'Social Mobility and Social Class in Industrial Communities', in M. Gluckman (ed.), *Closed Systems and open Minds*, Edinburgh, Oliver & Boyd, 1964, p. 174.
5 A. Bowers, 'Surrey on the Fringe', *Sunday Telegraph*, 1 August 1971.

Notes to pages 112–49

6 The term was first used by R.E. Pahl, 'The Social Objectives of Village Planning', *Official Architecture and Planning*, 29 August 1966, pp. 1146-50.
7 J.B. Cullingworth, *Housing and Local Government*, London, Allen & Unwin, 1966, p. 121.
8 J. Connell, Aspects of Housing and Migration in Central Surrey, unpublished PhD thesis, University of London, 1973, pp. 281-316.
9 *Surrey Advertiser*, 5 June 1974.
10 J. Tucker, *Honourable Estates*, London, Gollancz, 1966, p. 12.
11 Individuals of unknown social class have been excluded from these calculations but not from the Tables. The high proportion of unclassified council-house tenants is partly a result of age structure—there are many widows, and several men have been retired for a long time. The classification is also dependent on often inadequate housing-office data.
12 J.W.R. Whitehand, 'The Settlement Morphology of London's Cocktail Belt', *Tijdschrift voor Economische en Sociale Geografie*, 58 (1), 1967, pp. 20-7.
13 J. Connell, Aspects of Housing and Migration in Central Surrey, unpublished PhD thesis, University of London, 1973, pp. 273-4.

Chapter 5 Country life

1 East Horsley Parish Council Minutes, March 1936.
2 I.C. MacPherson, East Horsley 1956, unpublished Diploma in Town Planning thesis, University of London, 1956; East Horsley Parish Council Minutes, October 1952.
3 C.S. Orwin, *Problems of the Countryside*, Cambridge University Press, 1945, p. 98.
4 H. Peake, *The English Village: The Origin and Decay of its Community*, London, Benn, 1922, p. 218.
5 E. Radford, *The New Villagers*, London, Cass, 1970, p. 41.
6 J.M. Pahl and R.E. Pahl, *Managers and Their Wives*, London, Allen Lane, 1971, p. 160, citing M. Stacey, *Tradition and Change*, Oxford University Press, 1960, p. 88.
7 See the review in D.C. Thorns, *Suburbia*, London, MacGibbon & Kee, 1972, pp. 127-34.
8 V.G. Pons, The Social Structure of a Hertfordshire Parish: A Study in Rural Community, unpublished PhD thesis, University of London, 1955, Chapter 11.
9 A. Tropp and L. Tropp, 'Some Aspects of the Social Structure of Surrey', in J.E. Salmon (ed.), *The Surrey Countryside*, Guildford, University of Surrey, 1975, pp. 205, 215.
10 R.E. Pahl, 'Class and Community in English Commuting Villages', reprinted in R.E. Pahl, *Whose City?*, London, Longman, 1970, p. 42.
11 M. Young and P. Willmott, *Family and Class in a London Suburb*, London, Routledge & Kegan Paul, 1960.

12 Exactly the same was found by Hall in the village of Spencers Wood in Berkshire. See P.G. Hall et al., *The Containment of Urban England*, London, Allen & Unwin, 1973, pp. 431-4.
13 R.K. Merton, 'Patterns of Influence: A Study of Interpersonal Influence and Communications Behaviour in a Local Community', in P.F. Lazarsfeld and F. Stanton, *Communications Research 1948-9*, New York, 1949, pp. 180-219.
14 Tropp and Tropp, *op.cit.*, p. 205.
15 R.E. Park, 'The City: Suggestions for the Investigation of Human Behaviour in the Urban Environment', *American Journal of Sociology*, 20, 1916, pp. 577-612.
16 W.H. Whyte, *The Organization Man*, New York, Simon & Schuster, 1956.
17 R.N. Morris and J.M. Mogey, *The Sociology of Housing: Studies at Berinsfield*, London, Routledge & Kegan Paul, 1965, p. 155.
18 A. Tod, 'Carpeted with Commuters', *Guardian*, 26 February 1968.
19 Young and Willmott, *op. cit.*
20 V. Bonham-Carter, *The Survival of the English Countryside*, London, Fairleigh Dickinson, 1971, p. 197.
21 S.F. Fava, 'Suburbanism as a Way of Life', *American Sociological Review*, 21, February 1956, pp. 34-7.
22 Thorns, *op.cit.*, pp. 149-50.
23 C. Bell, *Middle-Class Families*, London, Routledge & Kegan Paul, 1969, p. 129.
24 R.E. Pahl, 'A Sociological Portrait: Friends and Associates', *New Society*, 18, 18 November 1971, p. 982.
25 Rev. E.C. Craft, *St Martin's Parish Magazine*, East Horsley, November 1969.
26 J. Pilger, 'Honesty, Loyalty and Decency on the Up Line to Effingham', *Daily Mirror*, 16 March 1971.
27 Mrs A. Rayner, letter to the editor, *Observer*, 20 February 1972.
28 Mrs G.B. Greenham, letter to the editor, *Observer*, 27 February 1972.
29 Cited in *Official Architecture and Planning*, April 1969.
30 R.E. Pahl, *Whose City?*, London, Longman, 1970, p. 10.
31 Pahl and Pahl, *op.cit.*, p. 241.

Chapter 6 Participation and planning: preservation and people

1 Committee on Public Participation in Planning, *People and Planning* (Skeffington Report), London, HMSO, 1969, p. 4.
2 *Ibid.*, p. 5.
3 J. Barr, 'The Amenity Protesters', *New Society*, 12, 1 August 1968, p. 152.
4 P. Levin, 'The Amenity Movement', *Official Architecture and Planning*, 34, November 1971, p. 846.
5 Barr, *op.cit.*, p. 152.

Notes to pages 177–202

6 V.W. Morecroft, Secretary to the Green Belt Council, personal communication, 23 August 1971.
7 V.W. Morecroft, Secretary to the Green Belt Council, personal communication, 15 September 1971.
8 Surrey Amenity Council, *Annual Report 1969*, Guildford, 1970.
9 Horsley Countryside Preservation Society, *Newsletter No. 1*, June 1956.
10 West Clandon Society, *Newsletter No. 1*, 1962.
11 *Clandon Society Constitution*, mimeo, n.d.
12 Clandon Society, *Newsletter No. 4*, February 1964.
13 H.R. Kenwright, *Conservation in East and West Horsley: An Account of Some of the Activities of Horsley Countryside Preservation Society, March 1956-March 1974*, Mitcham, 1975, p. 3.
14 *Surrey Villager*, December 1968.
15 P. Jennings, *The Living Village*, London, Hodder & Stoughton, 1968, p. 134.
16 A.D. Cooper, chairman, Horsley Association, personal communication, 2 August 1971.
17 *Ibid.*
18 L.T. Velde, chairman, Glendene Avenue Residents' Association, 27 July 1971.
19 Five Villages Association, *The Route 37 Motorway*, mimeo, 1968.
20 A.H. Cope, chairman, Five Villages Association, personal communication, 9 June 1970.
21 Extending the system of forty-five area stewards pioneered by the Horsley Countryside Preservation Society, newsletters were delivered and liaison maintained with each street.
22 A.H. Cope, cited in *Surrey Advertiser*, 6 September 1968.
23 A.H. Cope, chairman, Five Villages Association, personal communication, 9 June 1970.
24 Miss M.L. Martin, personal communication, 26 July 1970.
25 Jennings, *op.cit.*, p. 104.
26 Kenwright, *op.cit.*, p. 3.
27 F.I. Masser and D.C. Stroud, 'The Metropolitan Village', *Town Planning Review*, 36, July 1965, p. 111; P. Hall, 'Thames Valley Tangle', *New Society*, 8, 1 December 1966, p. 822.
28 J. Simmie, 'Public Participation: A Case Study from Oxfordshire', *Journal of the Town Planning Institute*, 57, October 1971, pp. 161-2.
29 This seems to be one conclusion of G. Hoinville, 'Evaluating Community Preferences', *Environment and Planning*, 3(1), 1971, p. 33.
30 Clandon Society, *Newsletter No. 11*, February 1968.
31 *Surrey Advertiser*, 9 July 1971.
32 H. Sachs, A Study of New Ash Green, Centre for Environmental Studies Seminar Paper (unpublished), March 1971.

33 C.S. Orwin, *Problems of the Countryside*, Cambridge University Press, 1945.
34 G.C. McDonald, *Social and Geographical Mobility: Studies in the New Towns*, Department of Geography Occasional Paper No. 12, University College, London, November 1970, p. 1.
35 N. Taylor, *The Village in the City*, London, Temple Smith, 1973.
36 R.E. Pahl, *Patterns of Urban Life*, London, Longman, 1970, p. 113.
37 R. Blythe, *Akenfield*, London, Allen Lane, 1969, p. 17.

Chapter 7 The end of tradition

1 D.B.S. Fitch and R.P. Power, 'The Green Belt: Its Origins, Development and Uses', in J.E. Salmon, (ed.) *The Surrey Countryside*, Guildford, University of Surrey, 1975, p. 77.
2 P. Hall, 'Anatomy of the Green Belts', *New Society*, 23, 4 January 1973, p. 12.
3 E.L. Jones, 'Environmental Buffers of a Marginal Peasantry in Southern England', *Peasant Studies Newsletter*, 3 (4), October 1974, pp. 13-16.
4 R. Parker, *The Common Stream*, London, Collins, 1975, p. 228.
5 P. Ambrose, *The Quiet Revolution: Social Change in a Sussex Village, 1871-1971*, London, Chatto & Windus, 1974.
6 Quoted in an anonymous article, 'Housing Layout in Theory and Practice', *Journal of the Royal Institute of British Architects*, 55, 1948, pp. 421-32.
7 Anonymous, 'Country Matters', *New Society*, 18, 28 October 1971, p. 815.
8 R.E. Pahl, *Urbs in Rure: The Metropolitan Fringe in Hertfordshire*, LSE Geographical Papers, no. 2, 1965, p. 14.
9 R.E. Pahl, 'The Two-Class Village', *New Society*, 3, 27 February 1964, pp. 7-9.
10 R.E. Pahl, *Patterns of Urban Life*, London, Longman, 1970, pp. 66-8.
11 J. Rex and R. Moore, *Race, Community and Conflict: A Study of Sparkbrook*, Oxford University Press, 1967, p. 36.
12 G. Weightman, 'Deviant Hunters?', *New Society*, 24, 5 April 1973, p. 5.
13 The arguments in this paragraph are derived from those of Michael Lipton, *Why Poor People Stay Poor*, London, Temple Smith, 1977, pp. 130-5.

Index

Abinger Hammer, 68, 159
Accountants, 106, 158, 166
Agricultural Labourers' Union, 26
Agriculture: farming to quit, 67; hobby farming, 68; mechanisation, 2, 17, 66-8, 206-7, 208, 213; wages, 17, 18-19, 21, 37-8, 47, 217; *see also* Surrey and the individual parishes
Albury, 17, 89
Aldershot, 67
Alfold, 5
Ambrose, P., 219, 224
Amenity Provision, 81-8
Amenity societies, 174-97, 210
Ancient Order of Foresters, 31
Arch, Joseph, 26, 33
Areas of outstanding natural beauty, 95
Arnold, Matthew, 6
Ashby, M.K., 56
Ashby, R.F., 83
Ashtead, 111
Austen, Jane, 213

Bagshot Heath, 4
Bankers, 3, 106, 166
Barnard, J., 216
Barr, J., 176, 222
Bashall, H.St J.H., 218
Bedfordshire, 20-1
Bell, C., 222

Bennett, Albert, 21, 55
Berkshire, 101
Bevan, Aneurin, 209
Bicycles, 30, 34-5, 79
Blythe, R., 204
Bonham-Carter, V., 161
Bookham, 194
Bourne, G., 6, 7, 20-1, 24, 31, 55
Bower, J.B., 70-1, 74
Bowers, A., 112
Bronze Age, 10
Brown, 'Capability', 13
Building societies, 127-8
Burbridge builders, 71
Bus services, 80-1

Camberley, 96
Camden, W., 215
'Captain Swing', 15, 26
Caravans, 123
Car ownership, 1, 9, 54, 79-81, 95
Car, use of, 36-7, 149, 162-3
Chamberlin, E.R., 218
Charity, Bishops Mead and Commonfield, 30
Charity, Lady Noel Byron's Nursing, 30
Charity, Smith's, 28-30
Cheam, 101
Chilworth, 162
Chown, F.H., 47, 70-2, 74, 75, 76, 89, 188

225

Index

Christie, Agatha, 153, 213
Churches, *see* Religion
Churt, 24, 218
Civic Trust, 175, 177-8
Civil Servants, 106
Clandon Park, 13, 42
Clandon Ratepayers' Association, 176
Clandon Society, 178-9, 181-7, 195, 197-8
Clare, John, 212
Class divisions, 7-8, 64-6, 130-1, 136-7, 153, 160, 195-7, 204, 211
Claygate, 72
Cobbett, W., 3
Cobham, 13, 87, 91, 110-11
'Cocktail Belt', 127
Commons, Open Space and Footpaths Preservation Society, 175, 178
'Community', 55-6, 91, 170, 214
Community organisation, 52-3, 148-9
Commuters, 2, 5, 112, 208
Commuting, 34, 62, 77-81, 95, 106-7
Conformity, 157-60, 164, 168, 172, 210
Connell, J., 216, 220, 221
Conservative Party, 94-5, 132, 134, 139, 192
Cornwall, 153
Coronation Celebrations, 51, 52-3
Cosmopolitans, 153
Cottages, 77, 92, 127, 211-12
Coulsdon, 111
Council for the Protection of Rural England (CPRE), 175-8
Council house residents, 155-6, 170, 203-4
Council housing: attitudes to, 48-50, 91-2, 119, 135, 155-6; estates, 48-50, 76-8, 94, 100-1, 148, 209;
Council houses: allocation, 49-50, 113-18; rents, 118-19; sales, 95, 129-30
Council structure, 126-31

Council tenants: migration, 120-6, 129; social composition, 118-20, 125-6
Country Life, 212
Countryside, attitudes to, 161-2, 165-72, 199-203, 212
Cracknell, B.E., 6, 10
Craft, Rev. E.C., 220, 222
Cranleigh, 78
Cricket, 38, 134, 185
Croydon, 10, 102, 111
Cullingworth, J.B., 221

Davies, M., 7, 218
Defoe, D., 4
Devil's Punchbowl, 6
Devon, 153
Dialect, 19-20
Dorking, 4, 67, 78, 83, 110, 112, 178, 192
Dorset, 113, 175
Drama, 138
Duke of Wellington (pub), 34, 48, 143, 161
Dury, G.H., 95
Dyos, H.J., 215

Ealing, 110
East Clandon: 12-13, 39, 48, 51, 54-5, 74, 82, 87-8, 108, 144-5, 153, 191, 204, 208; agriculture, 44, 67-9, 208; economy, 12-13, 62-5; education, 24-8, 36, 83-4; health, 25; housing: council, 48, 76-8, 88, 100-1, 113-31, private, 90-2, 112, 127, rented, 54-5, 126-7, tied, 100, 112-13; migration, 100, 102, 152; Parish Council, 34-7, 44-5, 46, 51, 190, 198; planning, 82, 181-3, 199, 201; population, 15, 98; social divisions, 8, 155
East Horsley: 12-13, 39-43, 46-7, 51, 80, 106, 134-7, 145, 189, 191, 205-6, 211; agriculture, 67-9; economy, 12-13, 62-5; education, 19, 26, 36, 83-4; housing: council, 48-9, 76-8,

Index

100-1, 113-31, private, 70-3, 89-92, 127, 188, rented, 127, tied, 112-13; migration, 16, 97-8, 102, 152; Parish Council, 32-3, 36, 48-9, 186, 189-90; planning, 50, 72-3, 179-81, 186-93, 198, 201; population, 14-15, 98; social divisions, 7-8, 91, 155-7, 188
Eden, Sir Frederic, 217
Education, 19, 22-8, 35-6, 55, 83-4, 89
Effingham, 16, 39, 68, 69, 89, 102, 110, 137, 166, 189, 191
Effingham Junction: 16, 78-9, 86, 89, 91, 108, 142, 166, 193, 216; housing, 39, 91
Elizabeth I, 57
Epsom, 4, 37, 80, 97, 102, 104, 217
Ernle, Lord, 55
Esher, 83, 91, 102, 107
Essex, 110
Estate agents, 128
Evelyn, John, 12

Farming, *see* Agriculture
Farmhouses, 68
Farmworkers, housing, 113
Farnham, 13, 21, 24, 31, 96, 217
Fava, S.F., 222
Feltham, 217
Field, M.J., 219
Fines, K.D., 6
First World War, 20, 42, 43-4, 60
Fitch, D.B.S., 219
Five Villages Association (5VA), 89, 187, 189, 190-4, 202
Floral groups, 87, 136, 139-40
Folksongs, 20, 25
Football, 38, 134, 138
Forests, 10-12
Friends, 109, 151, 157-60
Frisch, M., 219

Gardening, 38, 161
Glendene Avenue Residents' Association, 188

Gloucestershire, 56, 153
Godalming, 6, 19, 111
Goldsmith, Oliver, 212
Goldthorpe, J.E., 97
Goodhart-Rendel, H.S., 23, 44, 54-5
'Good Neighbours', 142-3, 149
Grayshott, 96
Greater London, 102, 104, 106-7, 143-5, 162, 193
Green Belt, 56-9, 67, 68, 74, 88, 95, 112, 163, 180, 183, 189, 201-6, 211
Green Belt Council, 177-80
Greenleigh, 161
Guildford, 1, 4, 6, 10, 16, 26, 34, 37, 42, 67, 78, 79, 80, 86, 87, 102, 104, 106-7, 110, 111, 112, 122, 148, 179, 189, 214
Guildford District Council, 89, 130, 182, 188
Guildford Rural District, 62, 80, 88
Guildford Rural District Council, 49, 50, 72, 76, 82, 88, 181, 186
Guildford Rural District Council housing, *see* Council housing

Hall, P.G., 206, 222, 223
Hampshire, 101, 122
Haslemere, 16, 110
Hatchlands, East Clandon, 13, 52, 54, 60, 73, 92
Health, 25, 36, 39, 71-2, 82, 101, 115
Hersham, 110
Hertfordshire, 8, 38, 166-7, 210
Hill, Octavia, 175
Hinchley Wood, 110
Hindhead, 5
Hobsbawm, E.J., 32, 217
Hoinville, G., 223
Home, G., 43
Horses, 68, 207
Horsham, 78
Horsley Association, 187, 188, 194
Horsley Conservative Association, 94
Horsley Countryside Preservation

227

Index

Society, 178-87, 191, 195-7, 198
Horsley Liberal Association, 89
Horsley New Town, 76
Horsley Towers, 13, 24, 52, 70
Horticultural societies, 38, 136, 139-40
Houses: prices, 55, 71, 89-92, 112, 127-8, 139-40, 165; rateable values, 91-3; styles, 70-4, 213
Housing: classes, 66, 130-1, 211; council, *see* Council housing; demand, 90, 130, 156-7; layout, 39-42, 53, 71-3, 74-6, 157; rented, 18, 54-5, 126, 128-9; structure, 126-31; tied, 112-13, 126-31, 211-12; *see also* under separate parishes
Howitt, W., 216
Huggett, F.G., 217
Huxley, T.H., 175

Infilling, 2, 74, 183-4

Jackson, A.A., 219
Jekyll, Gertrude, 20, 21
Jennings, P., 132, 195
Jervis, C.R., 7
Jones, E., 2
Jones, E.L., 207
Journey to work, *see* Commuting

Kent, 13, 61, 122, 202, 208
Kenwright, H.R., 223
Kingston, 56, 86, 110, 111, 214

Labour Party, 87, 94-5, 134
Laker, Sir Freddie, 108
Lancaster, Osbert, 213
Land: ownership, 2; sales, 69-70, 73, 75; use, 10-13, 39-41, 66-9, 212
Laslett, P., 217
Leatherhead, 10, 16, 79, 80, 83, 87, 102, 107, 110, 111, 144, 148, 176, 189, 190, 193
Le Carré, J., 60
Leveson-Gower, G., 20

Levin, P., 222
Liberal Party, 94, 134, 139, 192
Libraries, 38, 46, 82-3
Life styles, change, 160-5
Lipton, Michael, 224
Lloyd George, D., 5
Local Authority housing, *see* Council housing
Locals, 153, 154-6
London: 4, 5, 6, 13, 56-9, 61, 67, 79, 91, 101, 143-5, 206; Central London, 106-7; County Council, 56-8; New Towns, 2, 209
Lousley, J.E., 219
Lovelace, Earl of, 13, 35
Lovelace Estate, East Horsley, 69-71
Lovelace, Lady, 22, 32
Low, S., 5

McDonald, G.C., 203
Mackinder, H.J., 1
MacPherson, I.C., 8, 221
Malcolm, J., 17
Malden, 110
Martin, E.W., 217
Marx, Karl, 66
Masser, F.I., 223
Merrow, 1, 38, 163
Merton, R.K., 153
Metropolitan villagers, 1-3, 75-6, 98-101, 112, 210
Middle class, 15, 171, 176, 188, 197, 204
Middlesex, 56
Migration: decision-making, 103-9, 112, 120-3, 125, 171-2; internal, 97, 99-101, 102-3; international, 20, 26, 102-3; regional, 3, 14, 17, 23, 101-3, 154-5; social composition, 98-9; *see also* Council housing
Mill, John Stuart, 175
Mobility, social, *see* Social mobility
Mogey, J., 222
Morris, J.E., 43
Morris, R.N., 222
Morris, William, 175

Index

Moul, D., 43

Nairn, I., 9, 215
National Farmers' Union, 67, 177
National Trust, 175, 178
Neighbours, 149, 157-9, 163
New Ash Green, Kent, 202
Newlands Corner, 6
Norfolk, 173
North Downs, 10, 91, 143, 193

Ockham, 16, 43, 47, 69
Ockham Road Protection Association, 189-90, 192, 194
Offices, 61, 63
Onslow Arms, 31
Onslow, Earls of, 13, 17-19, 21, 22, 74, 194
Organization Man, The, 157
Orwin, C.S., 146, 203, 215
Overbrook, West Horsley, 150, 163
Oxfordshire, 134, 137, 197, 209
Oxshott, 102
Oxted, 67

Pahl, J.M., 137, 221
Pahl, R.E., 2, 8, 137, 148, 171, 210, 215, 221, 222, 224
Parish councils: activities, 28-31, 34-7, 36-7, 46-7, 49-54, 89, 185-7, 197-8; composition, 32-4, 197
Park, R.E., 154
Parker, E., 218
Parker, R., 219, 224
Parton, A.G., 216
Peake, H., 135, 215
Peasants, 17, 50, 55, 207
Perry, P.J., 218
Pevsner, N., 9, 215
Pilger, J., 222
Pigs, 19, 134
Pitt, D., 220
Planning: attitude to, 46-7, 173-204; participation, 179, 182, 188, 189, 191-3, 194-5, 197-204
Ploughman, 18, 20, 22, 217
Poaching, 211

Police, 34-5, 54, 113, 158
Politics, 94-5
Pons, V.G., 38
Population change, 12, 14-15, 51, 78, 98-101
Portsmouth, 16, 27
Poverty, 16-17, 20-1, 28-31, 37-8, 210-12, 217-18
Power, R.P., 219
Preservation societies, 136 *see also* Clandon Society; Horsley Countryside Preservation Society
Public houses, 31, 38, 145-7
Public transport, 34-5, 44, 45-6, 77-81, 162

Radford, E., 221
Railway stations, 5, 16, 70, 73, 91, 166
Railways: construction, 16, 69, 77-8; use, 16, 34, 45-6, 71, 77-81, 95, 176
Raleigh, Sir Walter, 13, 84
Ramsey, Sir Alf, 8
Rats, 47
Read, Miss, 213
Recreation, 38-9, 143-50, 161, 212; *see also* Cricket; Football; Sport
Reigate, 16, 67, 112
Relatives, 109, 159, 161
Religion: church attendance, 140-3; churches' role, 28-31, 51, 86-7; education, 22-3, 28
Residential satisfaction, 165-72
Rex, J., 224
Ripley, 16, 42, 89, 102, 159, 162
Rounding off, 2, 74, 183-4
Rudé, G., 32, 217
Russell, B., 5, 205

Sachs, H., 223
St George's Hill, Weybridge, 91
Scott, J.W.R., 50, 218
Second World War, 29, 51-2, 61, 66-7, 176, 208
Selsdon, 71-2, 96
Send, 10, 89, 127, 216

229

Index

Sevenoaks, 111
Sewerage, 47, 82, 87
Shaw, M., 220
Sheail, J., 13
Shepherds, 18-19
Shere, 89, 159
Shopping, 76, 84-6, 209
Shops, 51, 72, 87, 183
Silver, O.B., 68
Simmie, J., 223
Simond, L., 17
Skeffington Report, 174
Smallholdings, 38, 44
Snow, U.H.S., 217
Social class, see Class divisions
Social divisions (in villages), 2-4, 7-9, 91-3, 127, 155-60, 204, 209-11
Social mobility, 104-5
Social organisations, 37-9, 132-40, 142-3, 178-97
Somerset, 153
Sopwith, T.O.M., 69
Spiralists, 104, 160, 220
Sport, 42, 134-5, 137-8
Stacey, M., 137
Staines, 101
Stamp, L.D., 12
Stockbrokers, 3, 95, 106, 152, 213
Stoke d'Abernon, 16
Stoneleigh, 149
Street lighting, 44-5, 185, 197-200
Stroud, D.C., 223
Sturt, G., see Bourne, G.
Suburbanisation, 2, 4-5, 13, 153, 161, 198-9
Suburbanism, 60, 152-3, 164-5, 201, 214
Suffolk, 162, 204
Sunbury, 101
Surbiton, 110
Surrey: 4-9, 87, 207; agriculture, 14-21, 47, 62, 66-9, 206-7; Amenity Council, 177, 178-9; Best-Kept Village competition, 88, 204, 212; County Council, 36, 76, 82, 88, 181, 190-3; employment, 60-5; industry, 4, 45, 60-5, 169; puma, 12; status, 95-6; University, 61, 107
Surrey, 168-9
Surrey Advertiser, 90, 168, 208
Surrey Life, 166, 168
Surrey Villager, 87
Sussex, 6, 113
Sutton, 101, 102, 104

Taylor, E.G.R., 215
Taylor, N., 224
Teachers, 23-8, 106-7
Television, 52-4, 145, 161
Tennyson, A., 5
Thames Ditton, 110
Theatres, 143-4
Thompson, G., 43
Thorburn, A., 220
Thorns, D.C., 221
Tillingbourne Valley, 4, 16, 63, 193
Tod, A., 160
Trade unions, 87, 203; see also Joseph Arch; National Farmers' Union
Tradition, 45, 88, 169, 205-14
Tree preservation, 180, 185
Tropp, A. and L., 220, 221, 222
Tucker, J., 221

Urbanisation, 1, 48-51
Urbanism, 47, 208

Village: concepts of, 151-7; metropolitan see Metropolitan villages
Village life, 18-19, 37-9, 51-6, 132-72
Villagers, 101, 151-7
Virginia Water, 95

Walton-on-Thames, 102, 107, 111, 112
Watson, W., 220
Weightman, G., 211
West Clandon: 10, 12-13, 18-19, 38, 39, 42, 43, 45, 52-3, 53-4, 55, 110, 147, 154, 181-2, 191, 216, 217-18; agriculture, 18-

230

Index

19, 21, 67-9; economy, 12-13, 62-5; education, 22, 83-4; housing: council, 78, 113-31, private, 73-4, 90-2, 127, rented, 127, tied, 112-13; migration, 15, 102; Parish Council, 33-4, 52, 83, 89, 186, 217; planning, 53, 181-3, 198-9; population, 14-15, 98; social divisions, 155-6, 160
'West Country', 154, 159, 172
West Horsley: 12-13, 39, 43, 47, 52, 53, 54, 56, 82, 106, 147, 191; agriculture, 67-9; economy, 12-13, 62-5; education, 83-4; housing: council, 49-50, 76-8, 113-31, private, 74, 90-2, 127, 176, rented, 127, tied, 112-13; migration, 102; Parish Council, 49-50, 53, 89, 185-6, 190, 198; planning, 179-81, 184-6, 192, 198-9; population, 15-16, 98; social divisions, 155
West Horsley North, 39, 74, 108
West Horsley Place, 13, 92
Wey and Arun Canal, 4
Weybridge, 61, 95, 102, 107, 110, 111, 156

White, H.P., 220
Whitehand, J.W.R., 127
Whyte, W.H., 157
Wibberley, G.P., 219
Wiggin, M., 54-5, 213
Willatts, E.C., 12
Williams, R., 219
Williams-Ellis, Clough, 176
Willmott, P., 149, 161
Wimbledon, 213
Wiltshire, 7, 218
Witley, 6
Woking, 16, 42, 78, 83, 102, 104, 110, 111
Women's Institutes, 39, 58, 88, 134, 135, 136-9, 140, 172, 192
Worcestershire, 135
Wordsworth, W., 212
Working Men's Clubs, 31, 38, 135
Worplesdon, 121

Young, A., 13, 16-17
Young, M., 149, 161
Young Farmers' Club, East Horsley, 88, 134, 137, 172
Youth clubs, 87, 135-6

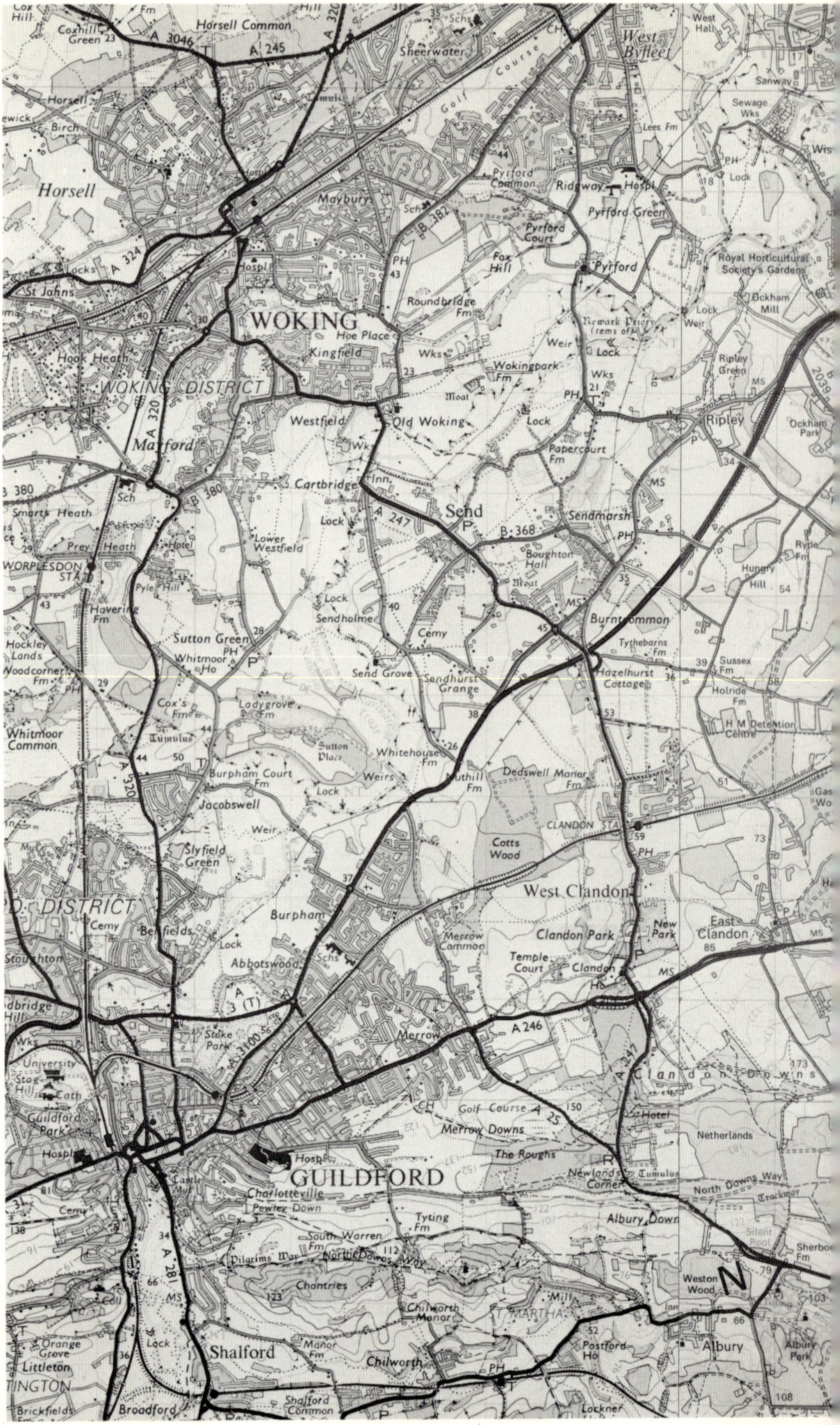
Horsell Common
Coxhill Green
Horsell
Horsell Birch
Sheerwater
West Byfleet
West Hall
Sanway
Sewage Wks
Golf Course
Maybury
Pyrford Common
Ridgway
Pyrford Green
Pyrford Court
Fox Hill
Pyrford
Royal Horticultural Society's Gardens
Ockham Mill
St Johns
WOKING
Hoe Place
Kingfield
Roundbridge Fm
Newark Priory (rems of)
Lock
Weir
Wokingpark Fm
Ripley Green
Ripley
Ockham Park
Hook Heath
WOKING DISTRICT
Westfield
Old Woking
Papercourt Fm
Mayford
Cartbridge
Inn
Send
Sendmarsh
Smarts Heath
Prey Heath
WORPLESDON STA
Lower Westfield
Boughton Hall
Hungry Hill
Pyle Hill
Havering Fm
Sendholme
Cemy
Burntcommon
Hockley Lands
Woodcorner Fm
Sutton Green
Whitmoor Ho
Send Grove
Sendhurst Grange
Tythebarns Fm
Hazelhurst Cottage
Sussex Fm
Holride Fm
H M Detention Centre
Cox's Fm
Ladygrove Fm
Whitmoor Common
Tumulus
Sutton Place
Whitehouse Fm
Muthill Fm
Dedswell Manor Fm
Burpham Court Fm
Jacobswell
CLANDON STA
Cotts Wood
Slyfield Green
West Clandon
D. DISTRICT
Burpham
Merrow Common
Clandon Park
New Park
East Clandon
Cemy
Bellfields
Stoughton
Abbotswood
Temple Court
Clandon Ho
Stoke Park
Merrow
Clandon Downs
University
Stag Hill
Cath
Guildford Park
Hospl
Golf Course
Merrow Downs
The Roughs
Hotel
Netherlands
GUILDFORD
Castle
Charlotteville
Pewley Down
Newlands Corner
Tumulus
North Downs Way
Trackway
Tyting Fm
Albury Down
South Warren Fm
Pilgrims Way
North Downs Way
Chantries
Silent Pool
Weston Wood
Sherbourne Fm
Orange Grove
Littleton
Lock
Chilworth Manor
St MARTHA'S
Postford Ho
Albury
Albury Park
Shalford
Manor Fm
Chilworth
Brickfields
Broadford
Shalford Common
Lockner
A 3046
A 245
A 324
A 320
B 380
B 382
A 247
B 368
A 246
A 25
A 3100
A 3 (T)
A 281
B 2039
M 25
N